Current Trends in Teaching Mathematics

Current Trends in Teaching Mathematics

Tim Hopkins

STATES
ACADEMIC PRESS
www.statesacademicpress.com

Published by States Academic Press,
109 South 5th Street,
Brooklyn, NY 11249, USA

ISBN: 978-1-63989-141-2

Cataloging-in-Publication Data

Current trends in teaching mathematics / Tim Hopkins.
p. cm.
Includes bibliographical references and index.
ISBN 978-1-63989-141-2
1. Mathematics--Study and teaching. 2. Mathematics. 3. Education. I. Hopkins, Tim.
QA11.2 .C87 2021
510.71--dc23

For information on all States Academic Press publications
visit our website at www.statesacademicpress.com

STATES
ACADEMIC PRESS

Contents

Preface

This book has been a concerted effort by a group of academicians, researchers and scientists, who have contributed their research works for the realization of the book. This book has materialized in the wake of emerging advancements and innovations in this field. Therefore, the need of the hour was to compile all the required researches and disseminate the knowledge to a broad spectrum of people comprising of students, researchers and specialists of the field.

Mathematics is an exact science related to measurements, calculations and determining relationships. It is a subject of great educational value and plays an important role in the lives of humans. It has numerous real-world uses and is required at every period of life. The study of mathematics disciplines the mind and develops reasoning power. It has great occupational and aesthetic value. Mathematics teaches economy in matters of time, money, speech and thought, and requires unique thinking. Many factors should be considered when teaching mathematics, such as the individual differences of the students, goals and purposes, selection of teaching methodology, etc. This book is a compilation of chapters that discuss the most vital concepts and current trends in teaching mathematics. It discusses the fundamentals as well as modern approaches of this field. This book attempts to assist those with a goal of teaching mathematics.

At the end of the preface, I would like to thank the authors for their brilliant chapters and the publisher for guiding us all-through the making of the book till its final stage. Also, I would like to thank my family for providing the support and encouragement throughout my academic career and research projects.

Tim Hopkins

1

Key Stage 3: An Overview

When designing a mathematics scheme of work for Key Stage 3, the obvious move would be to try to adapt the official programme of study.[1]

However:

- the programme of study incorporates some startling omissions of essential content that simply cannot be skipped (to give just two examples: there is no reference to the subtleties of teaching the arithmetic of negative numbers, or of combining negatives and 'minus signs' in algebra; nor is there any explicit mention of isosceles triangles, or of deriving and using their properties in other settings);
- many of the officially listed themes require careful interpretation in other ways;
- in the official programme of study the connections between topics are rarely elaborated; and
- the grouping and sequencing of, and the progression through, topics is far from clear.

In short, the programme of study needs to be supplemented and 'fleshed out' (and sometimes corrected). Moreover, unlike the programmes for Key Stage 1 and Key Stage 2,

> **the programme of study for Key Stage 3 has no year-by-year structure and no accompanying *Notes and guidance*.**

---

[1] National curriculum in England: mathematics programmes of study, https://www.gov.uk/government/publications/national-curriculum-in-england-mathematics-programmes-of-study; https://www.gov.uk/government/uploads/system/uploads/attachment_data/file/239058/SECONDARY_national_curriculum_-_Mathematics.pdf

The fact that we need to think more carefully about mathematics teaching at Key Stage 3 has been a theme of the Ofsted triennial reports on mathematics:

Mathematics: Understanding the score (2008)[2]

and

Mathematics: Made to measure (2012).[3]

These reports have not been as widely read as they deserved. Their analysis is unusually forthright for official documents, and provides a sobering starting point for any school seeking to review its mathematics provision at Key Stage 3. The reports summarise observations from hundreds of inspections—but they do so in an unusually constructive spirit. For example, having classified half of secondary maths lessons, and more than half of the schemes of work, as being either 'inadequate' or 'requiring improvement', Ofsted went out of their way to provide down-to-earth advice.[4]

This down-to-earth Ofsted DIY guide begins with a four-page table contrasting

- the general features of "good mathematics teaching"

with

- those of "mathematics teaching deemed to require improvement".

The Ofsted guide then presents a string of specific examples chosen to clarify the differences between 'weak' and 'more effective' mathematics teaching, and to challenge schools to reflect on, and to improve, their own teaching. Hence this collection of examples and advice should probably

---

[2] http://webarchive.nationalarchives.gov.uk/20141124154759/http://www.ofsted.gov.uk/resources/mathematics-understanding-score

[3] https://www.gov.uk/government/publications/mathematics-made-to-measure

[4] http://webarchive.nationalarchives.gov.uk/20141124154759/http://www.ofsted.gov.uk/resources/mathematics-understanding-score-improving-practice-mathematics-secondary

be taken seriously by any school seeking to revise its published scheme of work for Key Stage 3.

Key Stage 3 mathematics teaching is important because it marks a transition from the more *informal* approach in primary schools to the formal, *more abstract* mathematics of Key Stage 4 and beyond. Hence those teaching Key Stage 3 classes need a clear picture of how the constituent parts of secondary mathematics interlock, and how Key Stage 3 work can best support progression—first progression to Key Stage 4, and then to Key Stage 5 (at ages 16-18). In this regard the 2012 report *Made to measure* highlights the uncomfortable fact that (p. 4):

> "More than 37,000 pupils who had attained Level 5 at primary school gained no better than grade C at GCSE in 2011. Our failure to stretch some of our most able pupils threatens the future supply of well-qualified mathematicians, scientists and engineers."

This illustrates the extent to which current provision at Key Stage 2 and Key Stage 3 fails to lay the necessary foundations for **subsequent** stages, and raises the question of how to improve provision at Key Stage 3. The question is especially relevant given that so many schools feel unable to allocate their strongest mathematics teachers to Key Stage 3 classes. So there is clearly a need to provide more detailed guidance for those who teach at this level.

The quality of existing support and guidance at school level is summarised in the key findings of the 2008 report *Understanding the score* (p. 6):

> "Schemes of work in secondary schools were frequently poor, and were inadequate to support recently qualified and non-specialist teachers."

The 'Executive Summary' (p. 4) noted:

> "Evidence suggests that strategies to improve test and examination performance, including 'booster' lessons, revision classes and extensive intervention, coupled with a heavy emphasis on 'teaching to the test', succeed in preparing pupils

> to gain the qualifications but **are not equipping them well enough mathematically for their futures**. It is of vital importance to shift from a narrow emphasis on disparate skills towards a focus on pupils' mathematical understanding. Teachers need encouragement to invest in such approaches to teaching." [emphasis added]

And the 'Recommendations' (p. 8) included:

> "Schools should [...]
>
> - enhance schemes of work to include guidance on teaching approaches and activities that promote pupils' understanding and build on their prior learning."

Pages 19–25 of the 2008 report provide useful additional details: Figure 4 on p. 19, and Figure 5 on p. 24 summarise the observed weaknesses in secondary schools, and the surrounding paragraphs make clear suggestions as to what needs attention.

The 2012 report *Made to measure* echoes, and reinforces the concerns expressed in the 2008 report:

p. 9:

> "Teaching was strongest in the Early Years Foundation Stage and upper Key Stage 2 and **markedly weakest in Key Stage 3**." [emphasis added]

p. 18:

> "Learning and progress [...] were **least effective in Key Stage 3**, where only 38% of lessons were good or better and 12% were inadequate" [emphasis added]

p. 19:

> "[...] Quick-fix approaches were particularly popular. Aggressive intervention programmes, regular practice of examination-style questions and extra provision, such as

> revision sessions and subscription to revision websites, **allowed pupils to perform better in examinations than their progress in lessons alone might suggest.**
>
> These tactics account for the rise in attainment at GCSE; this is not matched by better teaching, learning and progress in lessons, or by pupils' deeper understanding of mathematics. In almost every mathematics inspection, inspectors recommended improvements in teaching or curriculum planning, in most cases linked to improving pupils' understanding of mathematics or their ability to use and apply mathematics.
>
> [...] It remains a concern that secondary pupils seemed so readily to accept the view that learning mathematics is important but dull." [emphasis added]

The analysis in this book may be seen as an attempt to help schools respond to one of the main 'Recommendations' in the 2012 report (p. 10):

> "Schools should:
>
> - tackle in-school inconsistency of teaching, making more of it good or outstanding, so that every pupil receives a good mathematics education
> - increase the emphasis on problem solving across the mathematics curriculum
> - develop the expertise of staff:
>   - in choosing teaching approaches and activities that foster pupils' deeper understanding, including through the use of practical resources, visual images and information and communication technology
>   - in checking and probing pupils' understanding during the lesson, and adapting teaching accordingly
>   - in understanding the progression in strands of mathematics over time, so that they know the key knowledge and skills that underpin each stage of learning

- ensuring policies and guidance are backed up by professional development for staff to aid consistency and effective implementation."

The seriousness of the current situation summarised in these two reports, and the weaknesses in the published Key Stage 3 programme of study may explain why these notes and guidance grew into an 'extended essay', rather than being effectively distilled into a punchy DIY manual. Despite (or perhaps because of) this, we hope that all teachers (from those just beginning their careers, or those aiming to take responsibility as Head of Department, to the most experienced practitioners), and those who train teachers will find that what follows provides food for thought, and that schools will find what is presented here helpful in reviewing their current provision in lower secondary school.

2

Key Stage 3: A Study Programme

Schools will naturally try to implement and adapt the published programme as it stands. It is therefore important to decide

- when it is safe simply to copy what is listed;
- when the given list of topics needs to be reordered or supplemented in some way; and
- when there are strong mathematical reasons to *reinterpret* an official requirement (and to clarify in one's own mind why it needs to be reinterpreted).

Hence the remaining sections of this book are presented in the form of a line-by-line commentary (where comment seems needed) on the published programme. The present part, Part II, concentrates

- on the *Aims* etc. which appear on page 2 of the published programmes of study (Section 1 below), and
- on the broad expectations discussed in the section headed *Working mathematically* on pages 4 and 5 of the published programmes of study (Section 2 below).

1. Aims

1.1. [*Aims* p. 2]

Mathematics is an interconnected subject in which pupils need to be able to move fluently between [different] representations and mathematical ideas.

Elementary mathematics derives its power from the way a simple idea sometimes has other interpretations, and from the way simple ideas from different domains can be *combined* to deliver more than one might expect. The published programme of study does not always make it easy to identify these connections and interactions. Hence it is important to consider how to sequence and to link the listed material in a way that clarifies and develops the interdependencies between topics and ideas.

For example, if we consider the most familiar idea of all—namely 'place value'—schools may recognise the need to reinforce:

- how the place value notation for integers works, and how it extends to decimals;
- that it does so in a way that links
  - the more familiar *positive* powers of 10 (tens, hundreds, thousands),
  - with $10^0 = 1$ (the 'units' or '1s' place), and
  - with *negative* powers of 10 (for places to the right of the decimal point);
- the fact that powers of 10 multiply together in a way that foreshadows the index laws for general powers;
- that the written algorithms of column arithmetic, which were developed in primary school for integers, extend naturally to decimals—giving plenty of opportunity to reinforce both the procedures themselves and *why they work*, and hence to strengthen pupils' sense of 'place value'.

Schools will benefit from identifying such recurring themes and important connections for themselves, and from organising the required Key Stage 3 content so that pupils come to appreciate these themes and connections. Some of these are very basic. The next ten bullet points indicate a few selected examples to illustrate the need

- to consider each of the requirements listed in the programme of study,
- to decide what links need to be explicitly mentioned, and
- where possible to include these in any scheme of work.

- The way work with *pure numbers* (that is, numbers like $1, 23, \frac{4}{5}$, or -67.8, stripped of any units), and the arithmetic of integers and decimals, links to simple applications—where purely numerical calculations allow one to solve problems involving *measures*, and to make sense of, and solve, all sorts of 'word problems'.

- The way multiplication and division of decimals and fractions hold the key to routinely solving almost any problem involving rates, or percentages, or ratios, or proportion.

- The way blind calculation gives way to *simplification* and "structural arithmetic", which links naturally to effective calculation in algebra.

- The way "I'm thinking of a number ..." problems should at first be tackled without algebra (as 'inverse mental arithmetic'), but can later be formulated as a simple equation in one unknown, then routinely solved.

- The way any linear *equation* in one unknown x reduces to $ax + b = 0$, with solution $x = -\frac{b}{a}$; and any linear *inequality* in one unknown x reduces either to

  (i) $ax + b > 0$ (or $ax + b \geqslant 0$) with $a > 0$, having solution $x > -\frac{b}{a}$ (or $x \geqslant -\frac{b}{a}$)—i.e. a 'half-line'; or alternatively to

  (ii) $ax + b < 0$ (or $ax + b \leqslant 0$) with $a > 0$.

- The way any linear *equation* $y = mx + c$ in two unknowns x, y corresponds geometrically to the set of all points (x, y) on a straight line, that the line divides the plane into two 'half-planes', and that the solutions of the corresponding linear *inequality* ($y > mx + c$, or $y \geqslant mx + c$) correspond to the set of all points (x, y) in one of these two half-planes.

- The fact that two simultaneous linear equations can be solved exactly, and that the solution is the point of intersection of the two lines corresponding to the linear equations (provided the two lines meet).
- The way short and long division (combined with a little algebra) shows that fractions correspond precisely to terminating or recurring decimals.
- The way the basic property of parallel lines forces the sum of the angles in a triangle to be equal to the sum of the angles at a point on a straight line.
- The way the congruence criterion and the parallel criterion allow us to justify the standard ruler and compass constructions, and to prove the basic facts about areas (of parallelograms and triangles), which lead to a proof that in any right angled triangle the square on the hypotenuse is miraculously equal to the sum of the squares on the other two sides, which then links with coordinate geometry by allowing us to calculate *exactly* the distance between any two given points in 2D or in 3D.

1.2. [*Aims* p. 2]

Pupils should build on Key Stage 2

This is excellent advice—provided it is suitably interpreted. Key Stage 3 has to start out from pupils' experience at Key Stage 2. But this prior experience also needs to be revisited and developed in fresh ways if it is to be used as a reliable foundation for further work. In commenting on this principle, we consider one example in modest detail (1.2.1), then digress to make three important general points (1.2.2–1.2.4), indicate some further examples more briefly (1.2.5), and end with a gentle warning about the likely impact of the Key Stage 2 programme of study on Key Stage 3 (1.2.6).

1.2.1 Mental calculation work should not end with Key Stage 2. It should continue in Year 7, but should increasingly use what pupils know in a way that **exploits structure**, rather than calculating blindly.

- Pupils need to learn to be on the look-out for ways of extracting 10s and 100s in additions such as

$$73 + 48 + 27 = \ldots;$$

  or in multiplications such as

$$14 \times 45 = 7 \times (2 \times 5) \times 9 = 630,$$

  or

$$75 \times 28 = 3 \times (25 \times 4) \times 7 = 2100.$$

- Decimal calculations (such as $7 \times 0.8 = \ldots$, and $12 \times 1.2 = \ldots$, and $0.7 \times 0.08 = \ldots$, and $1.2 \times 1.2 = \ldots$) should be routinely related to their familiar integer equivalents, exploiting opportunities to reflect on how multiplying and dividing by powers of 10 affects the decimal point.

- Common factors among a list of added terms should be seen as an opportunity to 'group' using the distributive law, as in

$$17 \times 23 + 17 \times 7 = 17 \times (23 + 7) = 17 \times 30,$$

  rather than to calculate the left hand side blindly. In general, common factors among terms which are to be added or subtracted, multiplied or divided, should be seen as an opportunity to simplify and to cancel.

- Lots of simple work involving fractions should include (a) switching to common denominators (by scaling up both numerator and denominator) in order to simplify the arithmetic, and (b) moving in the opposite direction when using cancellation to simplify fractions.

Written calculation with integers also needs to be strengthened and extended to decimals—but we shall have more to say on this in Section 1.2.5 below.

1.2.2 In Part I we saw clear evidence (in the two Ofsted reports) of the unfortunate consequences when a Key Stage seeks to maximise performance on immediately impending assessments, and forgets

> that our primary responsibility is always **to prepare pupils for the Key Stages that follow.**

Pressure to "achieve" in the short-term often encourages pupils to become dependent on (and teachers to allow) 'backward-looking' methods that deliver answers in easy cases, but which sooner or later become an obstacle to progress. Hence any internal scheme of work needs to make a clear distinction between

(a) **backward-looking methods** that get answers in the short-term, but which trap pupils in old ways of working (as with finger counting, or idiosyncratic calculation methods, or reducing multiplication to repeated addition, or modelling questions about fractions in terms of pizzas—all of which may have transitional value, but which are known to block later progress if they become too strongly embedded), and

(b) **forward-looking methods**, that may seem unnecessary if the perceived goal is merely to get answers to simple problems at a given stage, but which are important because of the way they reflect the inner structure of elementary mathematics, and are often essential for *progress at the next stage.*

It is not easy for a mere listing of curriculum *content* to capture this crucial distinction. An effective *primary* school is one whose pupils are taught in such a way that allows them to flourish at Key Stages 3 and 4. Similarly, effective teaching at Key Stage 3 prepares the ground for, and leads to solid achievement at Key Stage 4 and beyond. Insofar as the revised programme of study incorporates this idea, it tends to do so in ways that are not immediately apparent, so we shall occasionally comment on how Key Stage 3 material impacts on mathematics at Key Stage 4 and beyond.

1.2.3 The previous subsection drew attention to the distinction between *backward-looking* and *forward-looking* methods. Another important distinction is that between

- a **direct** operation (such as addition, or multiplication, or evaluating powers, or multiplying out brackets), and
- the associated **inverse** operation (such as subtraction, or division, or identifying roots, or factorising).

The distinction may be easier to appreciate if we consider a strictly artificial example—namely the "24 game". Four numbers are given, and each is to be used once. These four numbers may be combined using any three operations chosen from the four rules (with brackets as required), with the goal being to "make 24".

If one is given the starting numbers "3, 3, 4, 4", then one scarcely notices the distinction between

- a 'direct' calculation (such as "Work out $(3 \times 4) + (3 \times 4) = \ldots$"), and
- the 'inverse' challenge of having to "invent for oneself a way to make 24" (let's try "$(3 + 3) + (4 \times 4) = 22$"— not quite; or "$(3 \times 3) + (4 \times 4) = 25$"—nearly; or "$(3 \times 4) + (3 \times 4) = \ldots$").

When faced with the inverse challenge to "make 24 using 3, 3, 4, 4", it is almost as easy to dream up a combination that works as it is to evaluate the expression once it has been invented. But

- evaluating the answer of a given sum is a *direct*, or mechanical, process, whereas
- juggling possibilities to come up with a calculation which produces the required answer of "24" is an *inverse* operation, which is far from mechanical (even if in this case it is rather easy).

The distinction between *direct* and *inverse* operations becomes slightly clearer if the given numbers are "3, 3, 5, 5". Here the *inverse* task of coming up with a sum that delivers the required answer of "24" is significantly harder. The relevant tools are the direct processes of arithmetic—except that it is not clear which to use, so one has to scan what one knows, and select approaches which seem to be the most promising. It is precisely this willingness to juggle intelligently with numbers, and to think flexibly with simple ideas that is needed in many everyday applications. But once one is told what calculation to carry out, then the *direct* calculation "$(5 \times 5) - (3 \div 3)$" is entirely routine.

This distinction between the *direct* operation (which is straightforward, and which requires only that one should implement a given calculation to check that the answer is equal to "24"), and the *inverse* operation (which is much harder, and which here requires us to invent a sum that has the required answer "24"), becomes markedly more clear if one is given the starting numbers 3, 3, 6, 6, and is left to find a way to "make 24" (or if one is given the starting numbers 3, 3, 7, 7; or 3, 3, 8, 8).

To sum up: the reasons why this distinction is important are that

- almost every mathematical technique one learns comes initially in a *direct*, or mechanical, form, but leads naturally to *inverse* problems (as addition leads naturally to subtraction);
- *inverse* problems are usually much more demanding than their *direct* cousins;
- mastery of the *inverse* form depends on a prior robust mastery of the *direct* form;
- **but in the long run, it is the *inverse* operation which is generally more important.**

Those who complain that pupils, or school leavers, cannot "use" what they are supposed to know, often fail to notice that what pupils have been taught (and what has been assessed) has usually focused on *direct* procedures, whereas what is required is the ability to think more flexibly when faced with some kind of *inverse* problem. Inverse problems often come in different forms, or variations something that has been a focal point of the recent teacher exchanges with Shanghai, where the idea of "exercises with variation" has emerged as a recurring didactical theme

Given this, one might expect formal assessments to include a strong focus on ensuring mastery of the many *inverse* operations and the ability to solve the standard inverse problems in elementary school mathematics. In reality, *inverse* processes have been neglected, or (worse) have been distorted by providing ready-made intermediate stepping stones that reduce every *inverse* problem to a sequence of *direct* steps. Why is this?

Direct operations are relatively easy to teach, and to assess. The associated *inverse* operations may be more important, but they are **harder to assess**. *Inverse* problems are more demanding, and cannot be reduced to deterministic methods. So they give rise to **low scores**, and they do so in a way that is hard to predict. This makes them distinctly awkward for those who devise test items within a target-driven and test-driven culture, where the assessors may be contractually obliged to return predictable results, and to avoid low scores. Hence, if such problems are set at all, they are usually adapted in some way to make pupil performance more predictable (for example, by breaking down the unpredictable *inverse* problem into a more manageable sequence of steps—each of which is essentially a routine *direct* task).

Teachers need to recognise the importance of such problems for pupils' subsequent progress, and then devote sufficient time to them for pupils to achieve a degree of mastery. But it would obviously help if assessments regularly required, and rewarded, such mastery!

1.2.4 The bald listing of content in the official programme of study is rather dry and formal—focusing on "what" rather than "how". In one sense, this emphasis is healthy. But it ignores the essential interplay between **content** and **didactics**.

Procedural fluency is rightly stressed. But this emphasis is too often repeated in isolation—as though a robust grasp of place value (for example) will emerge spontaneously as a result of banging on about fluency in specified procedures. It won't. So something more is needed. If it is to serve as a useful guide, a content list or programme of study needs to be constructed in a way that indicates, and supports, a clear underlying "didactical architecture". In contrast, the given programme of study routinely misses the opportunity to convey key central principles (such as the contrast between *backward-looking* and *forward-looking* methods, or between *direct* and *inverse* operations), and important details (such as the key didactical stages which can lead from:

(a) talking about "half a pint" or "half an hour" in Year 2, to competence with the arithmetic of fractions in Year 9; or
(b) from meeting negative quantities for the first time in Key Stage 2, to calculating freely with negative numbers, and simplifying expressions

which combine subtraction and minus signs in algebra at Key Stage 3/4).

1.2.5 In early Key Stage 3 we need to reinforce Key Stage 2 work on the familiar written arithmetical procedures for *integers* in order to extend them to more serious long multiplication, to division, and to decimals. Column arithmetic for integers provides an excellent opportunity to cement number bonds and multiplication tables. It also develops the ability to carry out a sequence of simple steps completely reliably. The extension of these procedures to decimals provides fresh opportunities to address 'place value'. At the simplest level, pupils need to understand why it is essential to align the units and tens "places" when carrying out column addition and subtraction of integers, so that the requirement to align the decimal points when adding and subtracting decimals is recognised as being essential (see example 1.2.2C "$42.65 + 5.748 = \ldots$" in Part III). The *logic* of short and long multiplication will also need to be clarified before these procedures are extended to decimals. Integer arithmetic (including mental arithmetic in both direct and inverse forms with all variations) also needs to be in good shape before we extend integer arithmetic to fractions.

The extension of long multiplication and division to decimals may need to be slightly delayed. When they are addressed, pupils need first to know how the decimal point behaves under multiplication and division by powers of 10, so that they can understand how this allows multiplication and division of *decimals* to be transformed into *integer* multiplication and division.

Short and long division develop *the inverse* of multiplication, in that they require pupils to use what they know about multiplication in a flexible way. When asked to divide 17 onto 918, the initial *inverse* question:

> "How many times does 17 go into 91? And what is the remainder?"

requires greater mental agility than the two *direct* questions:

> "What is 17×5?", and "What is $91 - 85$?".

Short and long division also require pupils to string together *a chain of steps*, each of which is accessible, but where the whole chain has to be implemented 100% reliably for the process as a whole to succeed. And the power of the process becomes apparent when one discovers how it extends naturally to allow division of decimals. Later the division process helps to establish the remarkable connection between fractions and decimals.

Some pupils will benefit from the challenge of tackling (or extending their prior facility with) serious long division. This topic is listed in Key Stage 2 *for all pupils*. It is unclear what effect this may have; but we may well find that serious long division is appropriate for only around half of the cohort, even at Key Stage 3.

1.2.6 In exhorting teachers at Key Stage 3 to "build on Key Stage 2" it is only fair to mention that the Key Stage 2 programme of study may prove problematic in some respects. A preliminary indication of the extent of this difficulty may be gleaned from an earlier paper.[5] In particular

- a significant amount of material has been included at Key Stage 2 in a way that is likely to prove premature; and
- some of the listed topics which are entirely appropriate in Year 5 and 6 have been specified rather poorly.

Hence one can anticipate that many pupils entering Key Stage 3 will have at best a superficial grasp of some of the listed content from Key Stage 2.

Among the listed topics that are inappropriate and unnecessary in Year 6, many are implicit in the early Key Stage 3 programme of study, so could be safely delayed until Year 7. Some primary schools may recognise this and concentrate on more age-appropriate material—leaving other content to be treated more effectively at Key Stage 3. But many schools will go by the book and will try to cover whatever is listed—with predictable consequences. For both groups, this problematic material will need to be revisited at Key Stage 3 in order to establish a secure platform for progression. Examples of topics which may have been 'covered' at Key Stage 2, but which will need serious attention in Years 7 and 8 include:

- the extension of place value to decimals;

---

[5] http://education.lms.ac.uk/wp-content/uploads/2012/02/DMG_4_no_3_2013.pdf

- the arithmetic of decimals;
- work with measures—especially compound measures;
- the arithmetic of fractions;
- ratio and proportion;
- the use of negative numbers;
- work with coordinates in all four quadrants;
- simple algebra.

1.3. [*Aims* p. 2]

> **Decisions about progression should be based on the security of pupils' understanding and their readiness to progress to the next stage.**

Secondary schools will need to know how this excellent principle of "readiness to progress" has been handled at Key Stage 2. We give just one example of many.

There is a general welcome for the requirement that pupils should learn (i.e. know, and be able to use) their tables. But there is unanimity that this will not be achieved by the end of Year 4 as specified in the official programme of study, and that a more realistic objective may be to expect most pupils to achieve this by the end of Year 5 or Year 6. Hence material listed in Year 5 and Year 6 that depends on '**prior** mastery of tables' will not be accessible at the expected stage, so will prove unrealistic at that level. (For example, until tables are secure, one is limited in what one can achieve in factorising integers, finding HCFs, working with prime numbers, with short division and long division, with squares and cubes, with equivalent fractions and with cancellation.)

If primary schools feel obliged to try to teach inappropriately ambitious material purely because it is officially listed, this will lead to problems that are entirely avoidable. Thus secondary schools may have to encourage their feeder primary schools to trust their professional judgement in such matters, and to recognise those aspects of the Year 6 programme where work should remain 'preparatory', with a serious treatment being delayed until Year 7.

Some of the material that is listed in Key Stage 2 seems inappropriate at that level—partly because we know that it is hard to teach it well even at Key Stage 3. For example, it may make sense at Key Stage 2 to use symbols to summarise familiar formulae: such as re-writing the verbal equation

"(area of a rectangle) = (length times breadth)" as "$A = l \times b$".

However, it would be premature to expect most primary pupils to learn more serious *elementary algebra* (and most primary teachers are in no position to teach it effectively). And while there is every reason to engage pupils at Key Stage 2 in tackling "I'm thinking of a number ..." problems, they are best addressed at that age by using '*inverse* mental arithmetic': that is, where the missing number is discovered by using intelligent, flexible, *inverse* mental arithmetic, rather than by prematurely trying to formulate such problems algebraically as *equations* (as suggested by the official Year 6 programme listed under *Algebra*).

Even where secondary schools liaise effectively with most of their feeder primaries, they should think carefully—as part of ensuring "readiness to progress"—how to consolidate key ideas and techniques from Key Stage 2 in early Key Stage 3, and should be prepared to clear up misunderstandings that may have arisen as a result of material having been introduced prematurely.

A key application of this crucial principle of "readiness to progress" arises because the Key Stage 3 programme of study is now an explicit part of the GCSE specification. Hence decisions about progress through the Key Stage 3 curriculum are bound up with *decisions about future GCSE entry*. The Key Stage 4 programme of study states explicitly:

> **Together the mathematical content set out in the Key Stage 3 and Key Stage 4 programmes of study covers the full range of material contained in the GCSE Mathematics qualification. Wherever it is appropriate, given pupils' security of understanding and readiness to progress, pupils should be taught the full content set out in this programme of study.**

In its understated way this both presents a challenge to teach *as much of the listed material as possible* to as many pupils as possible, and at the same time leaves considerable scope for teachers to use their professional experience to decide *where this aspiration may not be "appropriate"*.

Those pupils who should progress comfortably to GCSE Higher tier may be able to swallow the complete Key Stage 3 programme **by the end of Year 9**. But those who may land up taking Foundation tier GCSE will often benefit from proceeding **more slowly** through Key Stage 3 in order to establish a solid foundation for those parts of the Key Stage 4 programme which they might subsequently manage to cover, and perhaps master. In other words, schools would seem to be free to interpret the Key Stage 3 programme *as part of GCSE*, and to allow some material to spill over into Year 10 where this seems appropriate. Those pupils heading for Foundation tier are far more likely to achieve mastery of some of this material if they are allowed to proceed more steadily (e.g. taking four years rather than three), than if they are forced to cover the material prematurely, and then have to repeat it.

1.4. [*Aims* p. 2]

> **Pupils who grasp concepts rapidly should be challenged through being offered rich and sophisticated problems before any acceleration through new content in preparation for Key Stage 4. Those who are not sufficiently fluent**

should consolidate their understanding, including through additional practice, before moving on.

The second sentence reinforces the comments made at the end of 1.3 above.

The first sentence advises against acceleration. It also highlights the fact that each listed topic can be treated on *many levels*, and states the important general principle that those who grasp a basic concept should be faced **with more challenging variations on the same material** before they move ahead. This is an extension of the idea of "readiness to progress": namely that

> **before allowing pupils to progress to more advanced topics, we should routinely expect a much deeper understanding on the part of those who might one day proceed further.**

At present we routinely let down large numbers of pupils by failing to establish a sufficiently robust mastery of important basic ideas. For example, the very first item under *Number* (*Subject content* p. 5: see Part III, section 1) states that pupils should

understand and use place value for decimals, measures and integers of any size.

Other requirements under the sub-heading *Number* relate to calculating with fractions, working with percentages, and simple algebra. But the evidence is that, even when teaching such basic material we in England have expected far too little—including from our more able pupils. Consider the following items, given to Year 9 pupils in around 50 different countries as part of the major international comparison TIMSS 2011:[6]

[6] http://timss.bc.edu/timss2011/

1.4A Which fraction is equivalent to 0.125?

A: $\frac{125}{100}$ B: $\frac{125}{1000}$ C: $\frac{125}{10000}$ D: $\frac{125}{100000}$

1.4B Which number is equal to $\frac{3}{5}$?

A: 0.8 B: 0.6 C: 0.53 D: 0.35

1.4C $\frac{4}{100} + \frac{3}{1000} =$

A: 0.043 B: 0.1043 C: 0.403 D: 0.43

1.4D The fractions $\frac{4}{14}$ and $\frac{\dots}{21}$ are equivalent. What is the value of $\dots$?

A: 6 B: 7 C: 11 D: 14

1.4E Which of these number sentences is true?

A: $\frac{3}{10}$ of $50 = 50\%$ of 3 B: 3% of 50 = 6% of 100

C: $50 \div 30 = 30 \div 50$ D: $\frac{3}{10} \times 50 = \frac{5}{10} \times 30$

1.4F Which shows a correct method for finding $\frac{1}{3} - \frac{1}{4}$?

A: $\frac{1-1}{4-3}$ B: $\frac{1}{4-3}$ C: $\frac{3-4}{3 \times 4}$ D: $\frac{4-3}{3 \times 4}$

1.4G Write $3\frac{5}{6}$ in decimal form rounded to 2 decimal places.

1.4H Simplify the expression

$$\frac{3x}{8} + \frac{x}{4} + \frac{x}{2}.$$

Show your work.

Success rates are never easy to interpret. But it seems sensible to compare the success rates for Year 9 pupils in England with those in Russia, in Hungary, in the USA, and in Australia rather than with countries from the Far East (for the released items and the corresponding results, see http://timss.bc.edu/timss2011/international-released-items.html). We note that:

- in Russia, children start school only at age 7, and in Hungary at age 6;
- the primary curriculum in Russia may include the idea of fractional parts, and the link with decimals, but calculation with fractions would seem to begin only in secondary school;
- tasks 1.4A–1.4F are multiple-choice questions with just four options, and some of the options could never be obtained as a result of making a mistake (which suggests that the English success rates for 1.4A–1.4C are already embarrassing).

1.4A Russia 86%, USA 76%, Hungary 74%, Australia 67%, England 62%;

1.4B Russia 84%, USA 83%, Australia 70%, Hungary 67%, England 59%;

1.4C Russia 83%, Australia 68%, Hungary 63%, USA 63%, England 57%;

1.4D Russia 62%, USA 55%, Hungary 49%, Australia 45%, England 43%;

1.4E Russia 58%, Hungary 53%, Australia 36%, USA 36%, England 33%;

1.4F Russia 63%, Australia 34%, Hungary 33%, USA 29%, England 28%;

1.4G Russia 39%, Australia 31%, Hungary 29%, USA 29%, England 24%;

1.4H Russia 35%, Hungary 34%, USA 19%, Australia 14%, England 9%.

The implication of these comparisons would seem to be that we in England

- are failing to achieve basic competence even for our more able pupils,
- that we routinely allow (or even encourage) pupils to move on to some "higher level" before basic material has been properly understood, and
- that we need to *slow down* and routinely use **slightly harder** and more varied problems to probe and strengthen pupils' understanding before they move on in this way.

This inference was supported by the recent ICCAMS study which set a sample of 15 year olds in English schools problems that had been used in a similar study in the late 1970s. We give just two examples:

> **1.4J** On the motorway my car can go 41.8 miles on each gallon of petrol. How many miles can I expect to travel on 8.37 gallons? [Six calculations involving 41.8 and 8.37 were given, and the relevant calculation was to be 'circled', not implemented.]

30 years ago **54%** of 14 year olds managed to circle 8.37×41.8; now **only 33%** manage this.

> **1.4K** Six tenths written as a decimal is 0.6. How would you write eleven tenths as a decimal?

30 years ago **36%** managed to write 1.1; now **just 16%** of 14 year olds respond correctly.

The message would seem to be clear. We need to do much more work with the **most basic** material to ensure that pupils grasp the relevant concepts. *The last thing our more able pupils need is to be accelerated.* They need to slow down, and to strengthen their understanding by tackling **harder**, and more varied, problems involving the same material as their peers. In particular, notwithstanding the wording of the requirement at the start of Section 1.4, able pupils may need challenges that are surprisingly basic, before they are confronted with material that is "rich and sophisticated".

The need to replace a philosophy of premature "acceleration" by a strategy of deepening and strengthening was strongly argued in the recent ACME report *Raising the bar.*[7] Any mathematics department which appreciates the importance of avoiding acceleration, but which anticipates being challenged by parents, or by senior management, will find valuable support in this report.

Ministerial advice regarding early GCSE entry has recently changed to reflect the same position. This change in official policy is partly based on overwhelming evidence. The instructive paper,[8] which was prepared by the Department for Education for the House of Commons Select Committee, contains some astonishing statistics that should also help to convince sceptical parents and management that acceleration incurs substantial human and resource costs with no evident benefits. Indeed, those who take GCSE early rarely benefit as a result.

This recent shift in policy is in line with the longstanding professional consensus, which was first stated in the analysis and the recommendations of the old report *Acceleration or enrichment*? (2000).[9]

2. Working mathematically

This section of the official programme of study contains eighteen bullet points under three headings: *Develop fluency, Reason mathematically,* and *Solve problems.* Many of these bullet points appear relatively unproblematic. Hence we restrict our remarks to those requirements that invite comment.

2.1. [*Develop fluency,* p. 4]

The list of themes referred to in the bullet points under this sub-heading in the official programme of study needs to be further supplemented: e.g. at

---

7 http://www.acme-uk.org/media/10498/raisingthebar.pdf

8 http://www.parliament.uk/documents/commons-committees/Education/MemoSelectCommitteeGCSEMultipleEntryFinal.pdf

9 http://education.lms.ac.uk/wp-content/uploads/2012/02/Acceleration_or_Enrichment_15Aug12.pdf

present there is no mention of measures, or of ratio and proportion, or of word problems, or of geometry.

In recent years those who decided what a typical pupil in England should be expected to learn have downplayed the importance of *memorisation*, and of *fluency*. Yet there are all sorts of reasons why we need to learn certain things **by heart**, and in general to achieve much higher levels of fluency. The word "fluency" is not quite the same as raw speed; but fluency, and the related notions of "learning by heart" and "automaticity", are useful indicators of understanding and mastery.

Memory contributes significantly to what we are, and to what we can do. We need to be completely on top of that limited collection of *basic facts* and techniques in terms of which most elementary mathematics can be understood. But we need to memorise far more than this. For example, when tackling an unfamiliar problem, one must be able

- to consider and choose between possible approaches and to compare the alternative intermediate steps in order to assess what seems to be the most promising strategy; and
- to achieve this, the possible steps or techniques need to be robustly internalised and immediately accessible.

Where a pupil struggles to use an idea, or fails to implement a learned procedure quickly and reliably, one can infer either that *the ingredient steps* need to be strengthened, or that more time needs to be devoted to *integrating these steps* into an effective method (or both).

When faced with routine inverse problems (such as "simplify $\frac{36}{54}$"; or "factorise $x^4 - 7x^2 + 1$"; or "make 24 with $3, 3, 5, 5$; or with $3, 3, 6, 6$; or with $3, 3, 7, 7$; or with $3, 3, 8, 8$"), one cannot begin unless the relevant direct facts are immediately to hand. Only then do we have a chance of recognising the relevance of those direct facts.

- We need immediate recognition that $36 = 4 \times 9$ and $54 = 6 \times 9$ in order to "simplify $\frac{36}{54} = \frac{4}{6} = \frac{2}{3}$".
- Given "3, 3, 5, 5 to make 24" we need to notice immediately that "5×5" is "close to 24", and then that "$3 \div 3$" makes up the difference.

- Later (at Key Stage 4 or beyond), unless the identity

$$(a^2 - b^2) = (a - b)(a + b)$$

is second nature, we are most unlikely to notice that

$$x^4 - 7x^2 + 1 = (x^2 + 1)^2 - 9x^2 = (x^2 - 3x + 1)(x^2 + 3x + 1).$$

That is, we need to memorise enough to enable us to respond flexibly.

What you don't know by heart, and so can't access instantly, you can't use.

This observation applies not only to facts (such as $36 = 4 \times 9$, and $5 \times 5 = 25$), but also to *procedures*. That is, we need to attain **fluency** in handling a wide range of arithmetical, algebraic, trigonometric and geometrical procedures, so that each new procedure can eventually be exercised *automatically*, quickly, and accurately. Once this level of **automaticity** is achieved, the brain is free to focus on those more demanding aspects of a problem that require genuine thought (such as trying to see whether $x^4 - 7x^2 + 1$ can be written as a difference of two squares).

2.1.1 [*Develop fluency* p. 4]:

- **consolidate their numerical and mathematical capability from Key Stage 2 and extend their understanding of the number system and place value to include decimals, fractions, powers and roots**
- **select and use appropriate calculation strategies to solve increasingly complex problems**

2.1.1.1 Consolidating Key Stage 2 work, and choosing and using appropriate calculation strategies should start immediately in Year 7. In particular, **mental** work should continue, but should move beyond idiosyncratic methods (which may have been quite rightly encouraged at some stage, but which should then have moved on to more efficient methods) towards *structural arithmetic* in preparation for algebra. (The meaning of "structural arithmetic" is explained briefly in Subsection 2.1.1.2.)

There should also be a continuing thread of *word problems*, through which pupils learn to extract information from given text and to

> "select and use appropriate calculation strategies to solve ...problems".

(What is meant by "word problems" is outlined in Section 2.3 *Solve problems*, and in particular in Subsection 2.3.3.)

Particular attention should be paid

- to pupils' facility in working with decimals as an extension of earlier work with integers, including a robust grasp of
  (a) the "transition across boundaries" (from 0.9 to 1.0, or from 1.19 to 1.20, or from 2.99 to 3.0, etc.),
  (b) multiplying by a suitable power of 10 to change decimals into integers and conversely,
  (c) translating decimals into fractions and vice versa,
  (d) adding and subtracting fractions and decimals (see the ICCAMS and TIMSS examples 1.4A–1.4K above, and example 1.2.2C in Part III);
- to consolidating long multiplication and short division, and *simple* long division for integers;
- to extending the standard written arithmetical procedures for *integers to decimals* (column addition and subtraction, short and long multiplication and short division)—using these procedures to reinforce the idea of place value, and to solve word problems and other problems involving measures;
- linking division to quotients, or fractions, so that pupils understand how decimal division can be effected by multiplying both divisor and dividend by a suitable power of 10 to change the divisor into an integer.

2.1.1.2 We end this subsection by explaining briefly what we refer to as *structural arithmetic*. One feature of mathematics teaching at all levels is the need to re-visit topics and methods which have been previously learned, in order to think about familiar things in new ways. As long as one avoids simply repeating what was done before, much may be gained from time spent revising and strengthening vaguely familiar ideas, language, and methods—even when the material has already been well taught. Where pupils failed to grasp a topic at the first encounter, subsequent re-visiting and revision is essential if they are to progress; and those pupils who appeared to understand things the first time round can always benefit from re-visiting basic material *in the right spirit*.

The 2003, 2007, and 2011 results from TIMSS (a 4-yearly study of school mathematics in different countries) revealed a significant improvement in *average* success rates among **Year 5** pupils in England when tackling internationally designed test items. The natural response was to see this as constituting resounding support for the extensive efforts that had gone into the early *Numeracy Strategy*. But closer inspection (for example, of those problems where English pupils performed less well) suggested that these improved average scores

- derived mainly from success on relatively simple tasks, where correct answers could be obtained using "backward-looking" methods, and that
- pupils in Year 5 struggled with precisely the material that is most relevant to subsequent progress at Key Stage 3.

This impression was reinforced by the fact that **the apparent improvement in average Year 5 scores was not reflected in any corresponding improvement at Year 9** (even though the 2007 Year 9 sample was from exactly the same cohort as the 2003 Year 5 sample; and the 2011 Year 9 sample was from exactly the same cohort as the 2007 Year 5 sample). If this analysis is correct, then we clearly need to focus our mathematics teaching rather differently, so that our approach to the content being taught in Years 5–8 *actively prepares the ground* for the way elementary mathematics will develop subsequently.

In particular, at the interface between Key Stage 2 and Key Stage 3 the approach to mental calculation needs to move beyond methods designed solely to "get the answer". As the range of numbers in calculations expands (to include arbitrarily large integers, decimals, fractions, and surds), most of the expressions one could conceivably be asked to calculate are so messy that they cannot be easily evaluated or simplified. Something similar occurs in algebra when, during Key Stage 3 and Key Stage 4, the possible algebraic structure of the expressions to be manipulated gets progressively more complicated. Attention then shifts away from working with "expressions in general" and concentrates on expressions whose "structure" allows them to be evaluated or simplified. Progress in mathematics then depends more and more on learning to use the *algebraic rules* which sometimes allow one to *simplify* unexpectedly. Hence from Key Stage 2 onwards, calculation should begin to move beyond bare hands evaluation, and should concentrate on developing

- flexibility in looking for ways to exploit *place value* (as in $73 + 48 + 27 = \ldots$, or $17.18 + 7460 + 22.82 = \ldots$), and
- an awareness of the algebraic *structure* lurking just beneath the surface of so many numerical or symbolical expressions [as in $3 \times 17 + 7 \times 17 = \ldots$, or $\frac{6\times 15}{10} = \ldots$, or $16 \times 17 - 3 \times 34 = \ldots$, or $6(a-b) + 3(2b-a) = \ldots$].

This habit of looking for, and then exploiting, **algebraic** structure in **numerical** work is what we call *structural arithmetic*.

2.1.2 [*Develop fluency* p. 4]:

> **use algebra to generalise the structure of arithmetic, including to formulate mathematical relationships**

Elementary algebra does not really "*generalise* the structure of arithmetic" as suggested in the above official requirement: algebra **copies** the structure of arithmetic *exactly* (that is, the four rules, together with the commutative laws, the associative laws, and the distributive law) and *applies it to a new "mixed universe"* of symbols (or letters) and numbers. Thus it is not the *structure* that is generalised, but the *universe* to which the old structure is applied.

This new domain of "elementary algebra" has several distinct aspects, or sub-domains, each of which sheds a slightly different light upon the subject.

Some of these sub-domains are more natural for beginners than others. The four most obvious ones—in approximate order of sophistication—are *formulae, equations, expressions,* and *identities.*

- *Formulae.* Here letters are used in place of familiar entities (e.g. $A = l \times b$ for the area A of a rectangle of length l and breadth b; or $C = 2\pi r$ for the circumference C of a circle of radius r). In each such formula, the letters can take different numerical values. The simplest formulae (such as $C = 2\pi r$) are rather like the simplest calculations that we meet at Key Stages 1 and 2, in that they tell us how the value of one entity (the circumference C) can be calculated once we know the values of certain others (the radius r).

- *Equations.* The first *equations* one meets involve a single letter (often denoted by "x"). This letter is usually referred to as the "unknown". An equation can be interpreted as a constraint which some unknown number "x" has to satisfy. Later one meets equations, and even pairs of equations, linking two or more "unknowns" (or "variables"). In all cases the strategy is the same: namely to transform the equations *using the rules of algebra* in a way that pins down the "unknown number (or numbers)" more precisely than was apparent in the original equation (or equations).

- *Expressions.* Given a formula, such as $C = 2\pi r$, we very soon want to move the letters around. For example:

  - Suppose we use string to measure the circumference C of a tall cylindrical lamp post and want to calculate the radius r (a length which we cannot measure directly). We then need to re-write the formula as $r = \frac{C}{2\pi}$ so that we can calculate r as soon as we know the value of the circumference C.
  - Or we may want to "expand" $(x+4)(x+2)$ or $(x+3)^2$; or to rewrite the quadratic equation "$x^2 + 6x + 8 = 0$" by "factorising" the LHS to get "$(x+4)(x+2) = 0$", or by "completing the square" to get "$(x+3)^2 - 1 = 0$".

In all these settings we need to know how to work with *expressions* made up of letters, and to transform them "as if the letters stood for numbers" (since this is exactly what the letters represent).

The fourth subdomain of elementary algebra—*identities*—is not mentioned explicitly in the Key Stage 3 programme of study. But it has already arisen in the previous bullet point; and it is highlighted by the later Key Stage 3 requirement (see Part III, section 2.4 below)

> "to simplify and manipulate algebraic expressions **to maintain equivalence**" [emphasis added].

Hence this subdomain is bound to arise in Key Stage 3, even if it is more evident at Key Stage 4 and beyond.

- *Identities*: In primary arithmetic the = sign at first tends to connect some required calculation such as "$13 + 29$" (on the left hand side) with the answer "42" (on the right hand side): $13 + 29 = 42$. But the = sign then broadens its meaning and is used to connect *any two numerically equivalent expressions*—such as "$13 + 29 = 6 \times 7$", or "$6^2 - 1 = 5 \times 7$", or "$\frac{28}{42} = \frac{10}{15}$". Something similar arises in the algebra of expressions, where pupils first learn that, given a jumble of symbols on the left hand side, one is expected to *simplify* it in some way and set it "equal" to something a bit like an "answer" (on the right hand side). For example one might be given an expression such as

$$\left(\frac{x}{x-1} - \frac{x+1}{x}\right)^{-1}$$

and be expected to rewrite it as "$= x^2 - x$" (or as "$= x(x-1)$"). However one later broadens this use of the equals sign so that "=" simply links two expressions that are "algebraically equivalent"—that is, where one side can be transformed into the other side via the rules of algebra. Any such equation that links two expressions that are algebraically equivalent is called an *identity*.

Pupils become aware of these four subdomains gradually, generally starting with formulae, then equations and expressions. The goal throughout should be to establish two main principles:

- letters are essentially placeholders for numbers, and so are subject only to the laws of arithmetic (or algebra);
- in formulae and equations, the letters can take any values that are consistent with the constraint expressed by the formula or equation; in an expression or identity the only constraints are the laws of arithmetic—so the x in "$\frac{1}{x}$" cannot be set $= 0$, but otherwise the letters can be replaced by any values whatsoever, as long as different instances of the same letter are given the same value.

2.1.3 [*Develop fluency* p. 4]:

> **substitute values into expressions, rearrange and simplify expressions, and solve equations**

2.1.3.1 The requirement in 2.1.3 reinforces the immediately preceding bullet point. In an equation, the letters are constrained, so can only take **particular** (as yet unknown) values.

- In contrast, the letters in an algebraic *expression* are only required to satisfy the rules of arithmetic (or of algebra), *so can be replaced by* ***any*** *numbers whatsoever* (provided they are not clearly "forbidden values"—such as those that would make a denominator equal to zero).

Many pupils never grasp this fact, and so move letters around without realising that they are little more than placeholders for numbers, and must be treated as such. Pupils need more experience of **substituting given numerical values for the letters in an expression**, in order to internalise the idea that a letter can be given any value *provided all occurrences of the same letter are given the same value*. The act of substituting and evaluating also provides opportunities

- to exercise mental arithmetic, and
- to check that standard algebraic notation (juxtaposition as multiplication, brackets, powers, the fraction bar notation, priority of operations, etc.) is translated correctly when calculating with numbers.

Moreover, evaluating expressions in this way begins to convey the key idea that

- each choice of *inputs* gives rise to a single, determined *output* value for the expression.

That is, such expressions provide the simplest examples of what we will later call a *function* (of its component variables).

2.1.3.2 The expression "rearrange and simplify" in the quote at the start of 2.1.3 gives a slightly misleading impression. Algebra almost never involves "rearranging" for the sake of it: one "rearranges" the terms of a compound expression for a reason—and that reason is almost always **to simplify** in some way. We are formally allowed to rearrange, or to manipulate, expressions in any way that respects the rules of algebra; but in practice we ignore almost all rearrangements, and focus on those which seem likely to lead to a more manageable, or "simpler", result. Hence "rearrange and simplify" might have been better expressed as

"rearrange *in order* to simplify".

In any event it is clear that pupils need more exercises (and *class discussion*) to help them learn what kinds of outputs are mathematically "simpler" (such as "fully cancelled" expressions, or those in "fully factorised" form), and to understand when and why the simpler forms are to be preferred.

2.1.3.3 The requirement at the start of Subsection 2.1.3 ends with three innocent-looking words: "and solve equations". In mathematics the expression "solve equations" strictly means "solve **exactly**"—by algebraic methods. We delay further comment on exactly what this means until Subsection 2.2.2.2. However, once this basic notion is understood, it can be modified, or re-interpreted in other fruitful ways.

The first such reinterpretation is to interpret the equations and the solving process *geometrically*. This reinterpretation does not help in the solution process itself, but it gives rise to interesting applications; it also provides a valuable alternative way of thinking about what is going on.

A different variation on the idea of "solving an equation" arises when we have no obvious way of finding an *exact* solution. It is then worth looking for effective ways of "getting close to" the elusive exact solution—that is, to find an *approximate* solution. The standard way to do this is to devise a process which allows us to "creep up on" a solution by generating a sequence which approaches the exact solution ever more closely. And the preferred kind of process is one which always takes the output from the previous step and operates on it in the same way to get the next approximation. This kind of repetition of a single process is called "iteration"—an idea which appears unannounced in the GCSE specification.[10] There, in item 20 under the heading *Number*, we read:

> **find approximate solutions to equations numerically using iteration;**

and in item 16 of *Ratio, proportion, and rates of change* we read:

> **work with general iterative processes.**

There is no officially required preparatory work at Key Stage 3. However, when finding approximate points of intersection of two straight lines, or of the graph of a curve and the x-axis, it may make sense to alert pupils to the desirability of having a deterministic numerical (rather than graphical) process that finds such solutions to any required degree of accuracy. At the same time one can prepare the ground as part of work with sequences, by exploring the behaviour of standard sequences that "converge" (such as $x_n = \left(\frac{1}{10}\right)^n$, or $x_n = \left(\frac{1}{2}\right)^n$, or $x_n = 1 - \left(-\frac{1}{2}\right)^n$, or $x_n = \frac{n-1}{n}$), and others that "diverge" (such as $x_n = 10^n$, or $x_n = 2^n$).

The geometrical interpretation of the meaning of "solve" arises because algebraic equations correspond to geometrical curves or surfaces. This important link between algebra and geometry was forged by Descartes (1596-1650), who in 1637 showed that solving an equation corresponds to

---

[10] https://www.gov.uk/government/publications/gcse-mathematics-subject-content-and-assessment-objectives

- looking for points on a curve or surface where some expression takes a particular value (as with contour lines on an Ordinance Survey map); or
- looking for points where a curve or surface intersects a line (such as the x-axis), or a plane.

Hence the solutions of an equation, or of a system of equations, can be thought of as the coordinates of some point or points where two or more curves, or surfaces, meet. This is a powerful idea which can help to explain, for example,

- why some quadratic equations, such as $x^2 + 1 = 0$, have no solutions (because the curve $y = x^2 + 1$ never crosses the x-axis—that is, the line "$y = 0$"),
- why other quadratic equations, such as $x^2 = 0$, have just one solution (because the curve $y = x^2$ *touches* the x axis "$y = 0$"), and
- why many quadratic equations, such as $x^2 - 1 = 0$, have exactly two solutions (because the curve $y = x^2 - 1$ cuts the x-axis "$y = 0$" in two points: $(-1,0)$ and $(1,0)$).

The geometrical interpretation makes it possible for pupils to engage the *hand* and the *eye* to draw the relevant curves and to find the approximate coordinates of the points which correspond to solutions of the given equation(s)—a process that can help the *brain* to make sense of the **exact** algebraic solution process, which might otherwise remain a purely abstract idea. Without the insights provided by this geometrical interpretation, pupils can all too easily misapply the rules of algebra—even with such simple examples as:

- $x = x^2$ (where thoughtless cancellation can easily lead one to lose the solution $x = 0$). If we interpret solutions of this equation as the two points $(0,0)$ and $(1,1)$ where the familiar curves $y = x$ and $y = x^2$ cross, this can illustrate the error, can underline the importance of only cancelling factors which are never zero, and can help to reinforce the reasons for the standard algebraic method (when dealing with quadratics and higher powers) of "taking everything to one side and factorising".

The same idea applies to less familiar equations such as

- $x = 2x^4$ (or $x = 3x^5$) where one can again consider the *two* points where the curves $y = x$ and $y = 2x^4$ cross (or the *three* points where the curves $y = x$ and $y = 3x^5$ cross).

Later one can apply the same idea to $\cos x = 1$, to $\sin x = \frac{1}{2}$, or to $x = \tan x$, to see that each equation has *infinitely many* solutions.

Sketching the lines or curves corresponding to two equations can allow one to find approximate solutions by estimating the coordinates of the points where the lines or curves intersect. This kind of geometrical visualisation is didactically and *psychologically* invaluable. But it is not a logical, or mathematical way of actually "solving the equation"—any more than the unknown length of the hypotenuse of a right angled triangle with legs of lengths 3 and 4 (or a and b) can be mathematically calculated by drawing an approximate 3 by 4 rectangle (or an a by b rectangle) and then *measuring* the diagonal.

2.2. Reason mathematically

2.2.1 [*Reason mathematically* p. 4]:

extend and formalise their knowledge of ratio and proportion

The words "ratio" and "proportion" are here used correctly! But they are so often used incorrectly that we go into considerable detail (here and in Part III, Section 1.9) to explain the background that is needed if pupils are to "formalise their knowledge of ratio and proportion". We should perhaps stress that our comments throughout are designed to provide food-for-thought for teachers, and are not intended to constitute a teaching sequence for pupils.

Elementary mathematics comes into its own (and needs to be seriously *taught*!) as soon as we take the step from addition to *multiplication*. Ratios are the quintessential "multiplicative relations", and work with ratios links naturally to work with fractions.

The basic "knowledge of ratio and proportion" which all pupils need to build on is relatively familiar and accessible to all: so all can make some progress. And this matters, because the topic is important, and has many applications. However, the step that leads from a "common sense" view to its mathematical analysis is more delicate; and though the art of teaching consists in finding ways to make such things easier to digest, one should not underestimate the challenge in this case.

The initial stage is purely numerical.

> A position is advertised at £8.30 per hour (including specified breaks).
>
> If my weekly schedule counts as 25 hours, then I expect to earn
>
> $$25 \times £8.30 = £207.50.$$

Here the given data includes the "**unit cost**" of "earnings per hour", and the calculation reduces to a single multiplication. Despite the disturbingly low success rate for problem 1.4J above, this kind of multiplication can be made accessible to almost everyone. So it should be possible (even if it takes time and care) to extend this idea to problems where the "unit cost" has to be extracted first, before it can be used to find the required answer:

> If **my** schedule counts as 25 hours per week and **I** earn £207.50, what would **you** expect to earn if **your** schedule counted as 30 hours?

All that is needed is to insert an extra reverse step, before repeating essentially the same calculation:

if 25 hours	$\longrightarrow$	earns £207.50,
then **1 hour**	$\longrightarrow$	earns £ ...
so 30 hours	$\longrightarrow$	should earn $30 \times £8.30 = £249$

In other words, all that is needed (once one has a template to organise one's thoughts and calculations) is to carry out **two** multiplications ("$\times \frac{1}{25}$" and

"$\times 30$") instead of one multiplication. This two-step process, where the **unit cost** is extracted first, is often referred to as "the **unitary method**".

The general situation of which the above is an example arises whenever two quantities, in this case

"hours worked" and "pay received (in £)"

vary together in such a way that, whenever we have *two linked pairs* of quantities, such as:

25 hours *corresponds to* £207.50,

and

30 hours *corresponds to* £249,

then the ratio between the two quantities of the first kind

25 : 30

is equal to the ratio between the two quantities of the second kind

207.50 : 249

This "equality of ratios" is called a **proportion**. We also say "the two quantities—hours worked, and pay received—vary in proportion to each other". (Slightly confusingly, this is sometimes referred to as "*direct* proportion"—to underline the contrast with "*inverse* proportion", where the two quantities x, y vary in such a way that the first quantity x varies in proportion to the *inverse* $\frac{1}{y}$ of the second quantity).

The "equality of ratios" can be re-written as an equality of *fractions*:

$$\frac{25}{30} = \frac{207.5}{249}$$

This is all very well, but each time we choose a different "linked pair of quantities" we get two new ratios. The new ratios are again equal, but they are *different from* the previous two ratios that were equal. **However**, if we rewrite the fraction equation in the form

$$\frac{25}{207.5} = \frac{30}{249}$$

then something remarkable happens: we obtain a quotient which is **always the same**—and which is called the **constant of proportionality**.

Teachers and schools will no doubt have their own ways of simplifying this idea. But there is no escaping from the need to prepare the ground by doing sufficient prior work with *word problems*, with multiplication and division, with *fractions*, and with *ratios*.

The teacher is like a midwife—using their own higher knowledge to coax ideas into pupils' minds. But to do this effectively, the teacher (like the midwife) needs to see the bigger picture—even if they then choose to suppress some of the details. *To generate a* ***ratio***, all that is needed is *a single class of pairwise* ***comparable*** *magnitudes* (that is, a class of magnitudes where any two given entities can be 'compared', so that we can decide which is the larger). The simplest examples of such a class of "comparable magnitudes" are the set of positive rational numbers, and the set of positive real numbers. In the context of ratios, real numbers generally arise as the set of possible numerical *measures* of some set of objects (relative to some chosen unit). *Numerical* ratios are easier to handle (replacing the class of *objects* by their *measures*). But ratios are not necessarily numerical. They arise naturally in mathematics whenever one has a class of "comparable entities" (such as line segments, or 2D shapes): we do not have to turn everything into numbers by measuring (for a very simple example, see Part III, Section 1.9.2).

The example above illustrates how a *proportion* arises whenever two **different** classes of entities are linked in a special (but very common) way. For example, suppose that one class consists of

"quantities of petrol"

and the other class consists of

"amounts of money in £".

If 1 litre of petrol	costs £1.50,
then we expect 2 litres	to cost £3 (= 2 × £1.50)

That is, for any two purchases from the same outlet at the same time, the ***quantities*** *purchased* (*in litres*)

are in the same ratio as

*the **amounts** paid* (*in £*).

If I buy a litres of petrol	and pay £c,
and you buy b litres of petrol	and pay £d,
then the ratio $a : b$	is equal to the ratio $c : d$.

The equality

$$\boldsymbol{a : b = c : d}$$

is what we call a *proportion*.

Note that since a, b, c, d are magnitudes, with a, b of one kind and c, d of another kind, then $a : b$ is a perfectly well-defined ratio; but "$a : c$" **makes no sense**, because a and c are not comparable magnitudes. One cannot have a ratio between a quantity of fluid and an amount of money. **However,** if we replace the different quantities and amounts by their numerical *measures*, then the equality of ratios "$a : b = c : d$" can be written as an *equation between fractions*, which can then be treated purely numerically (or algebraically), to give an equality of quotients, or fractions:

$$\frac{a}{b} = \frac{c}{d} \qquad (*)$$

The two quotients in equation $(*)$ are always equal, but can take any positive value. You could consider buying

$b = 2a$ litres of petrol	and pay $d = 2c$ pounds,

and the quotients would then both take the value $\frac{1}{2}$. Or you could buy

$b = \frac{1}{2}a$ litres of petrol	and pay $d = \frac{1}{2}c$ pounds,

and the quotients would then both take the value 2.

However, if we now treat the equation $(*)$ purely algebraically, then we can rewrite it in the form

$$\frac{c}{a} = \frac{d}{b}$$

This equation looks very similar to equation $(*)$, but it is completely different. The two sides do not represent ratios, but specify the *constant of proportionality* (relative to the two chosen units: litres and pounds (£)).

That is, once we choose units and give numerical values a and c to the basic pair of corresponding magnitudes—one from one class and one from the other

$$\mathbf{a \text{ litres}} \longrightarrow \mathbf{\text{cost } \pounds c}$$

the value of the quotient $\frac{c}{a}$ is a **constant**, the **constant of proportionality**. That is, it has the same value as the corresponding quotient $\frac{d}{b}$ *for any other pair* of corresponding magnitudes b, d (one from one class and one from the other).

This is the simplest, and perhaps the most valuable, application of school mathematics—to life, to science and to mathematics itself. It applies whenever two quantities are related so that if one quantity doubles, or triples, so does the other: that is, where the numerical measures a, c or b, d of the two quantities have a **constant ratio**. Two quantities that vary in such a way as to preserve a constant ratio between their values are said to be "in **proportion**".

The fact that "$\frac{c}{a}$ is a constant" means that the *number lines* corresponding to the two families of measures "line up" in such a way that one scale is simply a multiple ($\times\frac{c}{a}$) of the other:

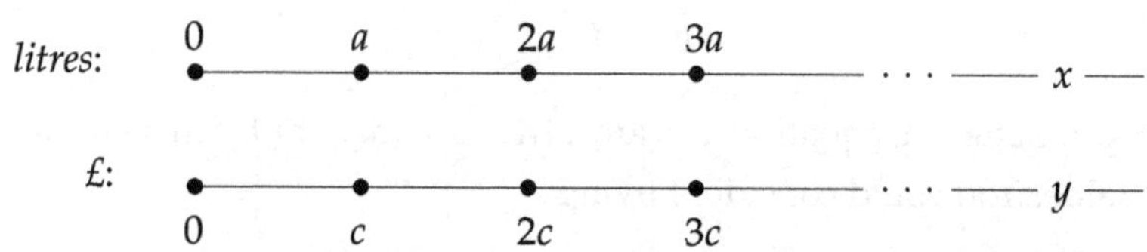

If we imagine a linked pair (x, y) of unknown variables—where "x litres costs £y"—then these variables are connected by the linear equation

$$y = \left(\frac{c}{a}\right) x.$$

Any particular proportion problem that pupils may be required to solve is likely to involve just two pairs (a, c) and (b, d),

- where a and b come from one class of magnitudes, and c and d come from the other class.

In a typical proportion problem, three of the four values are given and the fourth is to be found. Hence one pair is completely known, and we take this as our "base", or "reference pair":

$$\textbf{\textit{a} litres} \longrightarrow \textbf{cost £\textit{c}}$$

One of the *other* two values b, d is "to be found". So the four ingredients can be thought of as the corners of a rectangular array, where three of the values are known and the fourth is to be calculated:

$$\begin{array}{ll} \text{If} \quad \textbf{\textit{a} litres} \longrightarrow & \textbf{cost £\textit{c}} \\ \text{then } b \text{ litres} \longrightarrow & \text{cost £??} \end{array}$$

Alternatively, the missing value may be the one in the bottom left corner:

$$\begin{array}{ll} \text{If} \quad \textbf{\textit{a} litres} \longrightarrow & \textbf{cost £\textit{c}} \\ \text{then ?? litres} \longrightarrow & \text{cost £}d \end{array}$$

This standard way of representing the four pieces of information in a proportion—with three known values and one generally unknown—is referred to here as the *rectangular template* for displaying *proportion* problems. We will revise and extend this example in Part III (p. 137ff).

2.2.2 [*Reason mathematically* p. 4]:

> – **make and test conjectures about patterns and relationships; look for proofs or counterexamples**
>
> – **begin to reason deductively in geometry, number and algebra, including using geometrical constructions**

Learning to distinguish between a plausible guess and a provable fact should be part of school mathematics from the earliest years. In Key Stage 3 this distinction takes on a new importance—but the requirement stated in 2.2.2 is difficult to interpret because the logical framework within which such deduction is to take place remains undeclared (e.g. for Euclidean geometry).

2.2.2.1 The problems begin already with the requirement to "reason deductively in number" when making sense of simple *numerical patterns.* At present the patterns pupils meet are often chosen in a way that misleads everyone into thinking that

patterns that ***seem*** *genuine,* ***always are*** *genuine.*

This makes it hard for pupils to discover the need for **proof.**

Consider, for example, the first 17 terms of what should be a familiar endless sequence:

$$2, 4, 8, 16, 32, 64, 128, 256, 512, 1024, 2048, 4096, 8192, 16384,$$
$$32768, 65536, 131072, \ldots$$

These are the successive *powers* of 2. Pupils can extend the sequence as far as they need simply by repeatedly multiplying by 2.

Now consider the two sequences that arise naturally from this sequence of "powers of 2" by looking at the two "ends" of each term of this sequence:

first the succession of *units* digits:

$$2, 4, 8, 6, \quad 2, 4, 8, 6, \quad 2, 4, 8, 6, \quad 2, 4, 6, 8, \quad 2, \ldots$$

then the succession of *leading* digits:

$$2, 4, 8, 1, 3, 6, 1, 2, 5, 1, \quad 2, 4, 8, 1, 3, 6, 1, 2, \ldots .$$

As one continues to extend the original sequence of powers of 2, it is hard not to notice that both these sequences of digits **seem** to *recur*.

But do they really? And if they do, are these two conjectures really similar?

It is relatively easy to **prove** that **the first sequence "2, 4, 8, 6, 2, 4, 8, 6, ..." really does recur**. For we know that when we carry out the short multiplication, multiplying by 2 each time,

- each ***new*** *units digit* arises *from multiplying the* **previous** *units digit* by 2.

  So each time we reach a units digit of **2,** we notice that

- the units digit of the next term is **4** (since "$2 \times \mathbf{2}$ ends in **4**");
- then "$2 \times \mathbf{4}$ ends in **8**";
- then "$2 \times \mathbf{8}$ ends in **6**";
- then "$2 \times \mathbf{6}$ ends in **2**"—and the sequence "**2, 4, 8, 6**" starts to repeat.

However, **the second sequence**

$$\mathbf{2, 4, 8, 1, 3, 6, 1, 2, 5, 1, \qquad 2, 4, 8, 1, \ldots}$$

is different. There is no obvious reason why the **leading** digits should recur as they seem to do.

> *Somehow pupils need to learn that what looks like a pattern may not be a pattern at all!*

So we have to insist that, in the absence of an acceptable proof, no pattern is simply "believed"—no matter how persistent it may seem to be.

2.2.2.2 The requirement to "reason deductively in **algebra**" is more interesting—and is explored surprisingly rarely. Proof in *algebra* has to be based on combining

- use of the commutative and associative laws of addition and multiplication, and the distributive law, to simplify *expressions*,

together with

- the idea that one is allowed to operate on the two sides of any equals sign in the same way without destroying the equality.

The most obvious example at Key Stage 3 and Key Stage 4 (about which the programme of study remains stubbornly silent) is the proof that

$$(-1) \times (-1) = 1.$$

There are all sorts of heuristic arguments that can be used to "justify" this crucial mathematical fact. One of the more plausible explanations is to consider *dieting* and *weight loss*.

- If I consistently *put on* 1kg per month, then

in 3 months time, I will be (3×1)kg *heavier* than now; and

3 months *ago*, i.e. "**in −3 months time**", my weight was $[(-3) \times 1]$kg more than now.

- If I consistently *lose* 1 kg per month (that is, if I "put on (-1)kg per month"), then I know that

in 3 months time, my weight will be 3kg less than it is now; and

(∗) 3 months ago, my weight would have been **3kg more** than it is now.

If we try to express these observations arithmetically we see that

in 3 months time, my weight will be $[3 \times (-1)]$kg more than it is now; whereas

(∗∗) 3 months ago, my weight must have been $[(-3) \times (-1)]$kg **more** than it is now.

Taken together (∗) and (∗∗) seem to suggest that: $(-\mathbf{3}) \times (-\mathbf{1}) = \mathbf{3}$.

Such linguistic plausibility is fine at Key Stage 3. But at some stage in Key Stage 4, those who may move on to A level need to know that the fact has a simple mathematical basis. All we need to use is that:

(i) *multiplying by* 1 changes nothing: $a \times 1 = a$ for all a;

(ii) *adding* 0 changes nothing: $a + 0 = a$ for all a;

(iii) the distributive law holds.

It then follows that

- $$a = 1 \times a$$
  $$\therefore \quad a = (1 + 0) \times a$$
  $$\therefore \quad a + 0 = 1 \times a + 0 \times a = a + 0 \times a$$
  $$\therefore \quad 0 = 0 \times a \text{ for all } a$$

- $$\begin{aligned} \therefore 0 &= 0 \times (-1) \quad (\text{putting } a = -1 \text{ in "} 0 \times a = 0 \text{ for all } a\text{"}) \\ &= (1 + (-1)) \times (-1) \\ &= 1 \times (-1) + (-1) \times (-1) \\ &= (-1) + [(-1) \times (-1)] \\ \therefore \quad & (-1) \times (-1) = 1. \textbf{ QED} \end{aligned}$$

The proof given here is for teachers, and is based on the fact that

(i) is the defining property of the multiplicative unit "1", and

(ii) is the corresponding defining property of the additive identity "0".

Some readers may judge that *for pupils* the initial step—the fact that "$0 \times a = 0$ for all a"—is so familiar that the first bullet point is best suppressed.

A quite different fact that is often confused with the above is the fact that "subtracting a negative is the same as adding":

$$a - (-x) = a + x.$$

However tempting it may seem, little is gained by summarising this and the result proved above as "two minuses make a plus". The two results are in fact rather different: in the above equation there is no multiplication in sight. Moreover, the symbol "$-x$" should not be referred to as "a negative", since its value depends on the value of x itself: it is simply the "additive inverse of x"; that is, "$-x$" is the "negative of x", or that number which cancels out "x" under addition and produces 0.

Claim $a - (-x) = a + x$ for all a, x

Proof

(i) $a + (-x) + x = a + 0 = a$

Now subtract x from both sides:

$$\therefore a + (-x) = a - x$$

(ii) $a - (-x) + (-x) = a$

Use part (i) to replace "$+(-x)$" by "$-x$":

$$\therefore a - (-x) - x = a$$

Now add x to both sides:

$$\therefore a - (-x) = a + x. \quad \textbf{QED}$$

At Key Stage 3 schools will need to develop their own ways of achieving fluency in using such algebraic rules—for they are far from obvious! If the proof is illustrated numerically, one must first establish part (i), so that it can be used in part (ii); and it is important to give three or four examples—e.g. replacing a and x first by 1 and 2, then by 1 and -2, then by -1 and 2, and finally by -1 and -2.

A rather different opportunity for pupils to "reason deductively in algebra" arises in the solution of equations. We pointed out in Subsection 2.1.3 that "to solve equations" really means to solve **exactly**—by algebraic methods. A given equation in a single unknown "x" has an imagined (but unknown) set of "solutions", or possible values for the unknown "x". The art of solving equations algebraically is a process which exploits exactly two kinds of moves.

- The first kind of move allows us to replace any constituent expression on either side of the equation by another expression which is *algebraically equivalent* to it. Because "algebraically equivalent" expressions are equal **for all values of x,** this kind of move is *reversible,* so **exactly the same values** of the unknown "x" satisfy the new equation as satisfied the old equation.

- The second kind of move is to subject both sides of the equation to the same operation.

- **If** this operation is *reversible* (such as adding or subtracting the same thing from both sides, or multiplying or dividing both sides by a given expression *that is never equal to zero*, or cubing both sides), **then** we can again be sure that **exactly the same values** of the unknown "x" satisfy the new equation as satisfied the old equation.
- However, we are also free to subject both sides of the equation to an operation which is not reversible, such as squaring both sides of the equation. In this case we can only be sure that

  any value of "x" which satisfied the original equation
  will also satisfy the new equation.

  That is, any solution of the original equation is also a solution of the new equation, so we can be sure that *we have not **lost** any solutions.* However, we may have **gained** some new solutions which did not satisfy the original equation. For example,

  if "$A = B$", then we can square both sides to get the new equation "$A^2 = B^2$";

  but the change may introduce new solutions, since $A^2 = B^2$ includes the possibility that $A = -B$, which is quite different from the original equation.

A third domain where pupils should learn to "reason deductively in algebra" arises with *inequalities*. In many ways equations are rather rare. In mathematics and in life *inequalities* are much more common. For example, a business never quite 'breaks even': it either makes a surplus, or it makes a loss. And for a production line to keep running, one can never order the *exact* amount of material that is required: one has to slightly over-order to make sure that the supply of what is needed *never runs out* (and one would like to do so in such a way that waste is reduced to a minimum). This means that real problems are often formulated in terms of *inequalities*.

Much of what holds for *equations* translates to *inequalities*.

- The solution of a **linear** *equation* in one unknown "x" is a single point on the x-axis; and the solution of the corresponding **linear** *inequality* consists of all values *on one side* of this point (a "half-line").

- The possible solutions of a **linear** *equation* in two variables x, y correspond to the set of all points (x, y) on a line, which divides the plane into two "half-planes"; and the solutions of the corresponding **linear** *inequality* in two variables x, y consists of all points *on one side* of the line—that is, in one of the two half-planes.

The algebraic rules for "solving inequalities" are very similar to the rules for solving equations. For example, one is allowed to add the same to both sides of an inequality, or to multiply both sides of a given inequality by a *positive* quantity. But there is a twist: a *negative* multiplier *reverses* the inequality!

The extent to which inequalities are neglected in England is clear from one of the 2011 TIMSS Year 9 items:

2.2.2.2A "Solve the inequality: $9x - 6 < 4x + 4$".

We can transform the given inequality by collecting terms (or more correctly, by "adding $6 - 4x$ to both sides") to get $5x < 10$.

We can then multiply both sides by the positive multiplier $\frac{1}{5}$ to obtain "$x < 2$".

The percentage of correct responses to this problem from a representative sample of 15 year olds in more than 50 countries was not encouraging, and included:[11]

2.2.2.2A Korea 60% Russia 46% Hungary 38% USA 21%
Australia 8% England 3%

This suggests rather starkly that our approach to deduction and calculation in algebra needs to change in order to establish a clear connection between the familiar processes used in solving *equations* and those required to solve *inequalities* (which are listed in the Key Stage 3 programme in the third bullet point of "Algebra", and which feature in the GCSE mathematics subject content list, so certainly warrant preliminary work at this level—even if a more formal treatment can be delayed until Key Stage 4).

[11] http://timss.bc.edu/timss2011/international-released-items.html

2.2.2.3 The requirement to "begin to reason deductively in **geometry**" and to include "geometrical constructions" is in some ways easier to achieve. But it is in other ways more delicate.

Geometry at Key Stage 1 and 2 is predominantly experiential and descriptive. However, once the basic repertoire of shapes and language has been established, one can begin to organise the subject matter at Key Stage 3 into a logical, or deductive, hierarchy. For example:

- once one knows that angles at a point P on a straight line add to $180°$,
- one can **prove** that, whenever two lines cross at a point P, any pair of *vertically opposite* angles A and A' at P are necessarily equal:

  [**Proof:** Let B be the angle "between" the two vertically opposite angles A and A'. Then $A + B$ is the straight angle on one line, and $B + A'$ is the straight angle on the other line.
  $\therefore A + B = B + A'$, so $A = A'$. **QED**]

This proof only depends on the assumption (which pupils and teachers alike accept without even noticing) that:

> **all 'straight angles'** (at possibly different points on two straight lines) **are equal.**

Plane geometry deals with imagined *points* and *lines*. Two points determine exactly one line, and two lines which are not parallel meet in exactly one point. This much should be clear—though it needs to be reinforced in Year 7 through appropriate drawing exercises.

More importantly, the methods and language of geometry require us to make a clear distinction between

- the *line* AB (which passes through the two points A, B, and which extends forever in both directions)

and

- the ***line segment*** AB (that starts at A, runs to B, and then stops), which in the UK is usually also written as AB.

For example, the sides of triangle ABC are not the "lines" AB, BC, CA, but rather the line *segments* AB, BC, CA. Geometrical experience prior to Year 8 needs to ensure that these ideas can be taken for granted without drawing explicit attention to them. However, to go further, one needs a clear framework within which the basic results of Euclidean geometry can be derived. And since such a framework remains largely implicit (or even hidden) in the programme of study, it may help if we give (here and in Part III, Section 3) a brief outline of the necessary background.

The whole of geometry in 2D and in 3D rests on one key idea, which needs to be cultivated at Key Stage 2, and strengthened at Key Stage 3 through drawing, and through making and examining standard structures. This is the discovery that **triangles** hold the key to the construction and analysis of more complicated shapes. Every integer can be factorised as a product of prime numbers, and this factorisation tells us important things about the original number, even though most of the details of this factorisation cannot be seen when one first looks at the starting number. In much the same way important properties of complicated geometrical configurations can be analysed in terms of their constituent *triangles*, even though these triangles may not be immediately apparent in the initial configuration. (This strategy of reducing geometrical reasoning in general to reasoning about *triangles* is also related to the fact that the rigidity of structures in engineering—such as cranes, or roof trusses, or bridges, or the Wembley arch—often comes down to the way triangles are built in to their design.)

Mathematics succeeds by translating sense impressions and language, or sounds, into symbols which allow *exact calculation*. "The sum of three consecutive even integers" makes perfect sense in English, but the words alone suggest nothing special. However, as soon as we translate the words into symbols and write this as

$$2n + (2n + 2) + (2n + 4) = 6n + 6$$

it is clear that the result is always a multiple of 6. The same is true in geometry. The English words "triangle" or "quadrilateral" may conjure up a visual impression in the mind's eye of an imagined shape. But one cannot calculate with such an impression. If we wish to refer to a particular triangle or quadrilateral, we may point it out; and others may notice things about the indicated shape; but they cannot talk, or reason deductively about a triangle or quadrilateral which has been indicated in this way. Just as "consecutive even integers" were given names in accordance with the rules of algebra, so **a triangle or quadrilateral has to be given a name** in accordance with certain conventions before we can begin to calculate with it.

Labelling conventions have to communicate reliably between individuals, and so are chosen to reflect the underlying geometric structure. For example, a polygon is a collection of line segments, where successive pairs meet at a shared vertex. Hence *the sequence in which the vertices are labelled matters*. A quadrilateral $ABCD$ has to be labelled **in cyclic order**, where the edges are the successive line segments, or edges, that make up the quadrilateral: AB and BC (meeting at B), BC and CD (meeting at C), CD and DA (meeting at D), and DA and AB (meeting at A). Just as the neglect of grammar and spelling makes it impossible for pupils to organise and to express their thoughts, and hence to be understood, so it is an indication of the anarchy in English school geometry that standard geometric conventions are routinely flouted without the serious consequences being recognised.

There is another oversight which may prove harder for some to swallow. The reader is invited to imagine (and to draw, and to label) two adjacent unit squares—$ABCF$, $FCDE$. The squares $ABCF$ and $FCDE$ are clearly different, but very much alike. But we would not usually quibble if I referred to the first square as $ABCF$ and **you** referred to it as $BCFA$ (or even $BAFC$—but **not** $AFBC$). However, $ABCF$ and $BCFA$ are in some sense *different*—whether they are different squares or just different *labellings* need not be decided immediately. The difficulty may be clearer if one considers the two rectangles $ABDE$ and $DBAE$: much of the time one may loosely think of these as "different ways of referring to the same rectangle". But life is much easier if one views them as *different*—though closely related. This becomes clear as soon as one tries to sharpen the feeling that the two rectangles are "the same", or "congruent"; for then the "sameness" one is trying to capture requires one to match them up in a way that essentially *changes* the labelling of the second rectangle, since "AB" (the first side mentioned in $ABDE$) is a short side, whereas "DB" (the first side mentioned in $DBAE$) is a long side. It does not matter whether the matching up leads one to think of the second rectangle as $ABDE$, or $BAED$, or $DEAB$, or $EDBA$; but it becomes silly to insist on calling it $DBAE$ while also insisting that it is "the same as $ABDE$". Even if we do not strictly insist on such precision all the time, each time we do some kind of "calculation" with a triangle, or a quadrilateral, we find that the **order** matters (as well as the sequential labelling of the vertices).

So there is a clear sense in which, whenever push comes to shove, a "triangle" is not just a three-cornered shape: it is a *labelled, or ordered, triple* ABC, where **the order matters**. (If one only knows the three vertices, but not the order, then this corresponds to several *different* triangles: $\triangle ABC$, $\triangle BCA$, $\triangle CAB$, $\triangle BAC, \ldots$.)

Each triangle involves *six* different pieces of data:

- the three side lengths: $AB = c$, $BC = a$, $CA = b$, and
- the three angles: $\angle ABC$ (often abbreviated as "B"), $\angle BCA$ (abbreviated as "C"), and $\angle CAB$ (abbreviated as "A").

There are three basic organising principles on which deductive reasoning in geometry is based. Two of these principles (relating to *congruence* and to *parallels*) belong naturally to Key Stage 3; the third organising principle (the *similarity criterion*) belongs slightly later—perhaps in Year 9 or Year 10.

The first organising principle is the *congruence criterion*. This underlines the central role played by triangles, and should arise naturally as a formal summary of pupils' extensive experience from drawing, where they should discover that:

> one does not need to know *everything* about a triangle in order to specify it *uniquely*.

The "congruence criterion" then summarises the information that is needed to specify a triangle uniquely.

Two (ordered) triangles $\triangle ABC$ and $\triangle DEF$ are *congruent* if the (ordered) correspondence

$$A \longleftrightarrow D, \quad B \longleftrightarrow E, \quad C \longleftrightarrow F$$

matches up each of the six ingredients of triangle $\triangle ABC$ with those of triangle $\triangle DEF$ in such a way that

- all three *corresponding* pairs of line segments are equal: $AB = DE$, $BC = EF$, $CA = FD$, and
- all three *corresponding* pairs of angles are equal: $A = D$, $B = E$, $C = F$.

We write this as: $\triangle ABC \equiv \triangle DEF$ (which we read as "Triangle ABC is congruent to triangle DEF").

"Congruence of triangles" only makes sense between **ordered** triangles. And it can help pupils to see more clearly which vertex of the first triangle corresponds to which in the second triangle, and which side of the first triangle corresponds to which in the second triangle, if pupils initially write:

$$\begin{array}{rl} & \triangle ABC \\ \equiv & \triangle DEF \end{array}$$

since this lines up

- corresponding vertices (with A directly above D, B directly above E, C directly above F), and
- corresponding sides (with AB directly above DE, BC directly above EF, CA directly above FD).

Pupils' experience of drawing should then reveal that, in order to guarantee congruence

"just three pieces of data suffice",

provided we avoid the two triples that don't suffice! Hence they need to understand

- that any of SSS, SAS, ASA determine the triangle uniquely,
- that "AAA" determines the shape, but says nothing about the scale, or size, of the triangle;

- that the appropriately named "ASS" criterion is different, in that it may give rise to two possible triangles (for example, a triangle with $\angle B = 30°$ and $BC = \sqrt{3}$, $CA = 1$ could have either $AB = 2$ with $\angle A$ acute, or $AB = 1$ with $\angle A$ obtuse).

The *congruence criterion* summarises the first of these three bullet points:

- triangles $\triangle ABC$ and $\triangle DEF$ are congruent (by SSS) if $AB = DE$, $BC = EF$, and $CA = FD$;
- triangles $\triangle ABC$ and $\triangle DEF$ are congruent (by SAS) if $AB = DE$, $\angle BAC = \angle EDF$, and $AC = DF$;
- triangles $\triangle ABC$ and $\triangle DEF$ are congruent (by ASA) if $\angle BAC = \angle EDF$, $AB = DE$, and $\angle ABC = \angle DEF$.

The RHS congruence criterion is not part of this basic congruence criterion, so does not really belong at this stage. It arises as the degenerate instance of the failed ASS criterion (where the angle "A" in "ASS" is a *right angle*, and so is neither acute nor obtuse). The fact that RHS guarantees congruence follows somewhat later (once we have proved *Pythagoras' Theorem*, since knowing two sides and a right angle then determines the third side. So RHS is a special case of SSS).

SSS, SAS, and ASA congruence allow one to prove such results as:

- The two diagonals of a square $ABCD$ are equal

  [**Proof** The two triangles $\triangle ABC$, and $\triangle BCD$ are congruent by SAS:

  $$\begin{aligned} &\triangle ABC \\ &\equiv \triangle BCD \quad (\text{since } AB = BC,\ \angle B = \angle C, \text{ and } BC = CD). \end{aligned}$$

  Hence AC (in $\triangle ABC$) $= BD$ (in $\triangle BCD$). **QED**].

- The base angles of an isosceles triangle are equal:

  [**Proof 1** Suppose $AB = AC$. Construct the midpoint M of the base BC. Then, by SSS,

$$\triangle AMB$$
$$\equiv \triangle AMC \quad \text{(since } AM = AM,\ MB = MC \text{ (} M \text{ is the midpoint of } BC\text{), and } AB = AC \text{ (given))}.$$

Hence $\angle ABM$ (in $\triangle AMB$) = $\angle ACM$ (in $\triangle AMC$). **QED**].

It is worth pondering on a different proof of this result, which exploits the fact that $\triangle ABC$ and $\triangle ACB$ are different triangles.

[**Proof 2** Suppose $AB = AC$. Then the two different ordered triangles $\triangle BAC$, and $\triangle CAB$ are congruent by SAS:

$$\triangle BAC$$
$$\equiv \triangle CAB \quad \text{(since } BA = CA,\ \angle A = \angle A, \text{ and } AC = AB\text{)}.$$

Hence $\angle B$ (in $\triangle BAC$) = $\angle C$ (in $\triangle CAB$). **QED**].

- Any triangle with equal base angles is isosceles:

[**Proof** Suppose $\angle ABC = \angle ACB$. Then the two different ordered triangles $\triangle ABC$, and $\triangle ACB$ are congruent by ASA:

$$\triangle ABC$$
$$\equiv \triangle ACB \quad \text{(since } \angle ABC = \angle ACB,\ BC = CB, \text{ and } \angle BCA = \angle CBA\text{)}.$$

Hence AB (in $\triangle ABC$) = AC (in $\triangle ACB$). **QED**].

- In an isosceles triangle, the bisector of the apex angle, the median to the base, and the perpendicular to the base are all the same.

Isosceles triangles constitute one of the simplest and most fruitful sources of geometrical deduction. For example, in a circle any chord AB forms an isosceles triangle OAB with the centre O, so isosceles triangles allow one to deduce all sorts of properties of circles (the so-called "circle theorems").

The congruence criterion is also needed to prove that the basic ruler and compass constructions do what they claim to do:

- to bisect a given angle,

- to bisect a given line segment,
- to construct a perpendicular to a given line from a given point, and
- to construct a line parallel to a given line through a given point.

For example:

- ***To bisect a given angle*** $\angle BAC$. Let the circle with centre A and passing through B meet the half line AC at the point B'. Let the two circles—one with centre B and passing through A, the other with centre B' and passing through A— meet again at D. Then AD ***bisects*** $\angle BAC$.

  [**Proof** We show that $\triangle BAD \equiv \triangle B'AD$ (by the SSS congruence criterion), since
  $BA = B'A$ (both are radii of the same circle with centre A).
  AD (in $\triangle ADB$) $=$ AD (in $\triangle ADB'$) (the one segment is part of both triangles)
  $DB = AB$ (both are radii of the same circle with centre B)
  $AB = AB'$ (both are radii of the same circle with centre A)
  $AB' = DB'$ (both are radii of the same circle with centre B')
  $\therefore DB = DB'$.
  Hence $\angle DAB$ (in $\triangle BAD$) $=$ $\angle DAB'$ (in $\triangle B'AD$), so DA bisects $\angle BAC$. **QED**]

The second organising principle in geometry is the criterion for two lines in the plane to be *parallel*.

Given any two lines in the plane, a *transversal* is a third line that cuts both of the two given lines. The *parallel criterion* declares that:

- two lines are *parallel* precisely when the *alternate angles* (or the *corresponding angles*) created by a transversal are equal.

This is a rather subtle criterion, but one which can be made thoroughly plausible. It immediately allows one to prove:

Claim The angles in any triangle $\triangle ABC$ add to 180° (i.e. a "straight angle").

Proof Construct the line XAY through vertex A which is parallel to BC (where X, B both lie on the same side of the line AC).
$\therefore \angle XAB = \angle CBA = \angle B$ (alternate angles)
and $\angle YAC = \angle BCA = \angle C$ (alternate angles)

$$\begin{aligned} \therefore \angle A + \angle B + \angle C &= \angle A + \angle XAB + \angle YAC \\ &= \angle XAY (\text{a straight angle at } A \text{ on the line } XY). \textbf{ QED} \end{aligned}$$

And this in turn provides access to hundreds of wonderful (non-obvious, multi-step) problems involving *angle chasing*. This term is a shorthand for any activity in which a 2D configuration is specified, with the sizes of certain angles given, from which the sizes of other angles are to be logically determined (by reasoning and calculation, not by measuring). If the required angle were the third angle in a triangle whose other two angles were given, then the required angle could be immediately deduced. In general the size of the required angles may not be immediately deducible, but may force one to first calculate certain intermediate results. That is, *angle-chasing* refers to a restricted (geometrical) class of problems that are *multi-step*, and that are also deductive exercises in using the basic angle properties (angles at a point, angles on a straight line, vertically opposite angles, angles in a triangle—and later alternate angles). See for example, *Extension mathematics Book Alpha* by Tony Gardiner (Oxford 2007), Sections T9 and E2, and *Book Beta* Sections T17, C11 and E4.

If we combine the *parallel criterion* with the *congruence criterion*, we can prove the basic facts about parallelograms, and derive the fundamental fact that the area of a triangle is equal to

$$\frac{1}{2}(\text{base} \times \text{height}).$$

This then allows us to prove *Pythagoras' Theorem*.

The congruence criterion and the parallel criterion allow one to transfer *exact* relations (such as *equality* of line segments or of angles) from one place to another. The third organising principle of secondary school Euclidean geometry, the *similarity criterion*, goes beyond this world of *exact equality* to allow one to deal with ratios, scaling, and enlargement. The introduction of this criterion is probably best delayed until the basic consequences of congruence and parallelism have been fully explored, and until pupils are sufficiently confident in working with ratio.

As with congruence, similarity in general is formulated in terms of "similarity of *triangles*". *The similarity criterion* summarises the minimum requirement for two given triangles to be "similar". Two (ordered) triangles $\triangle ABC$ and $\triangle DEF$ are *similar* (which we write as $\triangle ABC \sim \triangle DEF$) if

- corresponding angles are equal:

$$\angle A = \angle D, \quad \angle B = \angle E, \quad \angle C = \angle F,$$

and

- corresponding sides are proportional:

$$AB : DE = BC : EF = CA : FD.$$

The *similarity criterion* may be thought of as a substitute for the (evidently false) "AAA congruence criterion", in that it states that each of the above bullet points **implies the other**:

if corresponding angles are equal:

$$\angle A = \angle D, \quad \angle B = \angle E, \quad \angle C = \angle F,$$

then corresponding sides are proportional:

$$AB : DE = BC : EF = CA : FD;$$

and

if corresponding sides are proportional:

$$AB : DE = BC : EF = CA : FD,$$

then corresponding angles are equal:

$$\angle A = \angle D, \quad \angle B = \angle E, \quad \angle C = \angle F.$$

Special cases of this can be proved using the *exact* relation of congruence. For example, one can prove the *Midpoint Theorem*, which says that:

> if in $\triangle ABC$, M is the midpoint of AB and N is the midpoint of AC,
> then MN is parallel to BC and $BC : MN = 2 : 1$.

That is $\triangle ABC \sim \triangle AMN$, with the corresponding scale factor $AB : AM = AC : AN = BC : MN = 2 : 1$.

Some further detail concerning geometry may be found in Part III, Section 3.

2.2.2.4 The requirements listed at the start of Section 2.2.2 suggest that during Key Stage 3 pupils should

> "make and test conjectures"

and

> "begin to reason deductively".

This should be interpreted as part of the (unstated) requirement that pupils should at all times expect the methods of elementary mathematics to *make sense*. But there are different kinds of "sense making": some involve *inference*; some involve plausibility arguments; and some are rooted in *deduction*. The requirement for pupils to "reason deductively" means that they need to be clear

- when they are experimenting or conjecturing, and when they are working "deductively";

and also

- when they are working in rough, and when they are writing for others to read.

That is, they need some way of demonstrating (to themselves and to others) which mode they are in at any given time. For pupils who are ready for the formal procedures of elementary mathematics at Key Stage 3, the calculations and methods should be increasingly justified in ways that are *exact* and deductive (rather than approximate, inferential, or based on the authority of the teacher). The essence of elementary mathematics at secondary level incorporates the twin facts

- that its domain is restricted and abstract, and
- that within this limited domain, the knowledge it delivers is **certain**—that is, *objective*, rather than subjective (or approximate, or based only on experience, or conjecture, or convention).

For such pupils calculations and solutions need to be increasingly presented in a way that constitutes a **proof** that the answer to the original problem is undeniably what emerges at the end of the calculation or solution. And this is best conveyed by laying out calculations and deductions **line-by-line**,

- with the given information, and any symbols representing "unknowns" declared at the outset,
- with each fresh step on a new line (and any explanation given alongside),

and

- with the final answer clearly displayed at the end.

The sequence of successive steps can then be grasped as a single *chain of reasoning*, in which each step follows clearly from those which went before. This logical structure is equally applicable

- to simple calculations,
- to the solution of an angle-chasing problem,
- to setting up and solving an equation,
- to proving that two algebraic (or trigonometric) expressions are identical,
- to a ruler and compass construction,
- to a **proof** (such as, that the angle in a semicircle is a right angle), or

- to the way pupils present their solutions to set problems.

It is hard to convey this style consistently in a discursive text such as this one. But it can be seen in the way we present short proofs. And it is also visible elsewhere—such as in the solution at the end of Section 2.3.5 below.

2.3. Solve problems

[*Solve problems* p. 5]:

> – **develop their mathematical knowledge, in part through solving problems and evaluating their outcomes, including multi-step problems**
>
> – **develop their use of formal mathematical knowledge to interpret and solve problems, including in financial mathematics**
>
> – **begin to model situations mathematically and express the results using a range of formal mathematical representations**
>
> – **select appropriate concepts, methods and techniques to apply to unfamiliar and non-routine problems**

These four bullet points are clearly meant to encourage pupils and teachers to see school mathematics as more than endless practise with dry-as-dust formal technique. But beyond this admirable aspiration, it is far from clear what exactly is being advocated. We base our commentary on three questions.

- What is meant by a "problem", rather than (say) an "exercise"?
- What does it mean to "solve problems"?
- And why are "multi-step" problems important?

2.3.1 We begin by clarifying the distinction between "exercises" and "problems".

An **exercise** is a task, or a collection of tasks that provide *routine practice* in some technique or combination of techniques. The techniques being exercised will have been explicitly taught, so the meaning of each task should be clear. Each sequence of exercises is designed to cultivate fluency in using the relevant techniques, and all that is required of pupils is that they implement the procedures more-or-less as they were taught in order to produce an answer. The overall goal of such a sequence of exercises is merely to establish mastery of the relevant technique in a suitably robust form. In particular, a well-designed set of exercises should help to avoid, or to eliminate, standard misconceptions and errors.

Exercises are not meant to be particularly exciting, or especially stimulating. But they can give pupils a quiet sense of satisfaction. Without a regular diet of suitable *exercises*, ranging from the simple to the suitably complex (including standard variations), pupils are likely to lack the repertoire of basic techniques they need in order to make sense of mildly more challenging tasks (as the examples 1.4A-1.4K above show). In other words,

> *exercises* are the bread-and-potatoes of the mathematics curriculum.

Pupils in England clearly need more (carefully prepared) "bread-and-potatoes" exercises than they currently get. However, bread and potatoes alone do not constitute a healthy diet. Pupils also need more challenging activities both to whet their mathematical appetites, and to cultivate an inner willingness to tackle, and to persist with, simple but unfamiliar (or "non-routine") **problems**. A *problem* is any task which we do not immediately recognise as being of a familiar type, and for which we therefore know no standard solution method. Hence, when faced with a *problem*, we may at first have no clear idea how to begin.

The first point to recognise is that a task does not have to be all that unfamiliar before it becomes a *problem* rather than an *exercise*! In the absence of an explicit problem solving culture, an exercise may appear to the pupil to be a *problem* simply because its solution method has not been mentioned for a week or so, or because it is worded in a way which fails to announce its connection with recent work. The second point is that the distinction between a *problem* and an *exercise* is not quite as clear-cut as we have made it look, and is to some extent time- and pupil-dependent. For example, an "I'm thinking of a number" *problem* from Year 5 or Year 6 should by Year 8 be seen to be a mere *exercise* in setting up and solving a simple equation.

Most useful techniques involve a *chain* of simple steps, and the technique as a whole is only an effective tool if *the complete chain* can be carried out **entirely reliably**—a requirement which may only be achieved after extensive practice. Examples include: any of the standard written algorithms; the process of turning a fraction into a decimal; the sequence of steps required to add or subtract two fractions, or to solve an equation or inequality, or to multiply out and simplify an algebraic expression. Hence each set of *exercises* should include tasks that force pupils to think a little more flexibly, and that require them to string simple steps together in a reliable way. Too many sets of *exercises* get stuck at the level of "one piece jigsaws"—with one-step routines being practised in isolation, ignoring key variations. Pupils need to learn from their everyday experience that the whole purpose of achieving fluency in routine bread-and-potatoes *exercises* is for them to learn to marshal these techniques to solve more demanding **multi-step** *exercises*, and more interesting, if mildly unsettling, *problems*.

2.3.2 This distinction between *exercises* and *problems* affects how we choose to introduce each new topic or technique. Should we concentrate on relatively simple examples that minimise pupil difficulties, and which seem likely to guarantee a quick pay-off? Or should we—when working with the whole class—move quickly on to examples that provide a significant challenge, and so require pupils from the outset to grapple with (carefully chosen) tasks of a more demanding nature?

How challenging one can safely be will depend on the pupils. But experience from those who observe lessons in other countries suggests that the English preference for concentrating the initial worked examples on easy cases **increases the extent of subsequent failure**. Easy initial examples lead to cheap apparent success; but this initial pupil success may be based on pupils' own inferred methods that appear to work in easy cases, but which are flawed in some way; or on backward-looking methods, that seem (to the pupil) to work in simple instances, but which do not extend to the general case. So we need to consider the benefits of starting each new topic with a harder "class problem" that brings out the full complexity of the method that we want pupils to master, and then to follow this up with *exercises* that may start simply, but which oblige pupils to think flexibly from the outset, and to handle standard variations including inverse problems.

2.3.3 The last 30 years have witnessed a consistent concern about pupils' ability to "use" the elementary mathematics they are supposed to know. Previous versions of the mathematics National Curriculum displayed an admirable determination to incorporate "Using and applying" within teaching and assessment. But such determination is not enough. The experience of the last 25 years in England is more useful as a guide to what does **not** work than to what does work. Much effort has been expended in trying to do better—but with limited effect. In particular, ambitious attempts to coerce change—using extended investigations, coursework, and "modelling"—have mostly served to demonstrate what should **not** be officially required at this level.

Somewhere along the line we seem to have lost sight of simple **word problems**. *Word problems* typically consist of two or three short sentences, from which pupils are required

- to extract the intended meaning and any required information,
- to identify what needs to be done,

and then

- to carry it out, and interpret the answer in the context of the problem.

Everyday uses of elementary mathematics tend to come in some variation of this form. Yet the simplest exercises, which might be solved routinely if they were presented *without words*, become powerful discriminators when given this gentle packaging. The need for pupils to read and extract the relevant data from two or three English sentences may appear routine—but it is a skill that has to be learned the hard way, and that constitutes the initial stepping-stone *en route* to the ultimate solution of almost any problem. This simple format can be tweaked to cover the standard variations of the underlying task (e.g. so that it appears both in *direct* and in the various *indirect* forms).

During Key Stage 1 *word problems* are important because they reflect the fundamental links between

- the world of mathematical ideas and mathematical reasoning,

and

- the world of language.

Indeed, for young children, the *logic* of mathematics is inextricably bound up with the *grammar* of language.

At later stages *word problems* continue to serve as an invaluable way of linking the increasingly abstract world of mathematics and the world where its ideas can be applied. That is, they constitute the simplest exercises and problems in any programme that seeks to ensure that elementary mathematics can be used.

The suggestion that improving mathematical literacy depends on rediscovering the world of carefully structured word problems is both more ambitious and more modest than what has been attempted in recent English reforms.

- It is *more* ambitious in that the evidence from other countries shows just how much more we might achieve were we to incorporate a *permanent thread* of such focused material from the earliest years.

- It is more modest in that it explicitly encourages *more focused* (and hence more manageable) tasks—short problems with a clearly specified beginning and end, but with the path from one to the other left for the solver to devise. Such problems have "closed" beginnings and "closed" ends, but are **open-middled**. Almost any mental arithmetic problem, or word problem, might serve as an example. Suppose we ask:

  "*I pack peaches in* 51 *boxes with* 16 *peaches in each box.*

  How many boxes would I use if each box contained just 12 **peaches?**"

  What is given and what is required is "closed"—i.e. specified uniquely. But the mode of solution is left entirely open:

- some pupils might calculate the total number of peaches and then divide by 12;
- one would prefer to see a more structural version of this representing the total number of peaches as "51×16" without evaluating, and the required number of boxes as $\frac{51\times16}{12}$ before cancelling

$$\frac{17 \times (3 \times 4) \times 4}{12} = 17 \times 4;$$

- others might notice that $3 \times 16 = 4 \times 12$, and look for the number x satisfying "$x : 51 = 4 : 3$";
- while some might remove 4 peaches from each of the 51 boxes and group the 4s in groups of 3×4 to get 17 additional boxes.

2.3.4 Pupils need a regular diet of problems and activities designed to strengthen the link between elementary mathematics on the one hand and its application to simple problems from the wider world on the other. *Word problems* are only a beginning.

Some have advocated using "real-world" problems. But though these may have a superficial appeal, their educational utility is limited. Problems which support the move towards using and applying beyond the limited world of *word problems* need to be very carefully constructed, so that the real context truly reflects the mathematical processes pupils are expected to use as part of their solution. (Problems which have to be carefully designed in this way are sometimes called "realistic".)

The related claim that technology allows pupils to work with "real-world problems" and with "real (or 'dirty') data" becomes important once the underlying ideas have been grasped. However, for relative beginners the claim too often ignores the distracting effect of the *noise* which is created by "real" contexts, by "real" data, and by the non-mathematical interface that so easily prevents pupils from grasping the underlying mathematical message.

2.3.5 The official programme of study makes repeated reference to the need to solve **multi-step** problems. A *multi-step* problem is like a challenge to cross a stream that is *too wide to straddle with a single jump*, so that the prospective solver is obliged to look for stepping-stones—intermediate points which reduce the otherwise inaccessible challenge of crossing from one bank (what is given) to the other (the completed solution) to *a chain of individually manageable steps*. In elementary mathematics, this art has to be learned the hard way. It should not be seen as optional, or as a matter of taste. It is central to what elementary mathematics is about, and to how it is used.

One might think that—given the original emphasis on *Using and applying*—this goal has been an integral part of the National Curriculum since its inception. But that is not quite true—for we have too often confused

- "solving problems", and tackling "multi-step" problems

with

- *real-world* problems, and *extended* tasks.

The limitations of "real-world" problems were outlined in the previous Section 2.3.4. An *extended* task allows pupils considerable freedom, and can be beneficial precisely because the outcomes lie to some extent outside the teacher's control. However, this lack of predictability and control means that extended tasks are **not** an effective way for most pupils to *learn* the art of solving *multi-step* problems. For most teachers, this art is much more effectively addressed through **short**, easily stated problems in a specific domain (such as number, or counting, or algebra, or Euclidean geometry), where

- what is given and what is required are both clear,
- but the route from one to the other requires pupils to identify one or more intermediate stepping-stones (that is, they are "open-middled")—as with
  - solving a simple number puzzle, or
  - interpreting and solving word problems, or
  - proving a slightly surprising algebraic identity, or
  - angle-chasing (where a more-or-less complicated figure is described and has to be drawn, with some angles given and some sides declared to be equal, and certain other angles are to be found—using the basic

repertoire of angles on a straight line, vertically opposite angles, angles in a triangle, and base angles of an isosceles triangle), or

- proving two line segments or two angles are equal, or that two triangles are congruent (where the method of proof is not immediately apparent).

The steps in the solution to a multi-step problem are like the separate links in a chain. And the difficulty of such problems arises from the need to select and to link up the constituent steps into a single logical chain. Suppose pupils are faced with:

> **Question:** "I'm thinking of a two-digit number $N < 100$, which is divisible by three times the sum of its digits? How many such numbers are there?"

In Year 7 pupils may see no alternative to guessing, or to testing each "two digit number" in turn. But by Year 9 one would like some to respond to the trigger in the question

> "three times the sum of its digits"

by gradually noticing some of the hidden stepping stones.

Steps toward a solution

1. The number has to be a multiple of 3 ("divisible by **three times** the sum of its digits").

2. Hence the sum of its digits must be a multiple of 3 (standard divisibility test).

3. But then the number is divisible by 9 ("divisible by three times a multiple of 3").

4. And so the sum of its digits must be a multiple of 9 (standard divisibility test).

5. So the number is divisible by 27 ("divisible by three times a multiple of 9").

6. So we only have to check 27, 54, and 81. **QED**

The sequencing of the steps, and the connections between the steps, are part of the solution. In short, *basic routines become useful only insofar as sufficient time is devoted to making sure they can be linked together to solve more interesting (multi-step) problems.*

2.3.6 Expecting pupils to select and to coordinate simple routines to *create* a chain of steps in order to solve simple multi-step problems should be part of mathematics teaching for all pupils. In contrast, recent efforts to improve the effectiveness of mathematics instruction in England have concentrated on:

- the teacher, textbook author, or examiner *breaking up* each complex procedure into easy steps, and then concentrating on teaching and assessing the easy steps, or atomic outcomes (one-piece jigsaws),
- monitoring centrally whether these atomic outcomes can be performed in *isolation*, and
- ignoring the fact that we have neglected the most demanding skill of all—namely that of *integrating* the separate steps into an effective *multi-step procedure*.

The evidence from international studies confirms what should have been obvious: this reductionist process of de-constructing elementary mathematics into atomic parts, combined with central monitoring that rewards partial success, has distorted the way pupils and teachers perceive elementary mathematics in a most unfortunate way. Improved problem solving and more effective mathematics teaching depend on enhancing the skill of the teacher. In contrast, the policy of focusing on *targets* and *testing*, and our misplaced dependence on crude measures of "pupils' progress", have tended to undermine the authority, the professional judgement, and the perceived long-term responsibility of the teacher.

Solving problems is hard. Any system that uses targets and testing to exert pressure on schools soon discovers the awkward facts that assessment items that require pupils to link two or more steps

- have a high failure rate, and
- generate pupil responses whose profile is at odds with the contractual demands placed on those who design centrally administered tests.

Such problems are therefore deemed unsuitable, and the tests tend to concentrate on more manageable *one-step* routines (or break down longer questions into a pre-ordained sequence of one-step "subroutines"). As long as teachers are judged on test outcomes, and as long as unfamiliar, multi-step problems are largely excluded from the official tests, teachers will continue to conclude that "in the (short-term) interests of their pupils" they dare not waste time developing the only thing that matters in the long run—namely:

> *to provide their pupils with the skills and attitudes they need for the* ***next*** *phase.*

In short, England has adopted an "improvement strategy" that guarantees neglect of the delicate art of solving multi-step problems, and that is therefore self-defeating. Central prescription, and political pressure to demonstrate relentless year-on-year improvement, have resulted in a national didactical blind spot, with curriculum objectives and assessment—and hence teaching—becoming atomised, so that pupils are only expected to handle "one piece jigsaws". Exams have routinely broken down each problem into a succession of easy steps—in order to minimise the risk of failure, and to ease "follow through marking" for the examiner. Teachers have then concluded that the delicate art of *interlinking* simple steps can be safely ignored. And we have all pretended that

- candidates who can implement (most of) the constituent steps separately
- have thereby achieved mastery of the *integrated* technique.

This is a delusion. The individual steps may be a starting point; but the power and challenge of elementary mathematics lies in learning *how simple ideas can be combined* to solve problems that would otherwise be beyond our powers. That is, the essence of the discipline lies not so much in the techniques themselves as in the *connections* between its ideas and methods. Hence the curriculum (and, where possible, its assessment) need to cultivate the ability to tackle *multi-step* problems without them being artificially broken down into steps.

A curriculum or syllabus can specify the individual techniques, or steps; but this is futile if one then forgets that it is the **linking** of the material which determines whether it can be effectively used to solve problems. This interlinking is an elusive property, *which depends entirely on the way the material is* **taught**: that is, it depends on the teacher. So we need a system in which teachers are free (nay, in which teachers feel professionally obliged) to value this activity in their classrooms, even though its value will only become apparent at *subsequent* stages—after their pupils have moved on to other classes.

2.3.7 Two further issues warrant comment before we move on to consider the listed *Subject content* requirements in Part III. The first is the matter of *exactness* and *approximation*, and the second is the repeated reference to "financial mathematics".

Mathematics used to be known as "the *exact* science". Mathematical objects sometimes have their roots in the world of human experience; but they become *mathematical* only when the underlying ideas are abstracted from these roots. Unlike disciplines that work with real data or objects, mathematics studies a world of idealised, *mental* objects. For example,

- *numbers* have their roots in experience;
- but they soon become "mental objects" with exact properties, and are manipulated in the mind.

In much the same way, a sheet of A4 paper, or a wooden door, may serve as a suggestive model for a rectangle, but

- a *mathematical rectangle* is a perfect mental object, whose diagonals are *exactly* equal—their length being given *exactly* (in terms of the sides) by *Pythagoras' Theorem*.

The mathematical universe consists of *imagined* objects, which are precisely defined, and hence uniquely knowable. In particular, mathematics, or "the art of exact calculation", belongs to a completely different conceptual universe from the practical world in which one might

> "draw a scale diagram of a rectangle and *measure* the approximate length of the diagonal".

Helping pupils to appreciate the difference between these two universes, and to see the advantages—even for the most practical of purposes—of engaging with the *exact* world of mathematics, should constitute a key (though often unstated) goal of any curriculum.

The process of developing internal methods of calculating with these exact *mental objects* (whether numbers, symbols, shapes, or functions) is much the same today as it ever was—and is rooted in mental work and written hand calculation. Once these ideas are suitably embedded in the mind, calculators and other tools have much to offer: but initially, the learning process proceeds more naturally without such distractions.

The fact that the world of mathematics operates on *ideal objects* allows its ideas, its notation, its methods of calculation, and its processes of logical deduction to be *exact*. This guarantees that the answers and conclusions produced in mathematics are as reliable as the information that was fed into the relevant calculation or deduction. The importance of this aspect of elementary mathematics has been considerably blurred in recent years—for example, by inappropriate and premature dependence on calculators, by reduced emphasis on the need to attain mastery of the art of exact calculation, and by the way "valuing children's own reasons" has been misconstrued.

In contrast to the *exact* mental universe of mathematics, the world of experience, of measurements, and of ideas is inescapably "fuzzy". It should be a goal of any curriculum to convey implicitly this key distinction between the *exact* world of mathematics, and the approximate world where mathematics is used and applied.

Mathematical *exactness* is quite different from *precision*. The very idea of "precision" recognises that, outside mathematics, all measurements incorporate a degree of error, and so are **approximate**. In contrast, *exactness* in mathematics allows no scope whatsoever for error; indeed, in an *exact* calculation an error of any kind undermines the validity of the whole process. Mathematical methods can be applied to values which are only known *approximately*; but the "exact answer" which mathematics then provides indicates the exact *range of values* within which the actual answer must lie. To achieve this, we first need to know

- the maximum extent of potential error in the given data, and

- how these potential errors accumulate when one carries out exact calculations with numbers that are only known *up to this level of accuracy.*

For pupils to master the art of approximating arithmetical calculations in integers, they first need to master the art of *exact* calculation. Only then can they use their knowledge of exactness as a fulcrum for thinking precisely about more elusive *approximation,* or *estimation.* (This matter is explored further in Part III, at the end of Section 1.7.) And when they come to analyse the errors introduced by such approximations, they will find that this is done via the exact calculations of elementary algebra. Thus, even when seeking to transcend the inherent exactness of arithmetic by cultivating the art of making *estimates,* there is no escape from the maxim:

> *Mathematics is the science of exact calculation.*

Finally, while it is perfectly fair to require that pupils be required to

> "develop their use of formal mathematical knowledge to interpret and solve problems",

this challenge applies to problems of many different kinds. So there is no possible excuse for adding the words "including financial mathematics" in the second bullet point of 2.3. There is no such subject area as "financial mathematics" at Key Stage 3; so its explicit inclusion can only reflect an enforced response to improper political lobbying. Some material relating to financial matters will inevitably be included (e.g. as an application of percentage increases and decreases, and of iterated powers as a model for the returns on long term investment or the accumulation of debt). But the precise words are no more worthy of special mention in a national curriculum than many other examples.

3

Key Stage 3: Number, Algebra, Geometry, Probability and Statistics

In Part III we examine the detail of the listed *Subject content*. To comment on each bullet point in turn would tend to reinforce the fragmentation that arises when a curriculum is reduced to a mere content list. So we have tried instead to group the bullet points in a way that allows us to identify common threads and underlying themes, and to indicate some of the linking that may be needed.

1. Number (and ratio and proportion)

1.1. [Subject content: *Number* pp. 5–6]

- **understand and use place value for decimals, measures and integers of any size**
- **order positive and negative integers, decimals and fractions; use the number line as a model for ordering of the real numbers; use the symbols** $=, \neq, <, >, \leqslant, \geqslant$
- **use standard units of mass, length, time, money and other measures, including with decimal quantities**
- **round numbers and measures to an appropriate degree of accuracy [for example, to a number of decimal places or significant figures]**
- [*Algebra* p. 6] **work with coordinates in all four quadrants**

At Key Stage 3 basic number work acts as an essential bridge, reaching back to Key Stage 2, and looking ahead to the more subtle multiplicative methods of Key Stage 3—with 'structural arithmetic' serving as a template for elementary algebra.

Within this context, the five requirements listed in 1.1 constitute a very simple beginning, since they focus on the size of numbers, and do not yet address *arithmetic*. But it would be unwise to assume that these ideas will therefore not require consolidation and strengthening. Consider these two released items[12] from TIMSS 2011 which were set to pupils in Year 5.

1.1A In which number does the 8 have the value 800?

A 1,468 B 2,587 C 3,809 D 8,634

1.1B Which number is 100 more than 5,432?

A 6,432 B 5,532 C 5,442 D 5,433

These are very basic questions; and the answer to each question is given as one of four options. One should therefore expect almost all pupils to answer correctly. But the results suggest that we in England may expect less than comparable countries (some of whom start school significantly later than we do). We have included here the results from Flemish Belgium (who took part in TIMSS 2011 at Year 5, but not at Year 9).

1.1A Russia 90%, USA 87%, Flem Bel 87%, Australia 75%, England 68%, Hungary 66%

1.1B Flem Bel 84%, Russia 82%, USA 80%, Australia 73%, England 73%, Hungary 73%

Moreover, the examples 1.4A, 1.4B, 1.4C, 1.4D, 1.4G, 1.4K in Part II above suggest that this weakness needs to be (and is often not) addressed between Year 5 and Year 9.

Given the fourth requirement listed at the start of 1.1 we include an additional item from TIMSS 2011 for pupils in Year 9:

---

[12] http://timss.bc.edu/timss2011/international-released-items.html

1.1C Write $3\frac{5}{6}$ in decimal form rounded to two decimal places.

Here one expects significantly lower scores—but the English success rate is nevertheless disappointing:

1.1C Russia 39%, Australia 31%, Hungary 29%,
USA 29%, (Ave. 25%), England 24%,

The second bullet point at the start of 1.1 refers to "the number line". At Key Stages 1 and 2 the number line provides a valuable image which allows the different forms of "number" to be seen as part of a *single number system*. Moving along the number line also provides a useful physical model for skip-counting and for addition and subtraction—including with negative numbers (though it is less helpful with multiplication and division). But during Key Stage 3 the number line gradually loses its separate existence and becomes identified with the x-axis (and y-axis) in a coordinate system. The ordering of real numbers is then needed on both axes to locate points in the plane, where pupils need to learn to work comfortably with coordinates "in all four quadrants".

At Key Stage 3 the family of real numbers extends to include not only decimals and fractions, but also *negative numbers*, and later *surds*. A lot of work is needed to ensure that negative numbers and their arithmetic become a natural part of pupils' mental universe of mathematics. For example:

- locating "−3" and "−2.5" on the number line, or x-axis, helps to underline the ordering (e.g. $-3 < -2.5 < -2$);
- common sense may suggest that "measures" and "quantities" have to be *positive*, but pupils need to learn to interpret *negative* quantities in practical situations, so that, for example, "−3 hours' from now" is routinely interpreted as "3 hours *ago*".

The inequality symbols mentioned in the second requirement listed at the start of 1.1 may appear unproblematic. We see $2 < 3$ as being entirely natural; and $-3 < 2$ may seem only marginally less obvious (though it still needs to become second nature). However $-3 < -2$ is nowhere near as obvious as one might think, and has clearly not been well handled in the past.[13]

There seem to be few TIMSS 2011 released items on ordering numbers. But one Year 5 item suggests a need for further work on ordering fractions.

1.1D Which of these fractions is larger than $\frac{1}{2}$?

A $\frac{3}{5}$ B $\frac{3}{6}$ C $\frac{3}{8}$ D $\frac{3}{10}$

1.1D USA 62%, Russia 62%, Flem Bel 58%, Australia 54%, England 50%, Hungary 48%

Each such set of responses needs to be assessed on its own merits—bearing in mind that there are many hidden details that make the raw data hard to interpret reliably. For example, as far as one can tell, the primary curriculum in Russia does not seem to include explicit work on fractions or their arithmetic; but the *idea* of a fraction is clearly addressed in some preliminary way. The success rates in other countries are therefore merely guides as to what might reasonably be expected. The success rate for English pupils in example 1.1D is in fact just above the "international average"; but this "average" is skewed by many countries whose education systems are much less well developed. So it makes sense to focus any comparison on systems that are more naturally comparable with England.

In helping pupils make sense of "$<$" and "$\leqslant$", we need to be aware that these are *relations*, which are true if used for certain *pairs* of real numbers, and are false for other pairs. The truth of "$2 < 3$" and "$2 \leqslant 3$" may seem obvious. But it can be harder for pupils to accept that "$2 \leqslant 2$" is equally true.

In many countries, the list of standard symbols in the second bullet point at the start of 1.1 would include a symbol (usually $\approx$) to stand for "approximately equal to". It is perfectly natural to stretch the use of "=" to include

[13] http://www.manchestereveningnews.co.uk/news/greater-manchester-news/cool-cash-card-confusion-1009701

"$2\pi = 6.28$ (2 d.p.)", or "$\sqrt{2} = 1.4$ (2 s.f.)", or "$\sin 60^\circ = 0.866$ (3 d.p.)".

But given the requirement to use symbols "correctly", and to work with *rounding, estimates* and *approximations,* it is worth introducing a special symbol "$\approx$", and using it consistently whenever one is "actively approximating", as in:

$$35{,}941 \times 273 \approx 33{,}333 \times 300 \approx 10{,}000{,}000 = 1 \times 10^7.$$

These matters are addressed in more detail in Section 1.7 below.

The reference to "measures" in the first, second, and fourth requirements must include *compound measures.* A "compound" measure arises when two basic measures are combined: *area* is a compound measure, where length is multiplied by length, measured in "cm^2" (say); *speed* arises when length is divided by time, and is measured in "metres per second" or "miles per hour"; *density* arises when mass is divided by volume, and is measured in "grams per cubic centimetre". Other compound measures include "rates of pay", "fuel consumption", and "unit prices". One might think that compound units will be familiar from Key Stage 2 (even if only implicitly), because any problem which involves "measures" and "multiplication" inevitably involves *compound* measures:

> **Question** "I travel at 60 mph for 4.5 hours. What distance do I cover?"
>
> **Answer** $4.5 \times 60 = 270$ miles
>
> **Question** "My car consumes 8 litres of petrol per 100km. How much fuel is needed to drive 170 kilometres?"
>
> **Answer** $8 \times 1.7 = 13.6$ litres.

Yet compound measures are not explicitly mentioned in the Key Stage 2 programme of study! So those teaching at Key Stage 3 must anticipate that time may be needed to ensure that pupils can work comfortably with compound measures.

We end by mentioning one topic that can contribute much to pupils' understanding of place value, but which has dropped out of the official curriculum. That is, to engage in numerical work in *other bases*. We particularly recommend work in *base* 2, in *base* 9, and in *base* 11. *Base* 2 lies behind the 0–1 of all electronic devices; but it has other pedagogical advantages (such as allowing a row of seated pupils to emulate the sequence of digits representing a number, and to enact a human numerical "counter", with each pupil standing for "1" and sitting for "0"). *Base* 9 and *base* 11 are closer to the familiar *base* 10; and it can be highly instructive for pupils to extend the standard written algorithms by inventing and working with a new symbol for the "digit 10"—say "X"—when working in *base* 11. They can also discover the thought-provoking fact that

> in *base* 11 a number is "divisible by ten"
>
> precisely when "the sum of the digits is divisible by ten",

which matches the base 10 rule for divisibility by 9 (see Section 1.4.4 below). For more confident pupils it can be highly instructive to extend the notation for integers to "decimals" in these other bases, and to realise that whether a fraction has a terminating "decimal" depends on the *base*, not on the fraction itself.

1.2. [Subject content: *Number* p. 5]

- **use the four operations, including formal written methods, applied to integers, decimals, proper and improper fractions, and mixed numbers, all both positive and negative**
- **use conventional notation for the priority of operations, including brackets, powers, roots and reciprocals**
- **recognise and use relationships between operations including inverse operations**

The final paragraph of Section 1.1 above illustrates how difficult it is to separate the notation for *place value* from arithmetic, or work with *operations* (the four rules, powers, etc.), which is the focus of the present section.

1.2.1 Throughout the official Key Stage 3 programme of study there is an unfortunate silence concerning *mental* and *oral* work with numbers. The increase in the variety of forms in which "numbers" are encountered (positive integers, fractions, terminating and recurring decimals, negative numbers, surds, etc.) *increases* the need for such oral work at this level.

- Work with integers needs to be continually exercised, and extended to negatives.
- The same mental procedures need to be actively extended to work with decimals.
- Work with integers needs to be extended rather differently to support work with fractions.
- The "algebraic" conventions (for powers, for fractions, for brackets, for priority of operations, and for roots) need to be exercised fluently and automatically *with numerical expressions*, so that they are clearly understood **before** these conventions are extended to symbols.

As the examples 1.4A–1.4K in Part II indicate, such mental work has clearly been undervalued in English secondary schools for some decades, with significant consequences for pupils' subsequent progression. Here we can only illustrate what is needed on the simplest level, where pupils should be routinely expected to evaluate mentally such expressions as:

> $1.2 + 0.8$, $2(14.3 - 3.8)$, 17×0.9, 1.2×80, $1.08 \div 1.2$, $1.7 \times 13 + 0.3 \times 13$, $(0.8)^2$, $(0.4)^3$, $(1.2)^2$, $(0.12)^2$, $\sqrt{2.25}$, $\sqrt{1.96}$, $\sqrt{6.25}$, $\sqrt{16}$, $(\sqrt{2})^3$, $\sqrt{27}$, $\sqrt{100}$, $\sqrt{1000}$, $\sqrt[3]{27}$, $\sqrt[3]{64}$, $0.625 + \frac{3}{5}$, $\frac{4}{100} + \frac{35}{10000}$ as a decimal, $\frac{3}{10}$ of 40% of $50 \div 60$, $\frac{1}{3} - \frac{1}{4}$, $3\frac{5}{6}$ as a decimal.

In addition to mastering simple calculation, mental and oral work is perhaps even **more** important, and even less common, in **thinking about** calculation, and numerical relations. This is indicated by the following three released items[14] for Year 5 pupils from TIMSS 2001.

1.2.1A □ stands for the number of pencils Pete had. Kim gave Pete 3 more pencils. How many pencils does Pete now have?

A $3 \div \square$ B $\square + 3$ C $\square - 3$ D $3 \times \square$

1.2.1B $4 \times \square = 28$. What number goes in the box to make this sentence true?

1.2.1C $3 + 8 = \square + 6$. What number goes in the box to make this number sentence true?

In all three cases English success rates are around, or below the international average.

1.2.1A Russia 91%, Flem Bel 85%, USA 83%, Hungary 82%, Australia 79%, England 75%

1.2.1B Russia 95%, Flem Bel 94%, Hungary 91%, USA 87%, England 82%, Australia 77%

1.2.1C Russia 80%, Hungary 50%, Flem Bel 49%, USA 47%, Australia 33%, England 29%

1.2.2 The standard *written* algorithms need further attention at Key Stage 3 to secure their reliability for integers. More confident pupils can avoid mere repetition by concentrating on *inverse problems* to test their understanding (the meaning of "inverse problems" was explained in Part II, Section 1.2.3). We offer two more released items from TIMSS 2011 for Year 5 pupils as evidence that there will still be plenty to do in Year 7.

1.2.2A $5631 + 286 = \ldots$

1.2.2B $23 \times 19 = \ldots$

---

[14] http://timss.bc.edu/timss2011/international-released-items.html

Some will find the English success rates acceptable. But these are exercises one should expect almost all pupils to get right—as the results from other countries tend to confirm. In all cases the English performance is either below or just above the "international average".

1.2.2A Russia 89%, USA 84%, Hungary 77%,
England 67%, Flem Bel 66%, Australia 57%

1.2.2B Russia 74%, USA 59%, Hungary 40%,
England 37%, Flem Bel 26%, Australia 11%

Schools who actively seek to strengthen arithmetic in Year 7 and who need harder "inverse" problems for pupils whose arithmetic is strong, could do worse than to include lots of "missing digit" problems (for example, see Tony Gardiner, *Extension Mathematics Book Alpha* p. 46, p. 61, p. 74, p. 125).

These written procedures then need to be extended to decimals. And the simplest calculations with *decimals* (such as 71.6×2.8, or $271.6 \div 2.8$) demonstrate that this extension to decimals needs the corresponding integer procedures to routinely handle *multi-digit inputs* (at the very least 716×28, and $2716 \div 28$). In the released TIMSS 2011 items at Year 9, decimal arithmetic mostly arises in context. But the following item tends to reinforce the suggestion that we currently expect too little.

1.2.2C $42.65 + 5.748 = \ldots$

1.2.2C Russia 90%, USA 89%, Hungary 88%,
Australia 82%, England 79%

1.2.3 At this level, calculation with fractions becomes increasingly pervasive (solving simple numerical problems involving multiplication; understanding how the standard written algorithms of column arithmetic for integers extend to those for decimals; rearranging equations and simplifying expressions; using percentages; working with ratio and proportion). And something clearly needs to change if many more pupils are to learn to calculate reliably and confidently with fractions: examples 1.4A–1.4K in Part II above suggest that we currently fail to lay the most basic foundations. Rather than offer a trite summary here, we postpone discussion of fractions until Section 1.6 below— where, as a tentative contribution to the re-thinking that is needed, we outline some of the relevant background.

1.2.4 All three of the official requirements listed at the start of 1.2 include the word "use"; but the intended scope of the word is left unexplained. The official intention here may be restricted to *technical* usage, rather than to "applications". But we take the opportunity to explore what it means for pupils to be able to use what they have learned.

The last 35 years have witnessed a stream of complaints that those leaving school cannot "use" what they have been certified as "knowing". This suggests that everyone may have misunderstood what is required if a learned technique is to become available for use.

The ability to use the mathematics one knows

- includes its use within other parts of mathematics; and
- extends to simple applications, or word problems (see Section 2.3.3 in Part II for an explanation of what is meant by *word problems*).

In both domains, pupils' inability to "use what they know" often has the same cause, and stems from

- the fact that a typical technique is first learned as a deterministic *direct* procedure,
- whereas applications frequently require a flexibility in using the procedure in the spirit of the corresponding *inverse* process (the distinction between *direct* and *inverse* is explained in Part II, Section 1.2.3).

In other words, pupils' difficulties often reflect our failure to recognise the gulf between

- fluency in the underlying easy *direct* skill, and
- what is needed to work flexibly with this direct skill, and to handle the related *inverse problems*, or variations, which is what is generally needed for most applications.

Mathematics teaching and assessment have focused too strongly on the easy *direct* skills, and have often overlooked the fact that fluency, flexibility, and "use" require that far more attention be given to simple *inverse* problems. A pupil may know how to

- "find 75% of £120"

yet fail to relate this *direct* operation to *inverse* variations, such as

- "A price of £90 is raised to £120. What percentage increase is this?", or
- "Calculate the original price if I got 25% off and paid £90".

For each direct process, we need to allow far more time to develop the flexibility that is needed if pupils are to use the process effectively to solve related *indirect* problems.

1.2.5 The distinction in the previous subsection is illustrated in its simplest form by the third requirement listed at the start of 1.2. Once one moves into Key Stage 3, the key to arithmetic (and later to algebra) lies in *simplification.* One no longer applies brute force to calculate with each expression as it is given. Instead one looks first for ways of *simplifying*. And the key to simplification lies in looking for

"complexifications that cancel each other out",

that is, for hidden instances of operations cancelled out by their inverses. For example, when faced with the question:

"How many weeks are there in 5040^2 seconds?"

one would like pupils to set up the relevant equations

$$\begin{aligned} 5040^2 \text{ seconds} &= \frac{5040 \times 5040}{60} \text{ minutes} \\ &= \frac{5040 \times 5040}{60 \times 60} \text{ hours} \\ &= \frac{5040 \times 5040}{60 \times 60 \times 24} \text{ days} \\ &= \frac{5040 \times 5040}{60 \times 60 \times 24 \times 7} \text{ weeks} \end{aligned}$$

without evaluating $5040^2 = \ldots$, and without carrying out long divisions (or using a calculator), and then to look for ways of *cancelling*.

When dealing with algebraic expressions:

- It is permissible (but usually silly) to split up a single term and to spread the parts around to change a given expression into one that looks much more complicated; it is more helpful to reverse such "complexifications" by "collecting up" similar-looking terms to produce a more compact expression, which is then much easier to comprehend at a glance.
- It is equally permissible (and usually equally silly) to multiply the numerator and denominator of a given (numerical or algebraic) fraction by the same non-zero expression, and then to multiply out to make a new rational expression that appears more complicated than the original; but it is generally more sensible to factorise, to identify (non-zero) common factors, and to cancel in order to simplify.

That is,

- operations come in linked "direct-inverse" pairs which cancel each other out (addition-subtraction; multiplication-division; powers-roots; multiplying out and factorising; etc.).

Simplification is essentially the art of spotting such combinations, and cancelling them out.

This key algebraic art needs to be exercised and mastered first within *arithmetic*—so that *numerical expressions* are no longer "blindly evaluated", but are routinely simplified, using what we have called *structural arithmetic* (see Part II, Section 2.1.1)—so that one routinely notices: that

$$28 + 186 + 72 = (28 + 72) + 186 = 286;$$

or that

$$\frac{36}{54} = \frac{4 \times 9}{6 \times 9} = \frac{4}{6} = \frac{2}{3}.$$

One is then in a position to be pleasantly surprised by equivalences that are less obvious (such as that $\sqrt{3 + 2\sqrt{2}} = \sqrt{(1 + \sqrt{2})^2} = 1 + \sqrt{2}$).

1.2.6 The first of the requirements listed at the start of 1.2 refers to "proper and improper fractions" and to "mixed fractions". The expressions "proper fraction" and "improper fraction" make sense in Key Stage 2, but they are no longer really appropriate at Key Stage 3.

Fractions are introduced in Key Stage 1 and Key Stage 2 as parts of a whole, and so are automatically *less than* 1; hence, **at that stage**, when one comes to refer to fractions that are *greater than* 1, it makes sense to call them "improper". But the distinction is not a mathematical distinction; it arises because of the way fractions are introduced.

From Key Stage 3 onwards all fractions, whether greater than 1 or less than 1, should be treated in the same way, as the quotient of two integers $\frac{p}{q}$, with $q > 0$. Hence the use of words like "proper" and "improper" should be left behind (along with such language as "timesing").

Similarly, though it may sometimes be appropriate to present an answer in "mixed" form (say as $3\frac{5}{6}$), the expression "mixed number" is out of place in secondary mathematics.

1.3. [Subject content: *Number* p. 6]

- **use a calculator and other technologies to calculate results accurately and then interpret them appropriately**

"Calculators and other technologies" were first advocated at secondary level some 40 or more years ago. Yet we still do not seem to have forged a consensus as to when their use is "appropriate", and when not.

The opening *Aims* (see page 2 of the National Curriculum programmes of study for Key Stage 3) include the sensible warning that calculators, etc.

> "**should not** be used as **a substitute** for good written and mental arithmetic" [emphasis added].

However, this sound advice still needs to be interpreted. And the positive guidance as to when calculator use is "appropriate" is only slightly more helpful. The general advice offered at the beginning of the programmes of study for Key Stages 1 and 2, on pages 3 and 4,[15] says that calculators should only be introduced

> "to support pupils' conceptual understanding and exploration of more complex number problems, **if written and mental arithmetic** are secure" [emphasis added].

The dilemma highlighted by this advice refers to *integer* arithmetic in *primary* schools. But the same dilemma recurs throughout Key Stage 3—with *decimal arithmetic,* with *fractions,* with *surds,* and so on. Secure calculation by hand and in the head is a crucial ingredient of *the way beginners internalise meaning, structures, and procedures.* So in each case the above instruction would seem to imply that

- pupils should achieve conceptual understanding and mental and written fluency before routinely using a calculator,
- but that once a suitable level of fluency has been achieved, one can safely delegate "more complex number problems" to the calculator, and exploit the power of the calculator to extend conceptual understanding into new realms (see the example at the end of this section).

The introduction to the programmes of study for Key Stage 1 and 2 and for Key Stage 3 both state that

> "In both primary and secondary schools, teachers should use their judgement about when ICT tools should be used."

But the wider community remains confused. The judgement in the previous paragraph (that "secure calculation is an important part of the way beginners internalise meaning") would seem to be a reasonable summary of views in many other countries. But teachers in England will know that the mathematics education community here remains divided. Hence teachers must be prepared to develop and to use their own judgement as they are exhorted to do.

---

[15] https://www.gov.uk/government/uploads/system/uploads/attachment_data/file/335158/PRIMARY_national_curriculum_-_Mathematics_220714.pdf

To illustrate the divide, we give just two recent examples. The first is a report published by the *Joint Mathematical Council*[16] and a riposte.[17] The second is a debate between a strong advocate of "computer based mathematics" in schools and an agnostic:[18] (see "Technology and maths") .

Technology is clearly seen as "sexy" by politicians and by enthusiasts. And its evident potential should certainly be explored. But it is not easy for ordinary teachers to see beyond the rhetoric in order to discern

- whether we have already discovered some magic "royal road" to elementary mathematics, that removes the need for beginners to master the art of hand calculation; or
- whether those who currently advocate increased use of technology by beginners are getting ahead of themselves, and are misleading the rest of us as to what is currently in pupils' interests.

Whatever may be the eventual impact of technology on the learning of mathematics, the present evidence from international studies (illustrated by examples 1.4A–1.4K in Part II) would seem to be that we in England have tended to delegate calculation to the calculator or computer *far too easily*. Instead of using technology to achieve *more*, we have used it as a convenient *alternative* to achieving meaning and mastery. That is, we have failed to heed the exhortation of the official programme of study, and have allowed technology to be "**used as a substitute for**" pupils' understanding of written and mental arithmetic.

Computation by hand, or in the head, has too often been repudiated as if it were merely outmoded drudgery, or some puritanical hangover. But the importance of calculation at all levels stems from the role played by mental and written procedures in the subtle process of human **sense-making**. So we should perhaps hesitate before discarding it until such time as we are sure that we have other ways of establishing the kind of meaning that will allow pupils to use elementary mathematics with confidence.

---

[16] http://www.jmc.org.uk/documents/JMC_Report_Digital_Technologies_2011.pdf

[17] http://education.lms.ac.uk/wp-content/uploads/2012/02/Gardiner_on_JMC.pdf

[18] http://www.cambridgeassessment.org.uk/news/playlist/view/maths-podcasts/

The requirement that pupils should "use calculators and other technologies"

> "to calculate results **accurately** and then interpret them appropriately" [emphasis added]

needs to be interpreted with care. A calculator certainly allows us all to work with messier numerical data than we could otherwise manage. But for most calculations, a calculator is the opposite of "accurate": its value lies in the fact that it is "quick and dirty", and produces an answer which is a very good **approximation**, but which may not be exact. The ubiquity of calculators, and their ease of use makes it important for pupils to develop their own internal sense of number so that they can use calculators intelligently, interpret the approximate answers which they produce, and use these tools to extend their own powers of analysis.

To give an example from within elementary mathematics (having one eye on the next subsection), one might invite more able pupils in Year 8 or Year 9 to work (initially *without a calculator*) to address these three questions:

(a) Find a prime number which is one less than a square.

(b) Find another such prime number. And another.

(c) How many such prime numbers are there?

Different teachers will exploit the proposed task in different ways. Pupils must first access whatever internal register of squares they have, and then reinforce and extend their internal list to generate:

$$(1^2 - 1 = 0,)\ 2^2 - 1 = \mathbf{3},\ 3^2 - 1 = \mathbf{8},\ 4^2 - 1 = \mathbf{15},\ 5^2 - 1 = \mathbf{24},$$
$$6^2 - 1 = \mathbf{35},\ 7^2 - 1 = \mathbf{48},\ 8^2 - 1 = \mathbf{63},\ 9^2 - 1 = \mathbf{80},\ 10^2 - 1 = \mathbf{99},$$
$$11^2 - 1 = \mathbf{120},\ 12^2 - 1 = \mathbf{143},\ 13^2 - 1 = \mathbf{\ldots}\ , \ldots$$

They must then decide which of these numbers are prime. The associated "noise" (of having first to think about squares, then to subtract 1) makes this more awkward than simply asking pupils to test given integers to see whether they are prime. So one can anticipate some surprising mistakes. For example: though 8, 15, 24, 35, 48 are unlikely to be labelled as primes, the surrounding "noise" means that part (b) may well lead to 63 and 143 being proposed as candidate primes.

There are challenges here for pupils on many levels. A calculator may at first be used simply to extend the list of squares. If so, then 168, 195, 224, 255, 288, 360, 440 are unlikely to be proposed as primes; but 399 and 483 might well be, and 323 will almost certainly feature.

However, once the proposed candidates 63 ($= 7 \times 9$), 143 ($= 11 \times 13$), and 323 ($= \cdots \times \ldots$) have been seen to fail, one would like pupils to think rather than just press buttons and guess. A mixture of patience and prodding should allow them to discover the apparent pattern

$$8 = 2 \times 4,$$

$$15 = 3 \times 5,$$

$$24 = 4 \times 6, \text{ etc.},$$

and they can then to use the distributive law to multiply out

$$(n-1)(n+1) = n(n+1) - 1(n+1) = n^2 + n - n - 1 = n^2 - 1,$$

and to discover

- the advantages of thinking and working with **symbols** ("$n^2 - 1$")
- rather than with words ("one less than a square").

1.4. [Subject content: *Number* p. 5]

- **use the concepts and vocabulary of prime numbers, factors (or divisors), multiples, common factors, common multiples, highest common factor, lowest common multiple, prime factorisation, including using product notation and the unique factorisation property**
- **use integer powers and associated real roots (square, cube and higher), recognise powers of 2, 3, 4, 5 and distinguish**

between exact representations of roots and their decimal approximations

This collection of topics related to integer arithmetic deserves to be taken more seriously than has perhaps traditionally been the case at secondary level. The following released item from TIMSS 2011 for pupils in Year 9 suggests that work on primes and factors from primary school is often not followed up.

> **1.4A** Which of these shows how 36 can be expressed as a product of prime factors?
>
> A 6×6 B 4×9 C $4 \times 3 \times 3$ D $2 \times 2 \times 3 \times 3$
>
> **1.4A** Hungary 69%, Russia 68%, USA 64%,
> England 51%, Australia 45%

Bare hands integer arithmetic may suffice for pupils to find HCFs (to cancel fractions), and LCMs (to add or subtract fractions by writing both with a common denominator). But if the official requirements are interpreted coherently, then the listed ideas constitute a valuable "Key Stage 3 introduction to *Number theory*", a subject which is increasingly important in a world dominated by "calculators and other technologies".

1.4.1 The second listed requirement in 1.4 "use integer powers" is perhaps the simplest starting point. Pupils should recognise and work with

> squares: $1^2 = 1$, $2^2 = 4$, $3^2 = 9$, $4^2 = 16$, $5^2 = 25$, $6^2 = 36$, $7^2 = 49$, $8^2 = 64$, $9^2 = 81$, $10^2 = 100$, $11^2 = 121$, $12^2 = 144, \ldots$;
>
> and
>
> cubes: $1^3 = 1$, $2^3 = 8$, $3^3 = 27$, $4^3 = 64$, $5^3 = 125$, $6^3 = 216, \ldots$, $10^3 = 1000$.

They should also recognise the powers of 10 in exponent form and know the corresponding values:

> powers of 10: 10, $10^2 = 100$, $10^3 = 1000$, $10^4 = 10000$, $10^5 = 100000$, $10^6 = 1000000$, etc.

And they should work with and recognise powers of small integers, such as:

> powers of 2: 2, $2^2 = 4$, $2^3 = 8$, $2^4 = 16$, $2^5 = 32$, $2^6 = 64$, $2^7 = 128$, $2^8 = 256$, $2^9 = 512$, $2^{10} = 1024$
>
> powers of 3: 3, $3^2 = 9$, $3^3 = 27$, $3^4 = 81$, $3^5 = 243$
>
> powers of 4: 4, $4^2 = 16$, $4^3 = 64$, $4^4 = 256$, $4^5 = 1024$
>
> powers of 5: 5, $5^2 = 25$, $5^3 = 125$, $5^4 = 625$.

Squaring is a "unary operation" or function (in that the *output* n^2 is uniquely determined by a single *input*). Once sufficiently many squares are known, they can be exploited to interpret the *exact* meaning of the *inverse* unary operation, that is the square root function $\sqrt{\ }$ where

> $\sqrt{n}$ denotes "the **positive** number whose square is equal to n".

Notice that, since $\sqrt{\ }$ is to be a *function*, $\sqrt{4}$ must denote a *unique* value—namely the positive number whose square is equal to 4: i.e. 2. In contrast, the quadratic equation "$x^2 = 4$" has **two** solutions, which are $\pm\sqrt{4}$. Later, appropriate groups of pupils can help to formulate and **prove**:

Claim If $a^2 = b^2$, then $a = \pm b$.

Proof Suppose $a^2 = b^2$.

$\therefore a^2 - b^2 = 0$

$\therefore (a - b)(a + b) = 0$

$\therefore a - b = 0$, or $a + b = 0$, so $a = \pm b$. **QED**

This shows that there is just one positive number whose square has a given positive value.

Provided n is a perfect square, pupils can find the *exact* value of $\sqrt{n}$: for small squares:

$$\sqrt{4} = 2, \quad \sqrt{9} = 3, \quad \sqrt{16} = 4, \quad \sqrt{25} = 5;$$

and for larger squares:

$$\sqrt{81} = 9, \quad \sqrt{100} = 10, \quad \sqrt{121} = 11, \quad \sqrt{256} = 16.$$

They may be encouraged to notice that

$$\sqrt{4 \times 9} = \sqrt{36} = 6 = 2 \times 3 = \sqrt{4} \times \sqrt{9},$$

and that

$$\sqrt{9 \times 9} = 9 = \sqrt{9} \times \sqrt{9}.$$

They can then use this as a short cut to find the square root of larger squares such as $\sqrt{16 \times 25}$.

[Later they can prove that:

Claim $\sqrt{a} \times \sqrt{b} = \sqrt{ab}$ whenever a and b are positive:

Proof $\sqrt{a} \times \sqrt{b}$ is clearly positive (since $\sqrt{a}$ and $\sqrt{b}$ are both positive).

And $(\sqrt{a} \times \sqrt{b})^2 = (\sqrt{a})^2 \times (\sqrt{b})^2 = ab$

$\therefore \sqrt{a} \times \sqrt{b} = \sqrt{ab}$. **QED**]

And once sufficiently many *cubes* are known, pupils can find $\sqrt[3]{n}$ when n is a perfect cube:

$$\sqrt[3]{8} = 2,\ \sqrt[3]{27} = 3,\ \sqrt[3]{64} = 4,\ \sqrt[3]{1000} = 10.$$

With help they may notice that

$$\sqrt[3]{8 \times 27} = \sqrt[3]{216} = 6 = 2 \times 3 = \sqrt[3]{8} \times \sqrt[3]{27}.$$

This basic repertoire of calculations using powers and roots can then develop in two very different directions—one focusing on *calculation*, and the other on *structure*.

1.4.2 Further calculation The notation $\sqrt{n}$ and $\sqrt[3]{n}$ for square roots and cube roots has many features in common with the notation for fractions.

Some fractions, like $\frac{8}{2} = 4$, or $\frac{1}{4} = 0.25$, stand for familiar numbers, and can be *exactly* evaluated. But most fractions one can write down (such as $\frac{1}{6} \approx 0.167$) do not stand for any otherwise familiar number, and cannot be evaluated exactly. The value of the fraction notation is that it provides a way of writing *exact expressions* for "ideas of numbers", which we often have no other way of writing exactly, such as "that number—six identical copies of which add up to 1".

Similarly, the functions $\sqrt{\ }$ and $\sqrt[3]{\ }$ allow us to write *exact* expressions for numbers, most of which cannot be evaluated exactly as decimals, or in any other way. We know that $\sqrt{4} = 2$. But what number is represented by $\sqrt{2}$? Or by $\sqrt{3}$? Or by $\sqrt{300}$? Or by $\sqrt{0.3}$? Or by $\sqrt{\frac{1}{3}}$?

Before we worry about the square root of fractions or decimals, there is plenty of work to be done to establish the meaning and the arithmetical rules for working with *surds*: that is numbers of the form $\sqrt{n}$ when n is an integer. For example, we need to ensure

- that $\sqrt{10}$ is understood formally to be "the (positive) number whose square is 10";
- that since 10 lies between 9 and 16, $\sqrt{10}$ is seen to be slightly bigger than $\sqrt{9} = 3$ (and a lot less than $\sqrt{16} = 4$);
- that pupils compare the side length of a square of area 10 square units, with that for a square of area 9, and one of area 16; and
- that they later compare the length of a *diagonal* of a 1 by 3 rectangle

(a) with the length (= 3) of the longest side, and

(b) with the length (= 4) of the route round the perimeter of the rectangle from one corner to the opposite corner.

These ideas can later be taken further. *Pythagoras' Theorem* shows that an isosceles right angled triangle with legs of length 1 has a hypotenuse of length exactly $\sqrt{2}$. The hypotenuse is clearly longer than each of the two legs; and the *triangle inequality* shows that the hypotenuse is less than the sum of the two shorter sides. So we know that $1 < \sqrt{2} < 2$. But to pin down the value of $\sqrt{2}$ more accurately requires us to use a little of what we know about integer squares:

$$14^2 = 196 < 200 < 225 = 15^2$$
$$\therefore 14 = \sqrt{196} < \sqrt{200} < \sqrt{225} = 15$$
$$\therefore 14 < \sqrt{100 \times 2} = \sqrt{100} \times \sqrt{2} < 15$$
$$\therefore 14 < 10\sqrt{2} < 15$$

$$\therefore 1.4 < \sqrt{2} < 1.5$$

[In short: $1.4^2 = 1.96 < 2$, and $1.5^2 = 2.25 > 2$.]

Similarly, *Pythagoras' Theorem* shows that an equilateral triangle of side 2 has height exactly $\sqrt{3}$, and that this height is less than the hypotenuse, so $\sqrt{3} < 2$; and the triangle inequality shows that $1 + \sqrt{3} > 2$. Hence $1 < \sqrt{3} < 2$. But to pin down the value $\sqrt{3}$ more accurately we have to use what we know about integer powers to find reasonable estimates:

$$17^2 = 289 < 300 < 324 = 18^2$$

$$\therefore 17 = \sqrt{289} < \sqrt{300} < \sqrt{324} = 18$$

$$\therefore 17 < \sqrt{100 \times 3} = \sqrt{100} \times \sqrt{3} < 18$$

$$\therefore 17 < 10\sqrt{3} < 18$$

$$\therefore 1.7 < \sqrt{3} < 1.8$$

[In short: $1.7^2 = 2.89 < 3$, and $1.8^2 = 3.24 > 3$.]

In the same way one can use what pupils know about perfect cubes to ensure

- that $\sqrt[3]{10}$ is interpreted as "the number whose cube is equal to 10";
- that this number is seen to be slightly bigger than $\sqrt[3]{8} = 2$ and considerably smaller than $\sqrt[3]{27} = 3$;
- that pupils compare an imagined cube of volume 10 cubic units with a smaller cube of volume 8 and a larger cube of volume 27 cubic units—noting and understanding how a modest increase in the edge length leads to a cube with *three times* the volume!

1.4.3 Structure: the index laws The *structural* (or *algebraic*) theme related to powers prepares the ground for the *index laws*. The index laws are not explicitly mentioned within the Key Stage 3 programme of study, but there are several reasons why they need to be squarely addressed at this level.

One reason is that, as we shall see in Section 1.5, zeroth and negative powers are needed to represent real numbers *in standard form*; and the way we define these powers only really makes sense if we think in terms of the advantages of "preserving the index laws".

A more basic reason is for pupils to understand why

> when we multiply a digit in the 10^m place (or column) by a digit in the 10^n place (or column), the answer belongs in the 10^{m+n} column.

For this to make sense, pupils already need to know in their bones how products of powers work: for example, that

$$10^2 \times 10^5 = (10 \times 10) \times (10 \times 10 \times 10 \times 10 \times 10) = 10^{2+5}, \text{ and}$$
$$2^2 \times 2^5 = (2 \times 2) \times (2 \times 2 \times 2 \times 2 \times 2) = 2^{2+5}.$$

Once pupils

- think of the *place value* of positions, or columns, in terms of the exponent of the "power of 10", rather than verbally as "units, tens, hundreds, etc.", and
- realise that "when we *multiply* powers, we *add* exponents",

it becomes natural to think of the **unit** as $\mathbf{10^0 = 1}$.

> The rightmost place when representing an integer then corresponds to the "(units digit) $\times 10^0$".

The fact that $10^0 = 1$ then fits in with the way powers multiply (since we want $10^1 \times 10^0 = 10^{(1+0)} = 10$).

Once the units column (*just to the* **left** of the decimal point) is associated with 10^0, it becomes plausible that the place *immediately to the* **right** of the decimal point might correspond to "10^{-1}". And the idea that "when we *multiply* powers, we *add* exponents" also helps to explain why we take "10^{-1}" to equal $\frac{1}{10}$ (since we want: $10^1 \times 10^{-1} = 10^{1+(-1)} = 10^0 = 1 = 10 \times \frac{1}{10}$).

1.4.4 Introduction to number theory It is easy to compare, and to add, two fractions with the **same** denominator; but it is not at all obvious how to compare, or to add, two fractions with **different** denominators m, n. However, as soon as we change each fraction to one that is equivalent to it, and which has denominator "$LCM(m, n)$", comparison is again immediate, and addition, subtraction and division can be carried out easily. Hence LCMs come into their own as soon as we wish to compare, or to add, subtract, or divide two fractions with different denominators m and n. In general HCFs and LCMs feature whenever a problem requires us to switch to a common unit that works for both m and n (whether a multiple of each, or a submultiple—or factor—of each).

The HCF and LCM of two given integers m, n are easy to find in a primitive way.

> **HCF**: Each of the given integers m, n has a finite number of *factors*, and these can be listed; the two lists can then be scanned to find the *"highest"*, or largest, factor *in both lists*.
> **LCM**: The LCM of the given integers m, n can be found by making a list of (positive) multiples of each number ($2m$, $3m$, $4m, \ldots$; and $2n, 3n, 4n, \ldots$) and looking for the *"least"* multiple that occurs *in both lists*.

These primitive approaches are easy to implement, but are slightly unwieldy. Moreover, they do not immediately suggest, or explain why it is always true that:

$$HCF(m,n) \times LCM(m,n) = m \times n.$$

For suitable groups of pupils it is worth making sure that this result is discovered, or at least noticed, and if possible proved.

[**Proof** Let $HCF(m,n) = h$.

$\therefore m = h \times m'$ and $n = h \times n'$, where m' and n' have no common factors.

$\therefore m' \times n = m' \times (h \times n') = (m' \times h) \times n' = m \times n'$ is a multiple of m and of n, so is a common multiple of both m and n.

The fact that it is the LCM follows from the important fact that every common multiple of both m and n is also a multiple of their LCM. (So if there were a *smaller* common multiple of m and n, say k, then it would have to be a proper factor of $m' \times h \times n'$ and the quotient would be a factor of both m' and n'.)

$\therefore HCF(m,n) \times LCM(m,n) = h \times (m' \times n) = (h \times m') \times n = m \times n.$ **QED]**

The observation that $LCM(m,n)$ is a factor of every common multiple of m and n is not hard, but cannot easily be proved at this level. However, it can be established as a "fact of experience" by listing the common multiples of suitable pairs, such as:

2 and 3: 6, 12, 18, 24, ...
6 and 8: 24, 48, 72, 96, ...
6 and 14: 42, 84, 126, ...
30 and 42: 210, 420, 630, ...

And the fact that

$$HCF(m,n) \times LCM(m,n) = mn$$

can be re-explained later when one is in a position to look at HCFs and LCMs in terms of the prime factorisations of the two integers m and n.

The Key Stage 3 requirements relating to prime numbers and prime factorisation extend what is expected at Key Stage 2. There we find that pupils (in Year 5) are supposed to

- "know and use the vocabulary of prime numbers, prime factors and composite numbers"
- "establish whether a number up to 100 is prime and recall prime numbers up to 19", and
- "recognise and use square numbers and cube numbers and the notation for squared (^{2}) and cubed (^{3})".

Although we have been told that "Key Stage 3 should build on Key Stage 2", it may be wise to revisit, and to reinforce, these ideas in Year 7 before ploughing ahead (especially with regard to the third bullet point, which seems unnecessarily premature). A sensible initial goal at Key Stage 3 is

- to get to know the twenty five prime numbers up to 100

by implementing the *Sieve of Eratosthenes* (Greek, 3rd century BC).

- Write out the integers 1–100 in ten columns. Cross out 1 (as 1 is **not** a prime).

- Circle the first uncrossed integer (the prime 2) and cross out all its larger multiples.
- Circle the first uncrossed integer (the prime 3) and cross out all its larger multiples.
- Circle the first uncrossed integer (the prime 5) and cross out all its larger multiples.
- Circle the first uncrossed integer (the prime 7) and cross out all its larger multiples.

Then check that all of the remaining uncrossed integers

$$11, 13, 17, 19, 23, 29, 31, 37, 41, 43, 47, 53, 59, 61, 67, 71, 73, 79, 83, 89, 97$$

are in fact primes. (The reason why should be revisited later when the "square root test" has been understood—see later in this section.)

As part of this exercise one would like pupils to learn that, although unfamiliar integers sometimes "smell like a prime", this may be simply because (like 51, or 91, or 323) they are not routinely encountered in the multiplication tables. Pupils will later need to develop a systematic way of testing any three-digit integer to see whether it is prime (the "square root test").

The programme of study includes "prime factorisation" as an explicitly declared goal. So it is important to explain why we do not count "1" as a prime number (and to make it clear that this has nothing to do with enforcing an arbitrary definition of a "prime" as an integer with "*exactly two factors*"). Pupils should understand (from their own extensive experience of factorising integers: see below) that

- *prime numbers* are the "multiplicative atoms" for integers.

Hence we can break up any given integer as the product of its constituent prime factors. Once we grasp this important property of prime numbers, it should be clear that "1 is different", e.g.

$$1 = 1 \times 1 = 1 \times 1 \times 1 = \dots,$$

and

$$2 = 2 \times 1 = 2 \times 1 \times 1 = 2 \times 1 \times 1 \times 1 = \ldots.$$

So "1" is not such a constituent atom, and it would simply get in the way if we made the mistake of calling it a prime.

Some thought is needed when choosing a systematic procedure for "factorising integers". "Factor trees" may have a place for beginners, but it is worth thinking carefully why they are best left behind when we come to Key Stage 3 (along with oblongs, timesing, improper fractions, and mixed numbers). The most suitable systematic algorithm for achieving prime factorisation of a given integer is to carry out successive short divisions—upside down:

"Write **2310** as a product of prime powers."

2 is clearly a factor of 2310: $\begin{array}{r|l} 2 & 2310 \\ \hline & 1155 \end{array}$

$\therefore 2310 = 2 \times 1155$

3 is clearly a factor of 1155: $\begin{array}{r|l} 3 & 1155 \\ \hline & 385 \end{array}$

$\therefore 2310 = 2 \times 1155 = 2 \times 3 \times 385$

5 is clearly a factor of 385: $\begin{array}{r|l} 5 & 385 \\ \hline & 77 \end{array}$

$\therefore 2310 = 2 \times 3 \times 5 \times 77$

7 is clearly a factor of 77: $\begin{array}{r|l} 7 & 77 \\ \hline & 11 \end{array}$

$\therefore 2310 = 2 \times 3 \times 5 \times 7 \times 11$

If we apply a slightly compressed version of the same procedure to less carefully chosen starting integers—such as 1234, or 12345, or 123456, or 4321, or 54321, or 654321, then we quickly discover the need for an efficient way of deciding whether "large" integers are prime.

1234: 2 is clearly a factor:

$$\begin{array}{r|l} 2 & 1234 \\ \hline & \ 617 \end{array} \qquad \therefore 1234 = 2 \times 617.$$ **But is 617 prime?**

12345: 5 is clearly a factor:

$$\begin{array}{r|r} 5 & 12345 \\ \hline 3 & 2469 \\ \hline & 823 \end{array} \qquad \therefore 12345 = 3 \times 5 \times 823.$$ **But is 823 prime?**

123456: 2 is clearly a factor:

$$\begin{array}{r|r} 2 & 123456 \\ \hline 2 & 61728 \\ \hline 2 & 30864 \\ \hline 2 & 15432 \\ \hline 2 & 7716 \\ \hline 2 & 3858 \\ \hline 3 & 1929 \\ \hline & 643 \end{array} \qquad \therefore 123456 = 2^6 \times 3 \times 643.$$ **But is 643 prime?**

These unanswered questions lead naturally to the square root test for deciding whether a given integer is prime:

Square root test: Suppose that 643 is not prime.

Then 643 factorises—say as $643 = a \times b$, where a, b are both "proper factors" (i.e. $a, b > 1$) We may choose a to be the smaller of the two proper factors: so $1 < a \leqslant b$.

Then

$$\begin{aligned} 643 &= a \times b \\ &\geqslant a \times a \quad (\text{since } b \geqslant a) \end{aligned}$$

$\therefore \sqrt{643} \geqslant \sqrt{a \times a} = a$, so the smaller factor $a \leqslant \sqrt{643} < 26$.

Hence **to test whether 643 is prime, we only need to test for factors up to 25.**

The first few short divisions can be done in the head:

2 is clearly not a factor of 643;

3 is not a factor (the simple 'divisibility tests' are discussed below);

(4 cannot be a factor—or else 2 would have been a factor);

5 is clearly not a factor;

(6 cannot be a factor or else 2 and 3 would have been factors);

7 is not a factor;

(8 cannot be a factor or 2 would have been a factor; similarly 9 and 10 cannot be factors);

11 is not a factor; and so on.

The reasons why we do not have to check 4, 6, 8, 9, 10, ... show that we only have to check for possible **prime** factors up to $\sqrt{643}$—that is up to 23. And once the easy short divisions have been checked, it makes perfect sense to use a calculator to test for larger possible prime factors (say beyond 7, or 11). Moreover calculator use makes the power and speed of the method even more evident:

$643 \div 13 = 49.46\ldots;$

$643 \div 17 = 37.82\ldots;$

$643 \div 19 = 33.84\ldots;$

$643 \div 23 = 27.95\ldots.$

$\therefore$ **643 is prime**

Pupils can now look back at the "sieve of Eratosthenes" for the integers 1–100 and understand *why it stopped at multiples of* 7:

Proof Any **non-prime** $\leqslant 100$ must have a **prime factor** $\leqslant \sqrt{\mathbf{100}} = 10$.

That is, every **non-prime** $\leqslant 100$ is a multiple of 2, or of 3, or of 5, or of 7. **QED**

Armed with this method, they can then complete a *"sieve of Eratosthenes"* to find all prime numbers **up to 500** (by following the same procedure—circling the first uncrossed number and crossing out all higher multiples—for primes up to $\sqrt{500} = 22.36\ldots$—that is up to 19). Hence, in order to extend the list from 100 to 500 we only need to carry out **four extra steps**, to eliminate multiples of 11, of 13, of 17, and of 19.

The fact that every positive integer can be factorised *in just one way* as a product of prime powers cannot be proved at this level. Instead the uniqueness of prime factorisation emerges as a "fact of experience": the factorisation procedure above churns out the prime factorisation each time, and the subtle question as to its uniqueness is unlikely to arise.

There is plenty of mileage in exploiting prime factorisation. For example:

- to recognise squares as precisely those integers whose prime factorisation only involves primes to *even powers*
- to recognise cubes as precisely those integers whose prime factorisation only involves primes raised to powers that are all multiples of 3
- to see how $HCF(m,n)$ is just the product of those prime powers that occur both in the prime factorisation of m and in the prime factorisation of n, and hence to re-prove

$$HCF(m,n) \times LCM(m,n) = m \times n.$$

Divisibility tests are not explicitly mentioned in the Key Stage 3 programme of study. However, the requirements to understand place value (Section 1.1) and to test for factors (Section 1.4) should highlight the need to discuss these excellent examples of *structural arithmetic*.

The fact that **multiples of 10** are precisely the integers having "units digit = 0" is an evident consequence of *place value*: for example

$$\begin{aligned} 3210 &= 3000 + 200 + 10 \\ &= 300 \times 10 + 20 \times 10 + 1 \times 10 \\ &= 321 \times 10 \end{aligned}$$

Any integer N can therefore be decomposed as "a multiple of 10" plus its "units digit". The first of these two terms "a multiple of 10" is also "a multiple of 2" (because $10k = (2 \times 5)k = 2 \times (5k)$).

∴ An integer N is a **multiple of 2** precisely when its units digit is a multiple of 2.

That is, when it ends in 0, 2, 4, 6, or 8. (Be prepared to have to insist that "$0 = 0 \times 2$" is a multiple of 2, and so is *even*.)

Similarly, any multiple of 10 is also a "multiple of 5" (because $10k = (5 \times 2)k = 5 \times (2k)$).

∴ an integer is a **multiple of 5** precisely when its units digit is a multiple of 5.

That is, when it ends in 0, or 5.

The same idea shows that multiples of 100 are precisely the integers having "both tens and units digits = 0".

Any integer N can be decomposed as "a multiple of 100" plus the number formed by its tens and units digits. The multiple of 100 is also a "multiple of 4" (because $100k = (4 \times 25)k = 4 \times (25k)$).

∴ N is a **multiple of 4** precisely when "the number formed by its *last two digits* is a multiple of 4".

Multiples of 1000 are precisely the integers having hundreds, tens and units digits = 0.

Any multiple of 1000 is also a "multiple of 8" (because $1000k = (8 \times 125)k = 8 \times (125k)$); so an integer is a **multiple of 8** precisely when "the number formed by its *last three digits* is a multiple of 8".

This shows how the rules for spotting multiples of 2, or 4, or 5, or 8, or 10 derive from our *place value* system for writing numbers.

The divisibility tests for multiples of 3, and of 9 depend on the *place value* system in a more interesting way, which obliges us to think about the *algebraic* structure of the place value system. The key here lies in the fact that

$10 - 1 = \ldots, 100 - 1 = \ldots, 1000 - 1 = \ldots$ etc. are all multiples of 9.

Later this can be seen as a special case of the beautiful factorisation

$$x^n - 1 = (x-1)(x^{n-1} + x^{n-2} + x^{n-3} + \cdots + x + 1).$$

Hence any integer such as 12345, can be deconstructed into

$$\begin{aligned}
\mathbf{12345} &= 1 \times 10000 + 2 \times 1000 + 3 \times 100 + 4 \times 10 + 5 \\
&= 1 \times (9999+1) + 2 \times (999+1) + 3 \times (99+1) + 4 \times (9+1) + 5 \\
&= (1 \times 9999 + 2 \times 999 + 3 \times 99 + 4 \times 9) + (\mathbf{1+2+3+4+5})
\end{aligned}$$

The first bracket is clearly a multiple of 9—and so is also a multiple of 3.

Hence, for 12345 to be **a multiple of 3** the second bracket—that is, its **digit-sum** "$1+2+3+4+5$"—must be a multiple of 3 (which it is!).

And for 12345 to be **a multiple of 9**, the second bracket—that is, its **digit-sum** "1+2+3+4+5"—must be a multiple of 9 (which it is not). This yields a simple (and intriguing) test for divisibility by 3 and by 9.

The test for divisibility by 6 is mildly different: an integer is divisible by 6 precisely when it is divisible both by 2 **and** by 3. Similarly, an integer is divisible by 12 precisely when it is divisible both by 4 **and** by 3. Here it is important that $HCF(3,4) = 1$. (Notice that 18 is a multiple of 6 and of 9; but 18 is **not** a multiple of $6 \times 9 = 54$, because $HCF(6,9) \neq 1$.)

Divisibility by $11 = 10 + 1$ depends on a simple variation of the reasoning for divisibility by $9 = 10 - 1$. The key here lies in the fact that

$$\begin{aligned}
10 + 1 &= 11, \\
100 - 1 &= 99, \\
1000 + 1 &= 1001, \\
10000 - 1 &= 9999,
\end{aligned}$$

etc. are all multiples of 11.

An interesting consequence of the prime factorisation of an integer is that it allows an easy way of **counting the number of factors** which the integer has *without listing them all first*. The idea depends on "the product rule for counting" which is needed at Key Stage 3—but is not explicitly mentioned. However, it is optimistically hinted at rather vaguely in the Year 6 programme of study under

> "*Algebra*: – enumerate possibilities of combinations of two variables".

And the product rule is explicitly required at Key Stage 4.

The simplest version of the *product rule* tells us that the number of dots in a rectangular array is equal to "the number of dots in each row times the number of rows".

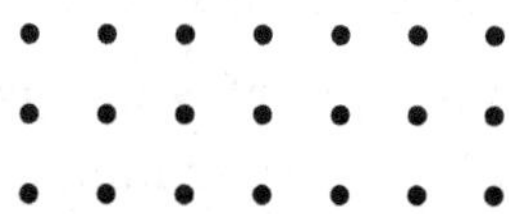

Instead of counting the dots individually, we note that there are 3 rows, each with 7 dots, so the total number of dots is "$7+7+7=\mathbf{3}\times\mathbf{7}$".

A similar situation arises whenever we are effectively counting "ordered pairs". When we roll two dice, one red and one blue, each outcome can be listed systematically as an *ordered pair*:

> (red score, blue score).

The key observation is that each possible first coordinate has the same fixed number of possible second coordinates, so the total number of outcomes can be counted very easily.

> There are 6 possible red scores;
> and each red score can occur with each of the 6 possible blue scores;
> so there are
>
> $$6+6+6+6+6+6=\mathbf{6}\times\mathbf{6}$$
>
> possible ordered pairs, or outcomes for rolling the two dice.

In the same way, if we want to count the possible factors of $12 = 2^2 \times 3$, then each factor must have the form $2^a \times 3^b$ with $a = 0, 1$, or 2, and $b = 0$, or 1. So

there are 3 possible choices for a;
and for each choice of a there are 2 choices for b. $\therefore$ **3 × 2 possible factors**:

$$2^0 \times 3^0 = 1, 2^0 \times 3^1 = 3, 2^1 \times 3^0 = 2, 2^1 \times 3^1 = 6, 2^2 \times 3^0 = 4, 2^2 \times 3^1 = 12.$$

1.5. [Subject content: *Number* p. 5]

- **understand and use place value for decimals, measures and integers of any size**
- **interpret and compare numbers in standard form $A \times 10^n$, $1 \leqslant A < 10$, where n is a positive or negative integer of zero**

The two requirements in 1.5 are closely intertwined—even if the second bullet point seems slightly premature from a purely mathematical viewpoint. (*Standard form* may have been included at this level to support the requirements of science teaching. Yet there is no mention of "standard form" in the Key Stage 3 science programme of study—unless the numerical significance of the "pH scale" as

> "the decimal logarithm of the reciprocal of the hydrogen ion activity in a solution"

is to be explained in detail, or the value of "Newton's gravitational constant" is to be pulled out of a hat as "$\approx 6.67 \times 10^{-11} N \cdot (m/kg)^2$".)

The sequence of topics related to the requirements in 1.5 would seem to include:

- understanding and working with positive integer powers
- recognising that multiplication of powers of 10 corresponds to "adding exponents" (i.e. the index laws)
- understanding that defining "$10^0 = 1$" is consistent with the place value notation for integers (so that the tens column is in some sense the 1st column, and the units column is the "zeroth" column), and that this

definition of 10^0 preserves the index laws for multiplication ($10^3 \times 10^0 = 10^{(3+0)} = 10^3$)

- understanding that defining "10^{-n}" to be equal to the reciprocal of 10^n then allows us to interpret the decimal places to the right of the decimal point in the same way (as the "$(-1)^{\text{th}}$" column, the "$(-2)^{\text{th}}$ column", the "$(-3)^{\text{th}}$ column", the "$(-4)^{\text{th}}$ column", and so on), and that this also respects the index laws
- learning to write any integer with $n+1$ digits as a decimal A ($1 \leqslant A < 10$) multiplied by 10^n (by moving the decimal point n places to the left to follow the leading digit), and learning to translate numbers which are given in standard form back into their more familiar guise
- extending this notation to numbers which are less than 1, so that it can be used for all positive real numbers
- learning to compare numbers given in standard form
- learning to interpret the conventions associated with rounding, where numbers are specified to so many "significant figures", or to so many "decimal places"
- learning how to multiply and divide, and to add and subtract, numbers given in standard form (bearing in mind the specified levels of accuracy).

Experience with different groups of pupils will determine which parts of this sequence are better delayed until Year 10 (or even Year 11). For example, some pupils may be able to compare relatively simple examples of numbers given in standard form, but will need to revisit and extend the idea in Years 10 and 11. However, the final bullet point in the sequence seems much too demanding at this stage, since it involves the interaction between standard form and rounding, or approximation. (Numbers given in standard form are almost never exact. So arithmetic with numbers given in standard form needs to be linked with an understanding of numerical data being "accurate to so many decimal places", and with the use of "significant figures".)

The first few bullet points in the above sequence were incorporated in our comments on powers in Section 1.4. On one level, in order to understand that

3.1×10 is equal to "31",

it is enough to know that

$3.1 \times 10 = (3 + 0.1) \times 10$, and that

0.1 is equal to $\frac{1}{10}$ (that is, that the "1" in the first decimal place corresponds to "tenths").

However, the *general* procedure for interpreting standard form makes much more sense once it is clear that the digit that is k places to the right of the decimal point corresponds to a multiple of 10^{-k}, so that multiplying by a suitable power of 10 simply "moves the decimal point" that number of steps *to the right* (or keeps the decimal point fixed and moves the digits the same number of steps to *the left*).

The same ideas are worth addressing because they are needed to understand

- the way **division** by a decimal can be transformed into division by an integer (by multiplying both the divisor and the dividend by a suitable power of 10), and
- the way **multiplication** of decimals can be transformed into a three-step process
  - first *multiplying* by a suitable power of 10 to transform the calculation into a familiar multiplication of integers,
  - then carrying out the multiplication of integers,
  - then *dividing* by the same power of 10 (that is, re-positioning the decimal point in the answer) to find the required answer.

Hence it may well be possible to convey something of the meaning of the standard form notation before the end of Key Stage 3—at least for those who are likely to need it elsewhere. But, in the spirit of the declared *Aims* of the mathematics programme of study, we urge mathematics teachers to avoid simply presenting standard form as an uncomprehended formalism. Instead we hope schools will lay the necessary foundations in Year 7 and 8 (through exercises that expand and then simplify powers such as

$$10^2 \times 10^5 = (10 \times 10) \times (10 \times 10 \times 10 \times 10 \times 10) = 10^{2+5},$$

linking this to an understanding of long multiplication), so that some modest version of the notation can be properly understood in Year 9 say. (The index laws offer a rare opportunity for pupils to experience at first hand the way meanings and definitions are extended in mathematics, though this opportunity is generally missed. For a systematic development at this level see *Extension mathematics Book Gamma* (Oxford 2007), Sections T14, C24, C31, C38.)

However, before launching into standard form, it would be good if pupils understood why it is often helpful to think in terms of "powers of 10", and why we focus on the exponent (or "baby logs") when dealing with very large or very small quantities or measurements. An easily available point of entry would be to watch the classic short movie *Powers of 10*, made many years ago by the Eames brothers.[19] (The film invites repeat viewing, stopping from time to time to discuss what is being shown.)

One everyday instance, where we focus on the exponent (or the logarithm) rather than the number itself, arises with the *Richter scale* for measuring the strength of earthquakes. This may already be familiar to some pupils. Here an **increase of 1** in the measurement used on the Richter scale corresponds to an earthquake which is **10 times more powerful**, and an **increase of 2** corresponds to an earthquake which is **100 times more powerful**. Other instances where such "log-scales" are used include the measure for the brightness of stars, and the pH scale.

1.6. [Subject content: *Number* p. 5]

- **use the four operations [...] applied to [...] fractions**
- **work interchangeably with terminating decimals and their corresponding fractions (such as 3.5 and $\frac{7}{2}$, or 0.375 and $\frac{3}{8}$)**
- **define percentage as 'number of parts per hundred', interpret percentages and percentage changes as a fraction**

[19] http://www.eamesoffice.com/the-work/powers-of-ten/

or a decimal, interpret these multiplicatively, express one quantity as a percentage of another, compare two quantities using percentages, and work with percentages greater than 100%

- **interpret fractions and percentages as operators**
- [*Ratio, proportion and rates of change* p. 7] **solve problems involving percentage change: including percentage increase, decrease and original value problems; and simple interest in financial mathematics**

As the last listed item here indicates, the boundary between this section and Section 1.9 below (on ratio and proportion) is blurred—so the two need to be considered together. The first listed requirement concerning calculation with fractions was also considered briefly in Section 1.2. However, since achieving fluency in calculating with fractions should be a central goal of Key Stage 3, this deserves to be addressed here in greater detail than was possible as part of Section 1.2.

1.6.1 Fractions as a unifying idea The central importance of calculation with fractions for all pupils only becomes apparent in late Key Stage 3 and early Key Stage 4. Before that pupils learn to work with division (sharing and grouping), parts of a whole, decimals, fractions, ratios, percentages, proportion, scale factors—first numerically and then within algebra. But at some stage pupils ideally discover that all of these apparently different ideas and procedures reduce to "calculation with fractions".

1.6.2 Prerequisites and follow-up When preparing to address the **arithmetic** of *fractions* in early Key Stage 3, the first move should be a check that the necessary prerequisites from *integer* arithmetic are firmly in place. These include: complete arithmetical fluency with integers; and flexibility in identifying common multiples (in order to switch to common denominators), and in identifying common factors (in order to simplify by cancelling).

The subsequent developments summarised below constitute a considerable challenge. But such examples as 1.4C, 1.4F, and 1.4H in Part II suggest rather clearly that the arithmetic of fractions needs to be given more time than has been usual in recent years. In particular, fraction work should be routinely included as part of solving equations, solving word problems, finding equations of straight lines through given points, and within other applications during the ensuing 2–3 years (where it has often been artificially avoided by restricting to problems with small integer solutions).

1.6.3 Fractions as operators and percentages The fourth requirement listed at the start of 1.6 reads as though pupils start out with a clear understanding of "fractions as numbers", and then need to interpret these "numbers" as "operators". This is potentially misleading.

Fractions are initially introduced (in Key Stages 1 and 2) as "parts of a whole"—that is, as [implicit] "operators". At that stage pupils have no conception of fractions *as numbers*, such as $\frac{1}{2}$ or $\frac{3}{4}$, but work only with "parts of an understood whole".

At some point these "parts of a whole", such as "half a pint" or "three quarters of a cake", have to give birth to the *numbers* $\frac{1}{2}$ and $\frac{3}{4}$. Exactly how this shift from working with "parts of a given whole" to "fractions as numbers" is supposed to be made is never clarified in the Key Stage 2 programme of study. So we may anticipate that many pupils entering Key Stage 3 will still think of fractions only as operators (so the word "fraction" will immediately conjure up the idea of "a fraction of" some whole).

The third, fourth and fifth requirements listed in 1.6 refer to percentages. The key here is to recognise that all work with percentages should eventually reduce to a particular instance of work with fractions (sometimes in decimal form). That is, "percentages" should eventually be no longer seen as a separate topic, and fractions (and their arithmetic) should become the unifying theme. We make three further comments on percentages.

First, once the transition from "fractions as operators" to "fractions as numbers" has been firmly established, pupils need to re-interpret fractions as "operators" once again, in order to implement the standard applications efficiently—so that, for example, a "20% increase" is naturally calculated by **multiplying by 1.2**, rather than by calculating 20% and adding.

The second comment on percentages has already been made in Section 1.2.3 of Part II, and in Section 1.2.4 above, but bears repetition in the context of percentages. Mathematics teaching and assessment too often focus on the easy *direct* skills, and overlook the fact that fluency, flexibility, and "use" generally require that far more attention needs to be given to simple *inverse* problems. A pupil may know how to

- "find 75% of (i.e. three quarters of) £120"

yet fail to relate this *direct* operation to the different *inverse* variations, such as

- "A price of £90 is raised to £120. What percentage increase is this? And what percentage decrease would then be required to revert to the original price?", or
- "Calculate the original price if I got 25% off and paid £120".

Pupils need to spend time tackling a suitable variety of problems on percentages ("including percentage increase, decrease and original value problems") in order to appreciate both the underlying direct process, and the slightly counterintuitive aspects of percentages that tend to arise only in connection with *indirect* variations.

The final comment is slightly awkward. It has become common in England to require pupils to treat "50%" as if it were a number equal to "$\frac{1}{2}$". This is not only false, but thoroughly confusing (and shows that textbook authors, editors, and examiners have themselves failed to distinguish between *numbers* and *operators*). The *number* "$\frac{1}{2}$" sits midway between 0 and 1. In contrast "50%" on its own has no more meaning than the "f" in $f(x)$: it is an operator, and gives rise to a quantity or value only when it is given a "whole" (or an "x") to act upon. "50% of" is another way of writing "$\frac{50}{100}$ of", which is in turn another way of writing "$\frac{1}{2}$ of". But this is an *operator*, and is not the same as the *number* "$\frac{1}{2}$". In particular, the arithmetic of fractions only applies to *numbers*: there is no similar way (at this level) of making sense of "adding and dividing operators".

1.6.4 The background to fraction arithmetic We noted in Section 1.6.1 that, by the age of 15 or so, it should be clear that large tracts of secondary mathematics come down to "fraction arithmetic". So we end Section 1.6 first with a uniform description of the mathematical *background* which underpins the **arithmetic of fractions**, and then look more closely at the link between fractions and decimals. This is not intended to be a "teaching sequence": its goal is to emphasise certain features of the arithmetic of fractions whose spirit needs to be incorporated into, and reflected in any teaching sequence which schools may adopt.

When introducing positive **integers**, we work at first in some detail with "copies of a concrete object" (such as sweets). Later we shift attention to the number "1" as a kind of abstract "*universal object*", which can itself be replicated (like the sweets, but more exactly, and wholly in the mind). Thus positive integers arise when we **replicate**, or take *multiples* of the unit 1:

$2 = 1 + 1$;

$3 = 1 + 1 + 1$; and so on.

In general, we may replicate the unit "1" n times to obtain

$$n = 1 + 1 + \cdots + 1.$$

All the facts of integer arithmetic follow from this "replication of the unit".

In a similar way, when introducing fractions, we begin by working in some detail with *concrete* objects and consider "parts of some given whole". That is, fractions are initially introduced as "parts of a whole", where the meaning depends on the particular "whole": in other words, the fractions are "fractions of" something, or operators. Before too long, we need to introduce the fundamental idea that if we take the number "1" to be the whole, and think of fractions as parts of this *universal object* "1", we obtain "fractions as numbers". That is, the unit "1" can be subdivided into n **equal** parts, each of which is equal to the **unit fraction** $\frac{1}{n}$. This opens the door to a uniform treatment of fractions—including working with fractions that are bigger than 1: the fraction $\frac{m}{n}$ can be made by taking m copies of this "unit fractional part" $\frac{1}{n}$.

To repeat this explicitly:

Integers were constructed by **multiplying** (or *replicating*) the unit to obtain "multiples of the unit 1":

$$n = 1 + 1 + 1 + \cdots + 1 \quad (n \text{ terms}).$$

Fractions as numbers arise as

> "that part of 1" that emerges when we treat the unit "1" as our "whole", and apply the fraction as an operator to it.

The *unit fraction* $\frac{1}{n}$ is obtained by **dividing** the unit, taking $\frac{1}{n}$ to be "a *submultiple* of the unit 1"—namely that "part" of which exactly n copies make 1:

$$1 = \frac{1}{n} + \frac{1}{n} + \frac{1}{n} + \cdots + \frac{1}{n} \quad (n \text{ terms}).$$

Thus $\frac{1}{2}$ is precisely that number of which 2 identical copies make 1:

$$1 = \frac{1}{2} + \frac{1}{2};$$

$\frac{1}{3}$ is precisely that number of which 3 identical copies make 1:

$$1 = \frac{1}{3} + \frac{1}{3} + \frac{1}{3};$$

$\frac{1}{4}$ is precisely that number of which 4 identical copies make 1:

$$1 = \frac{1}{4} + \frac{1}{4} + \frac{1}{4} + \frac{1}{4};$$

and so on.

In the end, this is what every justification for calculation with fractions comes down to.

- The fraction $\frac{1}{q}$ is defined as above: namely that number of which q copies make 1.

  In the spirit of arithmetical *division*, this is interpreted as the result of dividing the unit 1 into q parts, and then taking one part. In other words, $\frac{1}{q}$ is the answer to the question

"$1 \div q = \ldots$?".

- The fraction $\frac{p}{q}$ is then defined to be $p \times \frac{1}{q}$ (that is,

$$\frac{1}{q} + \frac{1}{q} + \cdots + \frac{1}{q}$$

with exactly p terms).

In the spirit of *division* of given quantities, this can then be **proved** to be equal to the result of dividing p units (or wholes) into q identical parts and then taking one of the q parts (which is easiest to see by dividing **each** of the p units into q equal parts [each part being equal to $\frac{1}{q}$], and selecting 1 of these parts from each of the p different units, to give $p \times \frac{1}{q}$). In other words, $\frac{p}{q}$ is defined to be $p \times \frac{1}{q}$, but turns out to be equal to the answer to the question

"$p \div q = \ldots$?".

- We know that $\frac{1}{nq}$ is the number of which nq identical copies make 1:

$$1 = \frac{1}{nq} + \frac{1}{nq} + \frac{1}{nq} + \frac{1}{nq} + \frac{1}{nq} + \frac{1}{nq} + \frac{1}{nq} + \cdots + \frac{1}{nq} \quad (nq \text{ terms})$$

Since there are exactly $n \times q$ terms on the RHS, we can bracket them into q successive groups with n terms in each bracket:

$$\begin{aligned} 1 \;=\; & \left(\frac{1}{nq} + \frac{1}{nq} + \cdots + \frac{1}{nq}\right) + \left(\frac{1}{nq} + \frac{1}{nq} + \cdots + \frac{1}{nq}\right) + \cdots \\ & + \left(\frac{1}{nq} + \frac{1}{nq} + \cdots + \frac{1}{nq}\right) \end{aligned}$$

There are now q equal brackets on the RHS, so (by the definition of $\frac{1}{q}$),

– each bracket must be exactly equal to $\frac{1}{q}$;

- and each bracket contains n terms equal to $\frac{1}{nq}$, so each bracket is also equal to $n \times \frac{1}{nq}$, which is precisely what we call $\frac{n}{nq}$.

$$\therefore \frac{n}{nq} = \frac{1}{q}$$

An entirely similar argument shows that

$$\frac{np}{nq} = \frac{p}{q},$$

so we can replace any given fraction by another fraction *equivalent* to it by "cancelling", or by multiplying numerator and denominator by the same integer n.

- Addition and subtraction of fractions needs to be linked to reality by combining fractional parts of a *fixed* object.

- Any two fractions $\frac{a}{q}$ and $\frac{b}{q}$ with the *same* denominator can also be added or subtracted by remembering what they represent—namely $a \times \frac{1}{q}$ (that is,

$$\frac{1}{q} + \frac{1}{q} + \cdots + \frac{1}{q}$$

with a terms) and $b \times \frac{1}{q}$ (that is,

$$\frac{1}{q} + \frac{1}{q} + \cdots + \frac{1}{q}$$

with b terms), so that

  - their sum is

$$(a + b) \times \frac{1}{q} = \frac{a + b}{q}$$

(that is,

$$\frac{1}{q} + \frac{1}{q} + \cdots + \frac{1}{q}$$

with $a + b$ terms), and

- their difference is

$$(a - b) \times \frac{1}{q} = \frac{a - b}{q}$$

(that is,

$$\frac{1}{q} + \frac{1}{q} + \cdots + \frac{1}{q}$$

with $a - b$ terms).

- Any two fractions $\frac{a}{n}$ and $\frac{b}{q}$ with *different* denominators can be **added** or **subtracted** by first transforming them both into equivalent fractions with the same denominator

$$\frac{aq}{nq}\left(= \frac{a}{n}\right), \quad \text{and} \quad \frac{nb}{nq}\left(= \frac{b}{q}\right)$$

so that

  - their sum is

$$(aq + nb) \times \frac{1}{nq} = \frac{aq + nb}{nq}$$

(that is,

$$\frac{1}{nq} + \frac{1}{nq} + \cdots + \frac{1}{nq}$$

with $aq + nb$ terms), and

  - their difference is

$$(aq - nb) \times \frac{1}{n}q = \frac{aq - nb}{nq}$$

(that is,

$$\frac{1}{nq} + \frac{1}{nq} + \cdots + \frac{1}{nq}$$

with $aq - nb$ terms).

- *Division* of fraction x by fraction y needs to be linked to reality by discovering that both forms of division give the same answer:

  - "How many times does y go into x?" (or "How many times can I subtract y from x?"), and

  - "What do we multiply y by to get x?"

- We can formally divide any fraction $\frac{a}{q}$ by one with the same denominator, say $\frac{b}{q}$, by remembering what they represent—namely $a \times \frac{1}{q} = \frac{a}{q}$ and $b \times \frac{1}{q} = \frac{b}{q}$, so that we can switch to the equivalent fraction by multiplying both numerator and denominator by "q" to see that the quotient is $\frac{a}{b}$.

- To formally divide any fraction $\frac{a}{n}$ by one with a *different* denominator $\frac{b}{q}$, we first change them both to equivalent fractions

$$x = \frac{aq}{nq} \quad \left(= \frac{a}{n}\right), \quad \text{and} \quad y = \frac{nb}{nq} \quad \left(= \frac{b}{q}\right)$$

  with the *same* denominator, and we can then evaluate the quotient by switching to an equivalent quotient by multiplying numerator and denominator by "nq" to see that the quotient is $\frac{aq}{nb}$.

- To *multiply* two *unit* fractions $\frac{1}{n}$ and $\frac{1}{q}$ we return to their definitions as submultiples of 1, and think about the product

$$1 \times 1 = \left(\frac{1}{n} + \frac{1}{n} + \cdots + \frac{1}{n}\right) \times \left(\frac{1}{q} + \frac{1}{q} + \cdots + \frac{1}{q}\right)$$

  [n terms in the 1st bracket, q terms in the 2nd].

  When we multiply out the two brackets we obtain nq equal terms, each equal to

$$\left(\frac{1}{n}\right) \times \left(\frac{1}{q}\right),$$

whose sum is 1. But that is precisely the definition of the unit fraction "$\frac{1}{nq}$".

$$\therefore \left(\frac{1}{n}\right) \times \left(\frac{1}{q}\right) = \frac{1}{nq}.$$

When we multiply two general fractions $\frac{a}{n}$ and $\frac{b}{q}$ we can write each fraction out as:

$$\frac{a}{n} = a \times \frac{1}{n} = \left(\frac{1}{n} + \frac{1}{n} + \cdots + \frac{1}{n}\right) \quad (a \text{ terms})$$

$$\frac{b}{q} = b \times \frac{1}{q} = \left(\frac{1}{q} + \frac{1}{q} + \cdots + \frac{1}{q}\right) \quad (b \text{ terms})$$

and then multiply out the two brackets 'long hand' to get

$$\frac{a}{n} \times \frac{b}{q} = \left(\frac{1}{n} + \frac{1}{n} + \cdots + \frac{1}{n}\right) \times \left(\frac{1}{q} + \frac{1}{q} + \cdots + \frac{1}{q}\right)$$

[a terms in 1st bracket, b terms in the 2nd] where the RHS gives rise to exactly ab separate terms, each equal to

$$\left(\frac{1}{n}\right) \times \left(\frac{1}{q}\right) = \frac{1}{nq}.$$

$$\therefore \frac{a}{n} \times \frac{b}{q} = ab \times \frac{1}{nq} = \frac{ab}{nq}.$$

1.6.5 Fractions and terminating decimals Pupils need exercises that clarify three features of terminating decimals.

The first is to use place value to interpret each decimal as a sum. Just as

$$375 = 3 \times 100 + 7 \times 10 + 5,$$

so place value tells us that 0.375 means precisely the sum

$$3 \times \frac{1}{10} + 7 \times \frac{1}{100} + 5 \times \frac{1}{1000}.$$

The second is to rewrite the constituent parts (from the separate "places") with a common power of 10 as denominator (here "1000") to obtain:

$$\frac{3}{10}+\frac{7}{100}+\frac{5}{1000}=\frac{300}{1000}+\frac{70}{1000}+\frac{5}{1000}=\mathbf{\frac{375}{1000}} \qquad (*)$$

In other words, pupils need to connect the *definition* of place value (which breaks up the number into a sum of several parts—tenths, hundredths, thousandths, etc.) with the alternative reading of 0.375 as $\frac{375}{1000}$.

The third feature is more subtle, namely to realise precisely which fractions correspond to *terminating* decimals, and which correspond to *endless* decimals.

- If a fraction is given with denominator a power of 10, then it is easy to write it as a terminating decimal, in exactly the same way that equation $(*)$ tells us that

$$\frac{375}{1000}=0.375. \qquad (**)$$

- But what do we know about $\frac{3}{8}$ and $\frac{3}{18}$ that should tell us *in advance* that the first has a terminating decimal, but the second does not?

The key lies in the previous paragraph (and properties of prime factorisation which were addressed in Section 1.4).

Suppose we are given some unfamiliar fraction.

- The first move is to *cancel* any common factors between the numerator and the denominator which may mislead us.

For example, we know that the decimal for $\frac{1}{2}=0.5$, and so it terminates. But if we were faced instead by $\frac{3}{6}$, we might be misled by knowing that the decimal for $\frac{1}{6}$ does not terminate. This first move of "cancelling" puts the given fraction into its "standard form", or "lowest terms", $\frac{p}{q}$, where p, q have no common factors (other than 1): $HCF(p,q)=1$.

We have seen that a fraction whose denominator is equal to a power of 10 can always be written as a terminating decimal (as in equation $(**)$). Pupils need to extend this to see that

- if a given fraction $\frac{p}{q}$ **can be re-written** in a form with denominator equal to a power of 10 (in the same way that $\frac{3}{8} = \frac{375}{1000}$),

  then it will be equal to a terminating decimal.

That is, given a fraction $\frac{p}{q}$, we need to know when it can be rewritten as an equivalent fraction $\frac{np}{nq}$ which has denominator a power of 10.

> If nq is a power of 10 for some multiplier n,
>
> then **the denominator** q of the given fraction must be **a factor of some power of 10.**
>
> Now $10 = 2 \times 5$, so a power of 10, such as $10^m = (2 \times 5)^m$, has the form $2^m \times 5^m$.
>
> And any factor of $2^m \times 5^m$ must have the form $2^a \times 5^b$ for some $a, b \leqslant m$.
>
> $\therefore$ If the fraction $\frac{p}{q}$ has a terminating decimal, then the denominator q must have the form $2^a \times 5^b$: that is, a power of 2 times a power of 5.

- Conversely suppose we are given any fraction with denominator q of the form $2^a \times 5^b$.

  If $a \geqslant b$, then we can multiply by $n = 5^{a-b}$ to make $nq = 2^a \times 5^a = 10^a$; and if $b > a$, then we can multiply by $n = 2^{b-a}$ to make $nq = 2^b \times 5^b = 10^b$.

  $\therefore$ Any fraction with denominator of the form $2^a \times 5^b$ has a terminating decimal.

Hence whether a given fraction $\frac{p}{q}$ (where p, q have no common factors) has a **terminating** decimal or not depends entirely on the prime factorisation of the denominator q:

$$q = 1, 2, 4, 5, 8, 10, 16, 20, 25, 32, \ldots$$

all lead to terminating decimals, but

$$q = 3, 6, 7, 9, 11, 12, 13, 14, 15, 17, 18, 19, 21, 22, 23, 24, 26, 27, 28, 29, 30, 31, \ldots$$

never do.

1.6.6 Fractions and recurring decimals

Section 1.6.5 shows that:

> every fraction $\frac{p}{q}$, where p, q have no common factors and q is **not** of the form $2^a \times 5^b$ has a decimal that does **not** terminate, and so must go on for ever.

In fact every such fraction has a decimal that "recurs": that is, its decimal consists of

> an initial sequence of digits (which can be of any finite length), followed by a "block of digits" that simply repeats over and over again *for ever.*

The most familiar examples are

$$\frac{1}{3} = 0.3333333\ldots$$

which recurs from the beginning with a repeating block "3" of length 1;

$$\frac{1}{11} = 0.090909\ldots$$

which recurs from the beginning with repeating block "09" of length 2;

$$\frac{1}{6} = 0.1666666\ldots$$

which recurs from the 2nd place with repeating block "6" of length 1;

$$\frac{1}{7} = 0.1428571428\ldots$$

which recurs from the start with repeating block "142857" of length 6.

The converse is also true, in that

> every decimal which recurs in this fashion is the decimal of some fraction.

The proofs of these statements are discussed briefly in Section 1.8 below.

1.7. [Subject content: *Number* p. 6]

> – **use approximation through rounding to estimate answers and calculate possible resulting errors expressed using inequality notation $a < x \leqslant b$**

In mathematics we calculate with *exact* "mental objects". But when mathematics is *applied*, the numbers often come from the real world. Discrete data from the real world (e.g. small counting numbers) can sometimes be "exact"; but most measurements are reliable only to a certain degree of accuracy. The approximate character of certain measurements is reflected in the "rounding conventions". When a digit is known to be, or is to be taken as being, just beyond the known or required limits of accuracy, the "rounding conventions" mean that

> "a digit of 5 or more is rounded **up**, and everything else is rounded **down**".

Hence a decimal like 37.45293 would be written as

> "37.45 to 2 decimal places", or "37.5 to 1 decimal place".

Conversely, if we are given a measurement "$x = 37.5$ to 1 decimal place", then all we know is that the "true" value of x lies somewhere *in an interval*: $37.45 \leqslant x < 37.55$. (The inequality given in the official requirement listed at the start of 1.7 should probably have been written as "$a \leqslant x < b$" to fit in with this convention.)

If the initial data is only known to a certain degree of accuracy, then any calculation with that data is approximate from the outset. Even when our data and our calculations are "theoretically exact", approximations may arise when exact terms (such as "$\sin 45°$" or "$\sqrt{2}$") are "evaluated" at some point using a decimal approximation. All approximations affect the accuracy of the final result; so pupils need to understand how potential errors "accumulate" as a result of calculation, so that they can tell exactly how inaccurate the final result could be.

When *adding* or *subtracting* approximate numbers, *the errors in the data* **add up**. Given two lengths of 2.15cm and 1.75cm—each correct to within 0.05cm—their calculated difference of 0.40cm is only correct to within 0.1cm, so could actually be as low as 0.30cm or as high as 0.50cm. And if we were to add four lengths, each of which was accurate to within 0.05cm, then the result would only be accurate to within 0.2cm either way (so we would only know that the answer lies in an interval of length 0.4cm).

When *multiplying* or *dividing* the story is a more complicated. For example, the area of a rectangle whose dimensions are given as "15cm by 12cm", where each measurement is accurate to within an error of 0.1cm, is equal to $15 \times 12\text{cm}^2$, or 180cm^2, but only **to within 2.7cm^2**. And if we know that a rectangle has area 180cm^2 accurate to within 5cm^2, and that its length is 20cm accurate to within 0.1cm, then its width may be as small as small as $(175 \div 20.1)\text{cm} \approx 8.7\text{cm}$ (to 1 d.p.), or as large as $(185 \div 19.9)\text{cm} \approx 9.3\text{cm}$ (to 1 d.p.).

The art of making **estimates**, or *approximate* calculations, is more subtle than is often thought. It depends on:

- robust fluency in *exact* calculation, together with a "feeling for calculation" that is willing to think flexibly about the effect of any errors,
- a willingness to change *global* units intelligently (replacing the given units by larger or smaller "blocks" so as to make the eventual calculation more manageable), and
- an ability to make sensible *local* approximations (to find the approximate size of one of these new 'blocks' and to estimate the number of "blocks").

Consider first approximating an exact arithmetical calculation, such as 35941×273.

- We need the kind of flexibility that can think of this as 35941 "blocks" of 273, and combine this with a clear understanding of how the *exact* calculation would proceed using the given units—with 35941 copies of a collection of size 273.

- Instead of 35941 blocks (each of size 273) we then may see the advantage of interpreting the number of blocks as "slightly **more** than **33**$\frac{1}{3}$ *thousand*", and compensate the block size of 273 by thinking of it as "slightly **less** than **3** *hundreds*".

- This then suggests that the required answer is "approximately 100 hundred thousands", or 10 million.

By increasing one factor in the product and decreasing the other we managed to produce an answer that is fairly close to the actual value (9 811 893) of the product. But the method used gave us no clue as to whether we had overestimated or underestimated, or what our maximum error might be. To get such assurance we would have to approximate *consistently*—perhaps to work out

first an overestimate such as $36000 \times 300 = 10800000$,

then an underestimate such as $35000 \times 250 = 8750000$.

Similarly, in seeking to estimate the size of a large crowd, one may divide the whole into a number of blocks of more-or-less the same size, count (or estimate) the number in a given section of the crowd relatively accurately (for example, by counting the number of rows and the number in each row), and then multiply the answer by the number of blocks. A striking historical example of this approach to estimation occurs in Herodotus, *The Histories*, Book 7:

> "As nobody has left a record, I cannot state the precise numbers provided by each separate nation [towards the Persian army that Xerxes was leading against the Greeks in around 480BC], but the grand total, excluding the naval contingent, turned out to be 1 700 000. The counting was done by first packing ten thousand men as close together as they could stand and then drawing a circle around them on the ground; they were then dismissed and a fence, about navel-high, was constructed round the circle; finally the other troops were marched into the area thus enclosed and dismissed in their turn, until the whole army had been counted."

1.8. [Subject content: *Number* p. 6]

> – **appreciate the infinite nature of the sets of integers, real and rational numbers.**

There is an awkward clash between the precise, procedural language which is appropriate for specifying the ideas and processes of a school curriculum and this highly unusual and rather woolly "requirement". Indeed, it remains unclear how it survived the extended editing process.

The underlying idea would be fine as part of an *internal* curriculum—for in some sense, the whole of elementary mathematics is the story of "how we tame infinity". But to include such a requirement in a *national* curriculum (especially in such a curiously worded form) runs the risk that some examiner may decide that they are obliged to invent some way of "assessing" each year whether it has been addressed!

1.8.1 Mathematics begins when we move beyond the particular to the general. Every culture develops some way of referring to the *size* of small collections of objects (one, two, three, ...), and to the *ordering* of its objects (first, second, third, ...). They either develop some semi-systematic counting process or adapt that of some neighbouring culture for their own use. Some cultures go further and invent an "arithmetic" based on their counting process; but this is almost always done without worrying whether their form of counting could "go on for ever".

For example, the numeration system of the Egyptians, and that of the Babylonians, were both semi-systematic. But both were restricted by the need to invent specific new symbols each time they wanted to refer to larger numbers; so it is unclear whether they appreciated "the infinite nature of the set of integers". In contrast, there is something truly remarkable about the ease with which our Hindu-Arabic numeral system combines the ten digits 0-9 and the idea of "place value" to convey the **idea** that counting

$$1, 2, 3, 4, 5, 6, 7, 8, 9, 10, 11, 12, 13, 14, 15, 16, 17, 18, 19, 20, 21, 22, \ldots, 98, 99, 100, 101, \ldots$$

can **continue for ever**, even though we soon run out of linguistic ways of "naming" the numbers whose numerals we can all write down so easily.

Despite their mathematical sophistication, the Greeks had no such systematic notation—a lack which may have forced them to develop their astonishingly modern approach to handling infinity and infinite processes. But it also meant that *Archimedes* had to go to considerable lengths to demonstrate (in his little book, *The Sand Reckoner*) that "the number of grains of sand in the universe is finite". This he did by repeatedly changing units in order to estimate a finite upper bound (around 8×10^{63}) based on constructing a large *power* of a number called (in Greek) a "myriad myriad"—in much the same way as Herodotus reported (Section 1.7 above) that the Persians counted the number of soldiers in Xerxes' army as a *multiple* of ten thousand.

Our numeral system avoids the inevitable finiteness of number *names*, and focuses instead on a **numeral** system based on place value, which allows us to write numbers *without giving them names*. It then seems clear that, using only the digits 0–9, our *written numerals* for counting numbers could go on for ever. (The truth is more delicate. In our numeral system we "deduce" the endlessness of the sequence of counting numbers by first *assuming* that the sequence of possible "places"—the units, tens, hundred, thousands, etc.—goes on for ever! However, this is unlikely to disturb anyone.)

In some sense, that is all there is to it. The counting numbers are the same as the positive integers, so the integers—both positive and negative—are also infinite (that is, "more than just finite"). The integers are precisely the "rational numbers with denominator 1", so the set of rational numbers is even bigger—and hence infinite. And the real numbers include all the rational numbers—so the set of all real numbers is also infinite.

1.8.2 Sequences: What else is there to be said at secondary level? Endless sequences use the counting numbers to label the successive *terms* of a sequence. The squares, the cubes, the powers of 2—all go on for ever, and all get larger and larger without bound (though some "grow" faster than others):

$$0^2 = 0,\ 1^2 = 1,\ 2^2 = 4,\ 3^2 = 9,\ 4^2 = 16,\ \ldots, n^2,\ \ldots;$$

$$0^3 = 0,\ 1^3 = 1,\ 2^3 = 8,\ 3^3 = 27\ ,4^3 = 64, \ldots, n^3,\ \ldots;$$

$$2^0 = 1,\ 2^1 = 2,\ 2^2 = 4,\ 2^3 = 8,\ 2^4 = 16,\ \ldots, 2^n,\ \ldots.$$

Some sequences eventually stop. Others go on for ever, with one such term for each positive integer n. It is hard to see that there is much to make a fuss about.

However, there are two clear candidates at this level, which show that indeed there is indeed something interesting here, to which one might draw attention—at least for suitable groups of pupils. The first concerns prime numbers; the second concerns the way we can be sure that fractions are precisely the real numbers whose decimals either terminate or recur.

1.8.3 Prime numbers: Prime numbers are the multiplicative building blocks for integers.

> There are 4 prime numbers up to 10; 25 up to 100; and 168 up to 1000.
>
> That is: prime numbers make up 40% of integers up to 10; 25% up to 100; 16.8% up to 1000.

It is thus apparent that prime numbers seem to be "thinning out" as one goes up. So one might ask:

> Do the prime numbers eventually "peter out"? Or do they go on for ever?

There is no indication that anyone considered such a question before the Greeks (4th century BC), who **proved** that

> "the prime numbers are more than any assigned multitude".

That is, that *the prime numbers go on for ever.* Euclid's original proof is highly memorable and has impressed many a young mind—but it is often misrepresented. We give it here in a form that is both close to the original, and in the spirit of modern constructive mathematics.

> We know a few prime numbers, so we can clearly pick one to start with—say p_1. (We could choose $p_1 = 2$, but we do not have to.)

We then set

$$N_1 = p_1 + 1$$

to be "1 more than the product of all the primes in our list so far".

$\therefore p_1$ is not a factor of N_1 (since it leaves remainder $= 1$); so **the smallest prime factor** p_2 of N_1 is a **new** prime number.

Then set

$$N_2 = p_1 \times p_2 + 1$$

to be "1 more than the product of all the primes in our list so far".

$\therefore$ Neither p_1 nor p_2 is a factor of N_2 (since both leave remainder $= 1$); so the smallest prime factor p_3 of N_2 is a **new** prime number.

Then set

$$N_3 = p_1 \times p_2 \times p_3 + 1$$

to be "1 more than the product of all primes in our list so far".

$\therefore$ None of p_1, p_2, p_3 is a factor of N_3 (since all leave remainder $= 1$); so the smallest prime factor p_4 of N_3 is a **new** prime number.

And so it goes on, for ever. **QED**

That is, once the list gets started, no matter how many primes we have listed so far, we have a bomb-proof way of finding a **new** prime.

Suppose we start with $p_1 = 2$, then $N_1 = 3$ is prime, so $p_2 = 3$;
then $N_2 = 7$ is prime, so $p_3 = 7$;

then $N_3 = 43$ is prime, so $p_4 = 43$.

It is important **not** to stop at this point, but to complete the next three stages in order to understand how the process really works.

Work out

$$N_4 = 2 \times 3 \times 7 \times 43 + 1,$$

and hence find its **smallest** prime factor $p_5 = \dots$.

Then work out

$$N_5 = 2 \times 3 \times 7 \times 43 \times p_5 + 1,$$

and hence find its **smallest** prime factor $p_6 = \dots$.

Then work out

$$N_6 = 2 \times 3 \times 7 \times 43 \times p_5 \times p_6 + 1,$$

and hence find its **smallest** prime factor p_7 .

It is also worth starting with various different "initial primes" p_1 to see how this affects the sequence which is generated each time.

Those who took up our earlier suggestion (Section 1.3) of challenging pupils to

"Find a prime number which is one less than a square. Find another. And another."

might also like to use the similar-sounding, but actually very different challenge:

"(a) Find a prime number which is one **more** than a square

(b) Find another such prime. And another."

If one tries this, then it quickly becomes clear that, except for the very first such prime $1^2 + 1 = 2$, one can restrict to looking for *odd* primes, and these must be "one more than an **even** square". Among the list of numbers that are "one more than an even square",

$$2^2 + 1,\ 8^2 + 1,\ 12^2 + 1,\ 18^2 + 1,\ 22^2 + 1,\ 28^2 + 1, \dots$$

are all multiples of 5.

If we eliminate these multiples of 5, we are left with a long list of candidate primes, starting:

(2,) $5, 17, 37, 101, 197, 257, 401, 577, 677, 901, \ldots$

Almost all of these 11 "*candidate* primes" turn out to be *genuine* primes (only one of those listed is not). This raises the question:

> Are there infinitely many prime numbers of the form "$n^2 + 1$"?
>
> Or does the list eventually peter out?

This is perhaps the simplest question one can pose at this level to which the answer is not yet known.

1.8.4 Recurring decimals: One other place where infinity features at Key Stage 3 and needs to be handled properly is the way the normal division process is extended to compute recurring decimals for fractions. We have seen that when we divide an integer p by another integer q, the process *terminates* precisely when the fraction $\frac{p}{q}$ is equivalent to a decimal fraction (one with denominator 10^n for some n)—as with

$$\frac{3}{24} = \frac{125}{1000},$$

or

$$\frac{5}{16} = \frac{3125}{10000},$$

and that this occurs whenever the fully simplified fraction has a denominator of the form $2^a \times 5^b$.

In all other cases, the division process continues indefinitely. For example, when one carries out the division for $\frac{1}{7}$, the output seems to recur: 0.14285714.... All too often pupils are left with the impression that

> the **output** to the division process "recurs" **because it seems to recur.**

This is like believing that the "leading digits" of the sequence of powers of 2 recur **because they look as though** they recur:

$$2, 4, 8, 1, 3, 6, 1, 2, 5, 1; 2, 4, 8, 1, \ldots .$$

The fact that the division of p by q recurs follows **not** from the apparent **output**, but from the **pattern of remainders**.

- The decimal for $\frac{p}{q}$ *terminates* precisely when at some point we obtain a remainder of 0.
- So if the decimal does **not** terminate, then the only possible remainders are

  $$1, 2, 3, \ldots, q-1.$$

  Hence, within at most q steps, we will always get a remainder r that we have seen before; and this remainder r becomes $10r$ in the next decimal place *as it did on the first occurrence of the remainder* r, so from then on the process simply repeats whatever happened after the previous occurrence of the remainder r.

For example, when calculating the decimal for $\frac{1}{7}$ we divide 7 into 1.000000... .

- **Forget about the output**, or the "answer", and **concentrate on the remainders**.
- The process begins with a remainder of "1", then "3", then "2", then "6", then "4" then "5", then "1" (the first repeat)—which becomes "10" in the next column, as it did at the first stage when the initial "1" became "10 tenths".
- The process must then repeat from here on (giving the answer

  $$0.14285714285714\ldots,$$

  with the block "142857" repeating for ever).

The converse claim—namely that

> every number x whose decimal recurs is the decimal of some fraction

can be appreciated at this level (say Year 9 or Year 10) via the procedure for turning any such decimal back into a fraction. For example:

$$
\begin{aligned}
&\text{Suppose } x = 0.37255555\ldots \text{ (for ever)}\\
&\text{Then } 10x = 3.72555555\ldots \text{ (for ever)}\\
&\therefore 9x = 10x - x\\
&\qquad = 3.353 = \tfrac{3353}{1000}\\
&\therefore x = \tfrac{3353}{9000}.
\end{aligned}
$$

$$
\begin{aligned}
&\text{Suppose } x = 0.72525252525\ldots \text{ (for ever)}\\
&\text{Then } 100x = 72.5252525252\ldots \text{ (for ever)}\\
&\therefore 99x = 100x - x\\
&\qquad = 71.8 = \tfrac{718}{10}\\
&\therefore x = \tfrac{718}{990} = \tfrac{359}{495}.
\end{aligned}
$$

1.9. [Subject content: *Ratio, proportion and rates of change* p. 7]

- **change freely between related standard units (for example time, length, area, volume/capacity, mass)**
- **use scale factors, scale diagrams and maps**
- **express one quantity as a fraction of another, where the fraction is less than 1 and [where the fraction is] greater than 1**
- **use ratio notation, including reduction to simplest form**
- **divide a given quantity into two parts in a given part:part or part:whole ratio; express the division of a quantity into two parts as a ratio**
- **understand that a multiplicative relationship between two quantities can be expressed as a ratio or a fraction**
- **relate the language of ratios and the associated calculations to the arithmetic of fractions and to linear functions**

- **solve problems involving percentage change, including: percentage increase, decrease and original value problems and simple interest in financial mathematics**
- **solve problems involving direct and inverse proportion, including graphical and algebraic representations**
- **use compound units such as speed, unit pricing and density to solve problems**

1.9.1 This is a mixed bag of requirements linked to multiplication, ratio and proportion, and scaling—and hence, ultimately to the application of fractions.

- The first two listed requirements (the ability to switch "between related units", and to work with "scale factors, scale diagrams and maps") clearly involve "multiplying factors" and an application of ratios.
- We have already noted the relative neglect of compound units. So the last listed requirement in 1.9 should be interpreted in the light of comments already made in Section 1.1 above and in Part II, Section 1.2.
- Percentage and percentage change has already arisen in 1.6, but reappears here for good reason.
- The requirements for pupils to "express one quantity as a fraction of another" and to "divide a given quantity into two parts" underline the connections between the work required here and work involving fractions (see Sections 1.6.1–1.6.3 above).

1.9.2 We repeat and expand some of the ideas touched upon in Part II, Section 2.2.1. Elementary mathematics comes into its own (and needs to be seriously *taught*!) as soon as we take the step from addition to *multiplication*. Ratios are the quintessential "multiplicative relations", and work with ratios links naturally to work with fractions.

All that is needed to generate a ***ratio*** *is a single class of* ***comparable magnitudes***—that is, a class of magnitudes

- where any two given entities can be "compared", so that we can decide which is the larger, and
- where one can also subtract the smaller from the larger, with the "difference" being another entity from the same class (as, for example, with line segments).

That is, one needs to be able to implement a version of the *Euclidean algorithm.*

The simplest example of a class of "comparable magnitudes" is the set of positive *real numbers*. In the context of ratios, real numbers normally arise as the set of *numerical measures* of some set of objects (relative to some chosen unit). Such *numerical* ratios are easy to handle (with the class of *objects* being replaced by their *measures*); but ratios also arise naturally in mathematics between comparable entities (such as line segments, or 2D shapes) without turning everything into numbers by 'measuring'.

For example, 3cm and 2cm are in the ratio "3 : 2". But we also have the same ratio between the *two line segments*, say AB and CD, that were measured as being of lengths 3cm and 2cm. Even if we do not know their exact lengths, there is often a natural way to be sure that "half of the second segment fits *exactly* three times into the first segment". For example, if we draw a circle with centre O passing through the point X, extend the radius XO to meet the circle again at Y, and construct the mid-point M of the segment OY, then we can be sure (without measuring) that

$$XM : XO = 3 : 2.$$

1.9.3 The rest of our comments in this section revisit and extend our previous remarks in Part II, Section 2.2.1. What follows explores further the background to *ratio and proportion*, which is the key idea that underlies most of the (rather vaguely worded) requirements listed at the start of Section 1.9. We repeat our earlier comment: this outline is intended for teachers, and is not a teaching sequence for pupils.

The word *proportion* has a colloquial usage, which is unfortunately copied in many mathematics texts and classrooms. People speak about "a proportion of the class", meaning exactly the same as "a fraction of the class". **This**

has nothing to do with mathematical "proportion". Sloppy language is neither helpful nor harmless: it confuses pupils, teachers, textbook authors, and examiners alike. In general, technical words are best used correctly and with care in the mathematics classroom (as is normal in many other countries). Because the underlying mathematics may not be second nature, it seems simplest to repeat the basic framework from Part II, Section 2.2.1, while adding a little more detail.

Given the notion of a class of comparable magnitudes, or quantities, a (mathematical) proportion arises when two different classes of entities are linked in a special (but very common) way. For example, suppose that one class consists of

"quantities of petrol"

and the other class consists of

"amounts of money in £".

If 1 litre of petrol	costs £1.50,
then we expect 2 litres	to cost £3 (= 2 × £1.50)

That is, for any two purchases from the same outlet at the same time,

the ***quantities** purchased (in litres)*

are in the same ratio as

*the **amounts** paid (in £).*

If I buy a litres of petrol	and pay £c,
and you buy b litres of petrol	and pay £d,
then the ratio $a : b$	is equal to the ratio $c : d$.

The equality

$$a : b = c : d$$

is what we call a *proportion*.

Note that since a, b, c, d are magnitudes, with a, b of one kind and c, d of another kind, then "$a : b$" is a perfectly well-defined ratio; but "$a : c$" makes no sense, because a and c are not "comparable magnitudes". One can have a ratio $a : b$ between two quantities of petrol both measured in litres (or a ratio $c : d$ between two amounts of money—both measured in £); but one cannot have a ratio between a quantity of fluid and an amount of money.

However, something miraculous occurs if we replace the different quantities and amounts by their numerical measures. The equality of ratios

$$a : b = c : d$$

can then be written as an *equation between fractions*, which can be treated purely algebraically. That is, *if we replace each ratio by the quotient of the corresponding measures* we get an equality of quotients, or fractions:

$$\frac{a}{b} = \frac{c}{d} \qquad (*)$$

The two quotients in equation $(*)$ are always equal, but can take *any positive value*. For example, we could buy

$b = 2a$ litres of petrol and pay $d = 2c$ pounds,
and the quotients would both take the value $\frac{1}{2}$. Or we could buy
$b = \frac{1}{2}a$ litres of petrol and pay $d = \frac{1}{2}c$ pounds,
and the quotients would both take the value 2.

The equation $(*)$ *between fractions* can be treated purely numerically (or algebraically) and can be rearranged to give

$$\frac{c}{a} = \frac{d}{b}.$$

This equation looks very similar to equation $(*)$, but *it is completely different*. The two sides do not represent ratios, but specify the **constant of proportionality** (relative to the two chosen units: litres and pounds (£)). That is, once we choose units and give numerical values a and c to the basic pair of corresponding magnitudes—one from one class and one from the other

$$a \ \textbf{litres} \longrightarrow \textbf{cost } £c$$

the value of the quotient $\frac{c}{a}$ is a **constant**: that is, it is the same as the value of the corresponding quotient $\frac{d}{b}$ *for any other pair* of corresponding magnitudes b, d (one from one class and one from the other). The purely numerical quotient $\frac{c}{a}$ can now be interpreted as the "multiplying factor" that links the two classes of related magnitudes.

This is the simplest, and perhaps the most valuable, application of school mathematics—to life, to science and to mathematics itself. It applies whenever two quantities are related so that if one quantity doubles, or triples, so does the other: that is, where the numerical measures a, c or b, d of the two quantities have a **constant ratio**. Two quantities that vary in such a way as to preserve a constant ratio between their values are said to be "in **proportion**".

The fact that "$\frac{c}{a}$ is a constant" means that the *number lines* corresponding to the two families of measures "line up" in such a way that one scale is simply a multiple ($\times\frac{c}{a}$) of the other:

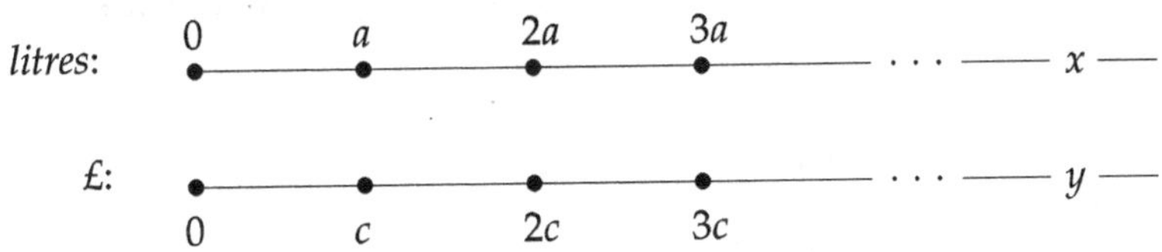

If we imagine a linked pair (x, y) of unknown variables—where

$$x \ \text{litres} \longrightarrow \text{cost } \pounds y$$

then these linked variables are related by the *linear equation*

$$y = \left(\frac{c}{a}\right)x.$$

Eventually (in late Key Stage 3 or Key Stage 4) one may want as many pupils as possible to appreciate this global picture, and to be able to

"formulate proportional relations algebraically"

as is required in the quote at the start of Section 2.2.1 in Part II. However, this is unnecessary, and probably inappropriate for beginners, who first need to learn how to solve the various standard problems involving proportion.

Any particular proportion problem that pupils may be required to solve is likely to involve just two pairs (a, c) and (b, d),

where a and b come from one class of magnitudes,

and c and d come from the other class.

In a typical proportion problem, three of the four values are known and the fourth is "to be found". This explains why the approach to solving this kind of problem is referred to in old texts as "the rule of three". Hence one pair is completely known, and we take this as our "base", or reference pair

$$\textbf{\textit{a} litres} \longrightarrow \textbf{cost £\textit{c}}$$

One of the *other* two values is to be found. So the four ingredients can be thought of as the corners of a rectangular array, where three of the values are known and the fourth is to be calculated, so we either have the unknown value in the bottom right corner:

$$\begin{array}{lll} \text{If} & \textbf{\textit{a} litres} \longrightarrow & \textbf{cost £\textit{c}} \\ \text{then} & b \text{ litres} \longrightarrow & \text{cost £??} \end{array}$$

or the missing value may be located bottom left:

$$\begin{array}{lll} \text{If} & \textbf{\textit{a} litres} \longrightarrow & \textbf{cost £\textit{c}} \\ \text{then} & \text{?? litres} \longrightarrow & \text{cost £}d \end{array}$$

This standard way of representing the four pieces of information in a *proportion*—with three known values and one generally unknown—is referred to here as the *rectangular template* for displaying *proportion* problems.

To repeat the earlier derivation, if we know the corresponding values a and c in our "reference pair"

$$a \longrightarrow c$$

then two unknown amounts x and y, which correspond to each other, provide the third and fourth vertices of our "rectangular template"

$$x \longrightarrow y$$

and so satisfy

$$x : a = y : c$$

If the two magnitudes of the first kind x, a, and the two magnitudes of the second kind y, c are replaced by their measures, then the proportion can be written as

$$\frac{x}{a} = \frac{y}{c}$$

and this can be rearranged to express the relationship between the two unknown values x and y as

$$y = \left(\frac{c}{a}\right) x$$

with multiplying factor $\frac{c}{a}$. If we are given the value of x, we can calculate the value of

$$y = \frac{c}{a} \times x;$$

and if we are given the value of y, then we can calculate the value of

$$x = \frac{a}{c} \times y.$$

For example:

if a = £100 **is worth the same as** **c = $150**

then

x = £200 will be worth exactly $y = \frac{c}{a} \times x = \$\ldots.$

And

if $a = 1kg$ **is the same as** **$c = 2.205lbs$**

then

$x = \frac{a}{c} \times y = \ldots kg$ is the same as $y = 5lbs$.

Earlier we showed how the "number lines" corresponding to the two families of magnitudes in a proportion problem can be lined up to form what is sometimes called a "double number line". We have since seen how the simpler "rectangular template" picks out two data points (a and b) on the first number line, and two points (c and d) on the second number line, and have suggested that this is sufficient for the beginner to solve problems. (To link the two representations one has to imagine that the double number lines run *vertically*, with a and b chosen from the left hand line and c and d chosen from the right hand line.)

We typically know one pair of corresponding values, such as that

£100 is worth $150;

and we want to know either:

"If I have £x = £768 how many $**y** can I expect in exchange?"

or

"How many £**x** should I expect in exchange for y = $1152?".

Pupils who become sufficiently confident may solve the first kind of *proportion* question directly—and in one of two ways:

(i) extract the ratio $\frac{b}{a}$ from two of the known quantities of one kind (e.g. $\frac{768}{100}$ in the above example), and apply it to the third known quantity c of the other kind, to find the unknown required value

$$y = c \times \frac{b}{a}$$

($150 \times \frac{768}{100} = \ldots$ in the above example); or

(ii) identify the *constant of proportionality* $\frac{c}{a}$ (= $\frac{150}{100}$ in our example) derived from two known corresponding quantities of different kinds, and apply it to the third known quantity b to find the unknown value

$$y = \frac{c}{a} \times b$$

($\frac{150}{100} \times 768 = \ldots$ in the above example).

However, for most students, the **unitary method** provides an essential stepping stone *en route* to this general method—a stepping stone which one can return to in any setting to re-explain, or to reinforce, the logic of the general method.

Given three of the four relevant values,

instead of using one of the two "magic multipliers" ($\frac{b}{a}$ or $\frac{c}{a}$) immediately, we use the two known corresponding values (one of each kind)—here £100 and \$150—to calculate:

- first that

  £1 (the *unit*) corresponds to $\$\left(\frac{150}{100}\right) = \$1.50$

- then to multiply the answer (\$1.50) by 768 to get the number of \$

  £768 = 768 × **£1** corresponds to $768 \times \$1.50 = \ldots.$

Thus

if	**£100**	⟶	**\$150**
then	£1	⟶	$\$\left(\frac{150}{100}\right) = \$1.50$
so	£768 = 768 × £1	⟶	$768 \times \$1.50 = \$\ldots.$

2. Algebra

2.1. Structure

We noted in Part II Section 2.1.1 that *elementary algebra* has its roots in *structural arithmetic*—the art of numerical calculation which exploits *structure* rather than brute force.

- At its simplest, this appeal to "structure" may go no further than to use *place value*—as in

$$73 + 48 + 27 = (73 + 27) + 48,$$

  or

$$17.18 + 7460 + 22.82 = (17.18 + 22.82) + 7460.$$

- This grows into an awareness of the algebraic *structure* lurking beneath the surface of many numerical or symbolical expressions—as in

$$3 \times 17 + 7 \times 17 = (3 + 7) \times 17,$$

or

$$\frac{6 \times 15}{10} = \frac{3 \times (2 \times 5) \times 3}{10} = \ldots,$$

or

$$16 \times 17 - 3 \times 34 = (16 - 6) \times 17.$$

- Eventually this instinct for "tidying up" applies the underlying *algebraic* rules in a way that allows us to simplify all manner of algebraic expressions—starting with the simplest examples, such as

$$6(a - b) + 3(2b - a) = \ldots .$$

But before this third stage, pupils must first internalise these *algebraic* rules by applying them to simplify *numerical* expressions, and then learn to see symbols as "placeholders for numbers" and to calculate with symbols in this spirit.

2.2. Technique

It is not easy to illustrate what we in England need to do differently with algebra at age 11–14. The complaints of those who teach the top 20% at the start of A level mathematics at age 16 are clear and consistent: these students—who are the most successful products of Key Stage 3 and Key Stage 4—**struggle with fractions, and with the simple algebra** they need for beginning A level. Other pupils are even more ill-served by the current approach to algebra up to age 16, where this key topic is either ignored, or treated far too superficially. We need to lay much stronger foundations in algebra for **all pupils** (even if some will inevitably go further than others).

The more focused demands of the new Key Stage 4 programme of study could provide a useful indication of what needs to be done—provided these demands are understood, and are taught with a view to mastery (rather than as mindless rules). Another useful pointer as to what needs attention may be found in the released items[20] from TIMSS 2011, which compared achievement in around 50 countries. English Year 9 pupils do tolerably well as long as they only need to use their common sense (e.g. "pattern spotting"). But once their performance depends on *technique* (i.e. something that has to be **taught**), the results are less encouraging. We saw in Part II (examples 1.4A–1.4K) how the bulk of Year 9 pupils in England struggle with simple problems involving *fractions* and *decimals*. In Sections 2.4, 2.5, and 2.7 below we include a selection of items intended to support the assertion that schools also need to re-consider how they approach *algebra* at Key Stage 3. We have again avoided making comparisons with countries from the Far East, and instead compare the results of pupils in England with those from Russia, from Hungary, from the USA, and from Australia.

2.3. [Subject content: *Algebra* p. 6]

- **use and interpret algebraic notation, including**

  ab in place of $a \times b$

  $3y$ in place of $y + y + y$ and $3 \times y$

  a^2 in place of $a \times a$, a^3 in place of $a \times a \times a$, a^2b in place of $a \times a \times b$

  $\frac{a}{b}$ in place of $a \div b$

  coefficients written as fractions rather than as decimals

  brackets

It would be hard to overstate the extent to which the algebraic *notation* summarised in these six bullet points makes elementary mathematics accessible to ordinary people.

The importance of *notation* should be clear if one considers the impact of our notation for writing integers and **decimals** *in base* 10. This was

20 http://timss.bc.edu/timss2011/international-released-items.html

proposed in 1585 by the Dutchman *Simon Stevin* in his little book *Die Thiende*. *Stevin*'s original notation was slightly unwieldy, but it soon evolved into the astonishingly compressed form that we use today, where a single succession of digits (and a decimal point) captures everything about a number, and does so in a way that allows routine calculation in a form that everyone can master. This notation was later extended by adopting our way of writing fractions or quotients (see the fourth bullet point above), and surds.

Our **algebraic** notation then emerged in almost modern form in Descartes' book on *Geometry* in 1637. This had an even greater impact. Before that time, even the best mathematicians struggled to express general calculations using symbols. Yet within 40 years, Descartes' new symbolism had revolutionised mathematics, allowing Newton and Leibniz to invent what we now call "the calculus". And within another 100 years, the language of algebra had been streamlined further by Euler into a form that made its potential power available to everyone.

But for ordinary mortals to access this power, the conventions summarised at the start of 2.3 have to be learned and respected. It seems not to be generally understood why these conventions make such a difference; but there is nothing difficult here, and beginners need to be absolutely clear that the conventions are not optional.

The whole purpose of algebraic notation as summarised above is

- to write algebraic expressions in a *compact* form, that can be apprehended at a glance, and
- to do so in a way that reflects the rules for *priority of operations*.

The genius of the *Descartes-Euler* conventions lies in the way they ensure that:

- Multiplication and division hold together tightly, allowing products (such as "$3ab$" or "$5a^2b$") to be spatially compressed, so that the eye and the brain perceive them as a single "term".
- In the same spirit, fractions—whether as coefficients, or as terms within the overall expression—must be written with a horizontal bar (as $\frac{1}{2}a$,

never in the misleading form "1/2a"); and decimals are best avoided whenever possible, since they undermine the goal of holding terms together compactly.

- Addition and subtraction link separate multiplicative "terms", but do so more loosely, so that the visual impression at a glance reflects the priority of operations.

The result is that the eye and brain can learn to read an algebraic expression at a glance in much the same way as place value allows one to grasp the meaning of numbers. But first one has to learn to routinely and reliably *translate* mildly complicated combinations into this new algebraic script. Thus one would like almost all pupils to be able to grasp the meaning of the simplest expression, such as "$xy + 1$"—especially if all they had to do was to choose between four mostly dodgy options.

2.3A What does $xy + 1$ mean?

A add 1 to y, then multiply by x B multiply x and y by 1
C add x to y, then add 1 D multiply x by y, then add 1

2.3A Russia 89%, USA 80%, Hungary 73%, England 72%, Australia 71%

Given the importance of algebra in elementary mathematics, we really do need to think how to get understanding at this most basic level up around 90%. So in Section 2.5 we stray from our usual "higher viewpoint" and risk a few specific suggestions to encourage schools to consider what we might be currently omitting.

One important point is obscured by the simple examples used in the requirements listed at the start of the current Section 2.3—namely that the ingredient constructions and conventions are often *combined*. Hence in a typical "sum" the terms being added may themselves already be **compound** *expressions* (as in "$(3x - 6y + 4) + (5y - 2x - 3)$"), and in a typical "square" the expression being squared may be a **compound** *expression* (as in "$(3x - 6y + 4)^2$"). Too often we stop short of adding this extra layer of complexity. In the short term, nothing may be lost; but such "layered complexity", or variation, is an integral part of the new algebraic language, which pupils need to get used to.

2.4. [Subject content: *Algebra* p. 6]

- **substitute numerical values into formulae and expressions, including scientific formulae**
- **understand and use standard mathematical formulae; rearrange formulae to change the subject**
- **understand and use the concepts and vocabulary of expressions, equations, inequalities, terms and factors**
- **simplify and manipulate algebraic expressions to maintain equivalence by:**
  - **collecting like terms**
  - **multiplying out a single term over a bracket**
  - **taking out common factors**
  - **expanding products of two or more binomials**

Section 2.4.1 addresses the content of these four requirements by providing some initial food for thought from TIMSS 2011, a study which compared the performance of Year 9 pupils in around 50 countries.

Section 2.4.3 is long and expands on our earlier remark that "Elementary algebra *copies* the structure of arithmetic (that is, the four rules, together with the commutative laws, the associative laws, and the distributive law), and *applies it to a new mixed universe of symbols* (or letters) and numbers."

Section 2.4.2 is relatively short, and refers loosely to some of the ideas from 2.4.3, so should perhaps follow it. But that would risk the basic message of 2.4.2 being obscured by the preceding detail. Since this message is simple and important, we present it *before* the details in Section 2.4.3.

2.4.1 We begin with six tasks taken from TIMSS 2011. The first three are simple exercises involving substitution, and so are directly relevant to the first listed requirement in 2.4. The last three—two of which are again simple exercises—are relevant to the second, third and fourth requirements (and especially the fourth).

2.4A $y = a + \frac{b}{c}$. $a = 8$, $b = 6$, and $c = 2$. What is the value of y?

A 7 B 10 C 11 D 14

2.4B $k = 7$ and $m = 10$. What is the value of P when $P = \frac{3}{5}km$?

2.4C Use the formula

$$y = 100 - \frac{100}{1+t}$$

to find the value of y when $t = 9$.

2.4D Which of the following is equal to $3p^2 + 2p + 2p^2 + p$?

A $8p$ B $8p^2$ C $5p^2 + 3p$ D $7p^2 + p$

2.4E Which expression is equal to $4(3 + x)$?

A $12 + x$ B $7 + x$ C $12 + 4x$ D $12x$

2.4F Simplify the expression

$$\frac{3x}{8} + \frac{x}{4} + \frac{x}{2}.$$

Show your work.

Once the conventions of elementary algebra are understood, substituting values should be entirely routine. Hence 2.4A, 2.4B, and 2.4C should be exercises in simple arithmetic—where we should expect a high level of success.

2.4D and 2.4E go beyond mere arithmetic, but remain the very simplest kind of algebraic exercises; so one should again expect success rates to be high.

The actual results for 2.4A, 2.4B, and 2.4C (see below) suggest either: that Year 9 arithmetic is weak; or that the conventions of elementary algebra are often not understood at this level. The results for 2.4D and 2.4E (multiple-choice questions with just four rather crude options) suggest that pupils' grasp of the basic algebraic conventions remains painfully weak.

2.4F is more searching. It is the simplest imaginable example of genuine algebraic simplification involving fractions (as opposed to an introductory textbook exercise); but it requires pupils to have understood that adding fractions requires one to reduce to a common denominator. This idea has to be applied in a mildly algebraic context—but it is hard to imagine what other standard principle might be elicited by the instruction to "simplify" such an expression. The results suggest that schools need to reflect on their current approach to the arithmetic of fractions and to elementary algebra.

2.4A Russia 91%, USA 81%, Hungary 81%, England 73%, Australia 71%

2.4B Russia 83%, USA 70%, Australia 46%, Hungary 46%, England 40%

2.4C Russia 80%, USA 55%, Hungary 51%, Australia 47%, England 45%

2.4D Russia 81%, Hungary 63%, USA 58%, Australia 56%, England 47%

2.4E Russia 81%, Hungary 57%, USA 53%, England 41%, Australia 40%

2.4F Russia 35%, Hungary 34%, USA 19%, Australia 14%, England 9%

2.4.2 "Substituting values into formulae and expressions" to highlight letters as placeholders for numbers The requirement to "substitute numerical values into formulae and expressions" draws attention to a basic characteristic of algebra which deserves more attention.

- In an **equation** the letters are constrained, so can only take **particular** (as yet unknown) values. So we are not free to "substitute arbitrary numerical values" for the unknown.

- A **formula** is essentially no different from an *equation* with two or more variables, in that it expresses the way one variable *depends on*, and *is determined by*, others. So we are only free to "substitute numerical values" for *certain* variables—and this then determines the value of some other quantity which depends on them.
- In contrast, the letters and numbers in an algebraic **expression** are only required to satisfy the rules of arithmetic (or of algebra), *so the letters can be replaced by* ***any numbers whatsoever****, provided all occurrences of the same letter are given the same value.*

Many pupils never grasp these facts, and blindly move letters around without ever realising that they are little more than "placeholders for numbers". The examples 2.4A, 2.4B, and 2.4C reinforce the impression that pupils need more varied, carefully designed experiences of "substituting given numerical values" for the letters in "formulae and expressions", so that they internalise the idea that each letter in an expression can be given any value.

The act of substituting and evaluating also provides opportunities

- to exercise mental arithmetic, and
- to check *in a numerical context* (and if necessary to correct) the way algebraic notation is understood—including brackets, the correct reading and evaluation of expressions involving exponents, the priority of operations, juxtaposition as multiplication, and the fraction bar as division.

Moreover, evaluating expressions in this way can begin to convey the idea that

- each choice of *inputs* gives rise to a single determined *output* value for the expression.

That is, that such expressions provide the simplest examples of what we will later call a *function* (of is component variables).

2.4.3 What is elementary algebra?

We saw in 2.3 how the *Descartes-Euler* notation for elementary algebra helps us to make sense of compound expressions as being made up from their atomic parts, which we call "terms". There is no strict definition of what counts as a "term", but it tends to refer to one of the products, or brackets, which are combined to make up the whole expression. For example, where an integer such as 35 can be written as a product of two integers ($35 = 5 \times 7$), the 5 and 7 are called *factors* of 35. Similarly, when a compound expression (such as $x^2 + 5x + 6$) can be written as a product of two or more brackets ($x^2 + 5x + 6 = (x + 2)(x + 3)$), each of the brackets on the RHS is a *factor* of the original expression. In the expanded form, "x^2", "$5x$", and "6" would be seen as separate terms; but in the factorised form, the separate brackets "$(x + 2)$" and "$(x + 3)$" might be referred to as constituent *terms*.

This new domain of elementary "algebra" has several distinct sub-domains, each of which sheds a slightly different light on the subject. Some of these subdomains are more natural starting points for beginners than others. The four most obvious subdomains—in approximate order of sophistication—are *formulae*, *equations* (and *inequalities*), *expressions*, and *identities*.

- *Formulae*. Here letters are used in place of familiar entities (e.g. $A = l \times b$ for the area A of a rectangle of length l and breadth b; or $C = 2\pi r$ for the circumference C of a circle of radius r). In each such formula, the letters can take different values. The simplest formulae are a bit like the simplest calculations that we meet at Key Stages 1 and 2, in that they tell us how the value of one entity can be calculated once we know the values of certain others. For a rectangle, $A = l \times b$ tells us that the area of a rectangle (measured in square units) is given by multiplying the length and the breadth: the entities l and b can take any value $\geqslant 0$, and the value of A is then determined.

  At Key Stage 3 it is important to stress that, even though symbols (like l and b) are often chosen so that the letters reminds us of what they represent, the symbols are not a shorthand for the *concepts* "length" and "breadth", but stand for *numbers*. Hence b stands for "the number of units in the breadth" rather than for the breadth itself, and the r in $2\pi r$ stands for "the length in units of the radius" (see Sections 2.4.1 above and Part II, Section 2.1.3).

[There may be a clash here with the way variables are used in science. In mathematics letters stand for pure numbers. But science teachers sometimes use letters to stand for *quantities*—including their units: so a letter may be used to stand for a length "3cm", rather than just for the number of centimetres—namely "3".]

- *Equations* (and *inequalities*). The first equations one meets involve a single letter (often denoted by "x"). This letter is usually referred to as the "unknown"—because an equation can be interpreted as an arithmetical constraint which some "unknown number x" has to satisfy. An equation can then be transformed using the rules of algebra to try to unmask this previously "unknown number". For example, the problem:

  "I'm thinking of a number.
  When I double it and add 3 the result is 15.
  What is my number?"

  can be formulated by saying:

  Let the unknown number be "x".
  Then x must satisfy the equation $2x + 3 = 15$.

  Once the equation has been set up, the secret is to forget where it came from and to transform the equation according to the laws of arithmetic (or the laws of algebra) in order to recover what information we can about "x": for example,

  adding "-3" to both sides we get $2x = 12$;
  then dividing both sides by 2 we get $x = 6$.

  These "transformations of an equation" set the scene for the way the "=" sign will be routinely handled when pupils work with *expressions* and *identities*.

Later we meet equations involving the square or the cube of the "unknown", or equations involving more than one "unknown". For example, suppose we are asked:

> "How can I transfer exactly 76 litres from a pond into an empty tank by using two buckets—one holding exactly 8 litres and the other holding exactly 7 litres?"

We can imagine filling and pouring the 7 litre bucket "x" times and the 8 litre bucket "y" times to get 76 litres, so that $7x + 8y = 76$. Notice that in the problem as described, the two unknowns x and y are both integers $\geqslant 0$. (We ignore for the moment the fact that one could also imagine pouring 12 full 7 litre buckets into the empty tank and then removing one full 8 litre bucket, or pouring 13 full 8 litre buckets into the empty tank and then removing 4 full 7 litre buckets—which correspond to solutions in which one of x and y may be negative.)

The third requirement listed at the start of Section 2.4 refers to *inequalities*. One should probably not try to go too far in exploring inequalities at Key Stage 3. However, we already saw at the end of Section 2.2.2 in Part II:

- that understanding and solving inequalities are important in applications of elementary mathematics,
- how solving inequalities relates to solving *equations*, and
- how badly neglected the topic has been in English schools.

The third bullet point here suggests that considerable thought needs to go into how to address this requirement in the course of Key Stage 3 and Key Stage 4. Work at Key Stage 3 needs to prepare for what will be needed at Key Stage 4, so one should hesitate to offer a general way of solving inequalities at this stage, and should focus instead on lots of examples. These examples should be given in different forms, and in different contexts, with both positive and negative coefficients, and with the unknown appearing on either, and on both sides of the inequality. The solutions should be expressed in words, marked on the number line (and eventually, for the bold, written using "set notation"—as is required in the GCSE *Subject criteria*).

To cut a long story short, every linear inequality in one variable can be reduced either

(a) to the form "$ax + b < 0$", or "$ax + b \leqslant 0$" (where a and b are constants, with $a > 0$), or

(b) to the form "$ax + b > 0$", or "$ax + b \geqslant 0$" (where a and b are constants, with $a > 0$).

To consider the first case only: we can add "$-b$" to both sides of the inequality, and then multiply both sides by the positive constant $\frac{1}{a}$, to conclude that the solutions in the two cases consist of

> "all values of x satisfying $x < -\frac{b}{a}$", or "all values of x satisfying $x \leqslant -\frac{b}{a}$".

These can be shown on the x-axis, or number line, by *shading*

> "all points x to the left of $-\frac{b}{a}$", or "all points x to the left of $-\frac{b}{a}$ **together with** $x = -\frac{b}{a}$".

For the more ambitious, the solutions can later be written in the form

$$\left\{x : x < -\frac{b}{a}\right\},$$

or

$$\left\{x : x \leqslant -\frac{b}{a}\right\}.$$

Quadratic inequalities in one variable, and linear inequalities in two variables, are more interesting, but probably belong at Key Stage 4.

- *Expressions*. Given a formula, such as $C = 2\pi r$, we very soon want to move the letters around. For example, suppose we use string to measure the circumference C of a tall cylindrical lamp post and want to calculate the radius r of the lamp post—a length which we cannot measure directly. We then need to re-write the formula as

$$r = \frac{C}{2\pi}$$

so that we can calculate r as soon as we know the circumference C. We therefore need to learn how to "calculate" with expressions consisting of letters and numbers, and to move the letters around "as if they were numbers" (since this is exactly what the letters represent).

As part of this process of collecting terms, adding, subtracting, multiplying and dividing, multiplying out brackets, factorising, cancelling common factors, etc. we have to learn to forget *temporarily* the meaning of the symbols and simply to respect the laws of arithmetic (or of algebra), and the meaning of "equality"—as we did

- with the equation "$2x + 3 = 15$" to get first "$2x = 12$" and then "$x = 6$"

and as we did

- when dividing both sides of the equation "$C = 2\pi r$" by "2π" to get "$r = \frac{C}{2\pi}$".

We can work in a similar way to discover how to obtain "exactly 76 litres"—but this time we have to exploit the fact that the unknowns have to be *positive integers*.

- We can start with $7x + 8y = 76$ and add "$-8y$" to both sides to get $7x = 76 - 8y$.
- We can then take out a common factor of 4 to get $7x = 4(19 - 2y)$,

which tells us that

- the LHS "$7x$" must be a multiple of 4, and hence x must be a multiple of 4.
- But we also know that, if x and y are integers $\geqslant 0$, then $7x$ is at most 76, so $x < 12$.
- So we only need to consider $x = 4$ (which yields a solution) and $x = 0$, or $x = 8$ (which do not).

It is this art of "calculating with expressions" that allows us to transform formulae and equations in a flexible way—and to derive information that may be far from obvious. And the art of calculating with expressions requires lots of carefully graduated practise if pupils are to become fluent in simplifying the kind of complicated-looking expressions that will arise naturally later.

The fourth subdomain of elementary algebra—namely *identities*—is in some ways the most important subdomain of the four. "Identities" are not mentioned in the third requirement at the start of 2.4—but they are implicit in other requirements, so cannot be entirely avoided at Key Stage 3 (even if they feature more strongly at Key Stage 4 and beyond).

- *Identities*: In primary arithmetic the = sign is at first used to connect some required calculation such as "13 + 29" (on the left hand side) with the answer "42" (on the right hand side):

  $$13 + 29 = 42.$$

  But the = sign then broadens its meaning and is later used to connect any two numerically equivalent expressions—such as

  $$\text{“}13 + 29 = 6 \times 7\text{”, or “}6^2 - 1 = 5 \times 7\text{”, or “}\tfrac{28}{42} = \tfrac{10}{15}\text{”}.$$

  Something similar arises in the algebra of expressions, where pupils first learn that, given a jumble of symbols on the left hand side, one is expected to simplify it in some way and set it "equal" to something a bit like an "answer" (on the right hand side). For example one might be given an expression such as

  $$\left(\frac{x}{x-1} - \frac{x+1}{x}\right)^{-1}$$

  and rewrite it as

  $$= x^2 - x.$$

  However one later broadens this use of the equals sign so that "=" simply links two expressions that are "algebraically equivalent"—that is, where one side can be transformed into the other side via the rules of algebra.

Any such equation that links two expressions that are algebraically equivalent is called an *identity*.

2.5. [Subject content: *Algebra* p. 6]

> – **model situations or procedures by translating them into algebraic expressions or formulae**

This requirement summarises what an idealist would like all pupils to be able to do *eventually*. However, at present very few pupils ever reach this level of fluency—even at Key Stage 4 (let alone at Key Stage 3: see examples 2.5B and 2.5C below). Hence the requirement needs to be interpreted with care.

One reason for our current limited success is that we fail to separate two stages which have here been combined in the same requirement:

- first learn to translate a numerical procedure, or a sequence of operations, into algebraic form *as an expression*;
- then learn to equate the results of two such procedures, or to take on board an additional constraint, to **derive an equation** (or a "formula").

That is, we pay too little attention to the more modest *prerequisite* requirement of getting pupils

– **to interpret descriptions, or situations, given *orally* in words and to write down the answers as expressions.**

The extent to which we need to rethink current practice is partly illustrated by the following five Year 9 tasks from TIMSS 2011. The first four tasks (2.5A–2.5D) are basic exercises. These are **not** sophisticated modelling tasks; but they indicate the kind of exercises that we may need to take more seriously, and engage with more systematically, if we are eventually to address the full-blooded requirement at the start of Section 2.5. The fifth example requires one to set up a very simple linear equation and to interpret its solution—and although the comparison countries show that this task is more demanding, the English performance on this problem is in some ways even more telling.

> **2.5A** There were m boys and n girls in a parade. Each person carried 2 balloons. Which of these expressions represents the total number of balloons carried in the parade?
>
> A $2(m+n)$ B $2+(m+n)$ C $2m+n$ D $m+2n$
>
> **2.5B** A taxi company has a basic charge of 25 zeds and a charge of 0.2 zeds for each kilometre the taxi is driven. Which of these represents the cost in zeds to hire a taxi for a trip of n kilometres?
>
> A $25+0.2n$ B $25\times 0.2n$ C $0.2\times(25+n)$
> D $0.2\times 25+n$
>
> **2.5C** What is the area of the rectangle shown? [A rectangle with *length* $x+2$ and *width* x is shown.]
>
> A x^2+2 B x^2+2x C $2x+2$ D $4x+4$
>
> **2.5D** What is the sum of three consecutive whole numbers with $2n$ as the middle number?
>
> A $6n+3$ B $6n$ C $6n-1$ D $6n-3$
>
> **2.5E** A piece of wood was 40cm long. It was cut into 3 pieces. The lengths in cm are: $2x-5$, $x+7$, $x+6$. What is the length of the longest piece?

The success rates among Year 9 pupils in our four comparison countries were as follows:

> **2.5A** Russia 90%, USA 88%, Hungary 80%, England 74%, Australia 73%
>
> **2.5B** Russia 70%, USA 61%, Hungary 50%, Australia 47%, England 45%

2.5C Russia 72%, USA 37%, England 35%, Hungary 30%, Australia 26%

2.5D Hungary 56%, Russia 53%, England 46%, Australia 45%, USA 37%

2.5E Hungary 23%, Russia 22%, Australia 7%, USA 7%, England 3%

Some observers might be satisfied with a 74% success rate for 2.5A. But the Russian, USA, and Hungarian scores should challenge such complacency. (This is a multiple choice question, and the 26% who chose options B, C, or D suggest that a significant number of pupils were simply guessing—so some of the 74% correct will have chosen option A by accident.)

The responses to 2.5B reinforce the impression that most Year 9 pupils in England are very rarely expected to formulate such simple expressions algebraically from a situation given in words. (Note that if 30% of pupils were fairly sure of option A, and the other 70% of pupils were reduced to guessing, then an additional 17.5% of the cohort would select option A by accident—so more than 45% would then have chosen the "correct" option.) Example 2.5C would seem to be even simpler—provided that pupils can read the simplest diagram and know that "area = length × breadth".

Setting up an "equation", or a "formula", is like writing a sentence. So pupils first need to learn how to "read", then how to "spell" the ingredient words and how to build up expressions (in a way that respects the conventions of elementary algebra—see Section 2.3). They then need to learn the basic art of naming a variable, and applying a sequence of arithmetical or algebraic transformations to it in a reliable way. We infer that this is either not done, or done in a way that does not allow these key skills to take root.

We have largely resisted the temptation to offer "solutions". However, as a contribution to the challenge for schools to develop the necessary extended sequence of stages that leads to algebraic fluency, we draw attention to three ingredients that seem to be relatively neglected. These stages relate the need to learn how to "match verbal descriptions with algebraic expressions" (see TIMMS example 2.3A above).

On the simplest level pupils need exercises of the following kind (see example 2.3A above to see why).

Match up each expression on the left with the corresponding English description on the right.

$4+2x$	Six less than four times x
$x-5$	Three times one more than x
$2x-4$	Two less than one quarter of x
$\frac{x+2}{4}$	Three times one less than x
$3(x+1)$	One quarter of two less than x
$4x-6$	One quarter of two more than x
$\frac{x}{4}-2$	Four less than twice x
$\frac{x-2}{4}$	Six more than half of x
$x+6$	One more than three times x
$3x+1$	Five less than x
$\frac{x}{2}+6$	Six more than x
$3(x-1)$	Four more than twice x.

Pupils then need to take the step from "matching up" verbal descriptions and *given* expressions to reading, or listening to verbal descriptions and reliably translating these into written expressions for themselves. So they need variations on the following activity to cultivate the art of *listening, thinking,* and *interpreting*. (We give two contexts for purposes of illustration—but many others can be imagined.) These are intended to be **oral** challenges, read slowly and clearly, leaving sufficient pauses between successive tasks—with pupils expected to **listen** and write down "answers" (preferably without the instructions being repeated).

(a) "I'm thinking of a number, which I multiply by 3. Write an expression for my final number."

"I'm thinking of a number, which I multiply by 3, and then add 2. Write an expression for my final number."

"I'm thinking of a number, to which I add 2 and then multiply the result by 3. Write an expression for my final number."

"I'm thinking of a number, to which I add 2, then multiply the result by 3, and then square the answer. Write an expression for my final number."

"I'm thinking of a number, to which I add 2, square the result, and subtract 4 times one more than the number I first thought of. Write a fully simplified expression for my final number."

(b) "A square has sides of length a. Write an expression for its perimeter. Write another expression for its area."

"A rectangle has sides of length a and b. Write an expression for its perimeter. Write another expression for its area."

"A rectangle has sides whose lengths differ by 1. Write an expression for its perimeter. Write another expression for its area."

"A rectangle has one side twice as long as the other. Write an expression for its perimeter. Write another expression for its area."

"A rectangle has sides in the ratio 3 : 2. Write an expression for its perimeter. Write another expression for its area."

Once pupils understand how *expressions* are constructed they may be in a better position to use this skill to translate a problem, or a result, given in words into an **equation** or *formula*, as with such variations on the above **oral** tasks as the following.

(a) "I'm thinking of a number, which I multiply by 3, and the result is 27. **Express this as an equation.**"

"I'm thinking of a number, which I multiply by 3, and then add 2. The result is 41. Express this as an equation."

"I'm thinking of a number, to which I add 2 and then multiply the result by 3. The result is 39. Express this as an equation."

"I'm thinking of a number, to which I add 2, then multiply the result by 3, and then square the answer. The result is 36. Express this as an equation."

"I'm thinking of a number, to which I add 2, square the result, and subtract 4 times one more than the number I first thought of. The result is 144. Express this as an equation."

(b) "A square has sides of length a. It perimeter is 108. **Express this as an equation.**"

"A square has sides of length $2a$. Its area is 144. Express this as an equation."

"A rectangle has sides of length a and b. Its perimeter is 108. Express this as an equation."

"A rectangle has sides of length a and b. Its perimeter is 10 and its area is 6. Express these facts as two equations in a and b."

"A rectangle has sides whose lengths differ by 1. Its perimeter is 62. Express this as an equation."

"A rectangle has sides whose lengths differ by 1. Its area is 56. Express this as an equation."

"A rectangle has one side twice as long as the other. Its area is 50. Express this as an equation."

"A rectangle has sides in the ratio 3 : 2. It perimeter is 130. Express this as an equation."

In the above examples, the numbers have been chosen so that the solutions may be accessed without requiring any special technique. This should allow pupils to check whether the evident *numerical* solution is consistent with their *algebraic* formulation. But pupils later need to progress to exercises where the solutions cannot be so easily discerned. The successful solution of any resulting equations will then depend on preparatory algebraic and arithmetical work done elsewhere (especially work with transforming algebraic expressions and with fractions).

In the official Key Stage 3 programme of study, the full version of the requirement given at the start of Section 2.5 is even more ambitious, in that it states that pupils should be taught to:

- "model situations or procedures by translating them into algebraic expressions or formulae **and by using graphs**." [emphasis added]

We have already suggested that increased success may depend on separating the art of "formulating a procedure as an algebraic expression" from, and treating it earlier than, "formulating equations". So the immediate juxtaposition of the two separate stages "expressions and formulae" could be misleading. The final four words above (in bold) would seem to constitute an even more unfortunate juxtaposition, in that two entirely separate requirements *that cannot be handled simultaneously* have been compressed into a single statement.

The reference to "graphs" suggests that the situation being analysed involves at least **two variables**. This in turn suggests that this requirement only becomes relevant much later. Long before one can think about "using a graph", one needs to be able to formulate the relevant algebraic equation in two variables entirely reliably—and this seems likely to take more time and effort than we have realised (see 2.5A–2.5C). Hence **schools must be prepared to use their judgement** as to when such apparently juxtaposed requirements in the official programme of study have to be separated in time, with the missing stages, or "stepping-stones", provided internally.

In this instance, the connection with graphs is likely to feature much later. Once pupils have learned to work with linear graphs, one could revisit

- "I'm thinking of a number, which I multiply by 3, and the result is 27."

and relate the algebraic solution:

> Let the unknown number be x.
>
> $\therefore 3x = 27$.

to the point of intersection $(9, 27)$ of the line $y = 3x$ and the ordinate $y = 27$. Later in Key Stage 3, or in early Key Stage 4 (see the third, fourth and fifth requirements in section 2.7 below), pupils might relate the problem

> "I'm thinking of a number, to which I add 2, then multiply the result by 3, and then square the answer. The result is 36. Express this as an equation."

to the intersection point $(2, 36)$ of the graph of $y = 9(x + 2)^2$ and the ordinate $y = 36$.

In the same spirit, the problem:

> "A rectangle has sides whose lengths differ by 1. Its area is 56. Express this as an equation."

could be linked to the *positive* intersection point $(7, 0)$ (after rejecting $(-8, 0)$) of the graph of $y = x^2 + x - 56$ with the x-axis $y = 0$.

And having learned to solve quadratic equations at Key Stage 4, pupils might relate

> "A rectangle has sides of length a and b. Its perimeter is 10 and its area is 6. Express these facts as two equations in a and b."

to the equation $x^2 - 5x + 6 = 0$ (whose roots are a and b). Some pupils could then explore the general question of whether knowing the sum $a + b$ and the product ab of two unknowns is always sufficient to determine a and b.

Teachers should know that this latter idea (namely that a rectangle is determined by its area and its semi-perimeter) is more important than one might think—both historically and at higher levels. The ancient

Babylonians and Greeks both tackled quadratics in this way (among others).

***Babylonian*: around 1700 BC** The Babylonian approach was eclectic, and essentially *algebraic*, but without symbols. The problems were expressed in words, and the solution methods were given as recipes applied to the particular numbers in the problem; but the recipes were so formulated that they would still work if the particular numbers were changed. They addressed a remarkable variety of problems which correspond to what we would call "quadratic equations". Otto Neugebauer, the leading historian of such matters in the first half of the 20th century, catalogued hundreds of examples in what he called "normal form", where two numbers were to be found if their *product* and their *sum* (or difference) were known. Neugebauer also found countless exercises designed to train young scribes how to reduce other sorts of quadratic problems to this "normal form".

***Greek*: around 300 BC** The Greek approach is harder to explain briefly, because it was expressed purely geometrically (for they had no way of writing algebraically). If we cheat a little and describe the steps in their method partly algebraically, their "normal form" for a quadratic problem was to imagine a line segment broken in to unequal lengths (so of length $a+b$, with $a>b$):

- to construct the midpoint and then construct the square on half of the complete segment
- to construct the "a by b" rectangle with the two unequal segments as sides
- to subtract the rectangle from the square
- to construct the square which was equal to this difference (whose side was therefore "$\frac{1}{2}(a-b)$")
- to combine the segments of length $\frac{1}{2}(a+b)$ and of length $\frac{1}{2}(a-b)$ to find a; then find b.

All of this was done strictly geometrically—though we would write the process algebraically as

(i) first find $\frac{1}{2}(a+b)$, and then $\left[\frac{1}{2}(a+b)\right]^2$;

(ii) find ab;

(iii) subtract $\left[\frac{1}{2}(a+b)\right]^2 - ab$ to get $\left[\frac{1}{2}(a-b)\right]^2$;

(iv) find $\frac{1}{2}(a-b)$;

(v) add to get

$$a = \frac{1}{2}(a+b) + \frac{1}{2}(a-b),$$

and subtract to get

$$b = \frac{1}{2}(a+b) - \frac{1}{2}(a-b).$$

When pupils proceed beyond GCSE, they will need to know that:

- If a quadratic $x^2 + dx + e$ has roots a and b, it can be factorised as

$$x^2 + dx + e = (x-a)(x-b);$$

and multiplying out the RHS shows that

$$d = -(a+b) \text{ and } e = ab.$$

Hence once we know the quadratic, we already know the sum and product of the roots, and "solving the equation" is a way of going from knowing "the sum and product of the roots" to finding the roots themselves.

- Though the Babylonians and Greeks did not know it, they had hit upon something important. For if a cubic $x^3 + dx^2 + ex + f$ has roots a, b and c, then it can be factorised as

$$x^3 + dx^2 + ex + f = (x-a)(x-b)(x-c);$$

and multiplying out the RHS shows that

$$d = -(a+b+c), \quad e = ab + bc + ca, \text{ and } f = -abc.$$

Hence once we know the cubic, we already know the sum of the roots ($-d$), the product of the roots ($-f$), and the sum of the products in pairs (*e*). So "solving a cubic equation" requires us to find a way of going from knowing "the sum of all three roots, the product of all three roots, and the sum of the products in pairs" to finding the three roots themselves.

2.6. [Subject content: *Algebra* p. 6]

> – **use algebraic methods to solve linear equations in one variable (including all forms that require rearrangement)**

Pupils will no doubt already be familiar with the way general results such as $C = 2\pi r$ can be expressed using letters; but in such a formula, the letters stand for familiar entities (the radius r of the circle, and its circumference C). In contrast, solving linear equations in one unknown may well be pupils' first encounter with symbols being used to encode information about completely unknown entities. So this is likely to be the setting in which key ideas about algebra are internalised—and where misconceptions may well take root.

We have seen (Part II, Section 2.2.2.2) that "to solve equations" means to solve **exactly**—by algebraic methods. We start out with an equation which has an unknown set of solutions, or possible values for the unknown "x". "Solving the equation algebraically" is a process which pins down the unknown "x" by exploiting two kinds of "moves".

- The first kind of move allows us to replace any constituent expression on either side of the equation by another expression which is *algebraically equivalent* to it (for example, we can "collect up" separate multiples of the unknown "x" into a single term). Because this kind of move is *reversible*, we know that exactly **the same values** of the unknown "x" satisfy the new equation as satisfied the old equation.

- The second kind of move is to subject both sides of the equation to the same operation (for example, we can add the same quantity to both sides, or multiply both sides by the same quantity). As long as this operation is *reversible* (as it always is if we add or subtract the same quantity to both sides, or if we multiply or divide both sides by a given expression *that is never equal to zero*), then we can again be sure that **exactly the same values** of the unknown "x" satisfy the new equation as satisfied the old equation.

Pupils need to learn not only to transform equations according to these rules of algebra, but also to recognise any pair of equations which are algebraically equivalent. Thus they should be faced with such tasks as:

Match up each equation on the left with the equation(s) on the right to which it is equivalent.

$x+6=11$	$7x=4$
$2x-3=5$	$2x+9=23$
$10=6+7x$	$2=-2x$
$\dfrac{x}{3}=4$	$14=2+x$
$3=2x-11$	$10+x=15$
$\dfrac{x}{3}-5=11$	$2x+2=10$
$5-2x=7$	$2x=14$
$13=x+6$	$16=\dfrac{x}{3}.$

Pupils also need lots of equations to solve, and standard contexts in which they learn to set up and solve equations which reveal things that were not previously clear and that are vaguely interesting. We offer a sequence of problems based on one idea—but there are dozens of other possible settings.

(a) *I start with the fraction $\frac{1}{6}$. I wish to add the same amount to the numerator and to the denominator so that the result is equal to $\frac{1}{5}$. What amount should I add?*

I then start with the fraction $\frac{1}{5}$. I wish to add the same amount to the numerator and to the denominator so that the result is equal to $\frac{1}{4}$. What amount should I add?

I then start with the fraction $\frac{1}{4}$. I wish to add the same amount to the numerator and to the denominator so that the result is equal to $\frac{1}{3}$. What amount should I add?

I then start with the fraction $\frac{1}{3}$. I wish to add the same amount to the numerator and to the denominator so that the result is equal to $\frac{1}{2}$. What amount should I add?

(b) *I start again with the fraction $\frac{1}{6}$. I want to* **add** *some amount a to the numerator and* **subtract** *the same amount from the denominator to make the result equal to $\frac{1}{5}$. Find a.*

I then start with the fraction $\frac{1}{5}$. I want to add some amount b to the numerator and subtract the same amount from the denominator to make the result equal to $\frac{1}{4}$. Find b.

I then start with the fraction $\frac{1}{4}$. I want to add some amount c to the numerator and subtract the same amount from the denominator to make the result equal to $\frac{1}{3}$. Find c.

I then start with the fraction $\frac{1}{3}$. I want to add some amount d to the numerator and subtract the same amount from the denominator to make the result equal to $\frac{1}{2}$. Find d.

I then start with the fraction $\frac{1}{2}$. I want to add some amount e to the numerator and subtract the same amount from the denominator to make the result equal to 1. Find e.

2.7. [Subject content: *Algebra* pp. 6-7]

- **work with coordinates in all four quadrants**
- **reduce a given linear equation in two variables to the standard form $y = mx + c$; calculate and interpret gradients and intercepts of graphs of such linear equations numerically, graphically and algebraically**

- **recognise, sketch and produce graphs of linear and quadratic functions of one variable with appropriate scaling, using equations in x and y in the Cartesian plane**
- **use linear and quadratic graphs to estimate values of y for given values of x and vice versa and to find approximate solutions of simultaneous linear equations**
- **model situations or procedures by translating them into algebraic expressions or formulae and by using graphs**
- **interpret mathematical relationships both algebraically and graphically**
- **find approximate solutions to contextual problems from given graphs of a variety of functions, including piece-wise linear, exponential and reciprocal graphs**

[Ratio, proportion and rates of change p. 7]

- **solve problems involving direct and inverse proportion, including graphical and algebraic representations**

2.7.1 This collection of requirements linked to graphs needs to be treated with extreme care. The first requirement makes perfect sense. The *first half* of the second requirement is equally standard; but the second half is already far from clear. And as one reads on, the meanings become more opaque and the stated goals appear progressively more optimistic, or overblown at this level. For example, we have already seen that direct proportion is hard, and that its "graphical and algebraic representation" may be more appropriate at Key Stage 4 (for more confident pupils); so the inclusion of this requirement for "inverse proportion" may need to be taken with a pinch of salt.

In short, we would urge schools **to sift out what clearly belongs to Key Stage 3 and to teach it well**. Where material seems out of place at Key

Stage 3, and where the listed material in standard type in the Key Stage 4 programme of study either repeats it verbatim or does not take it much further, work at Key Stage 3 should perhaps be limited to "preparatory" experience that can then be built on in Years 10 and 11.

2.7.2 The first requirement could be interpreted as being limited to work with individual points. However, one of the characteristic features of coordinate geometry and equations is that they are ways of working with *groups* of points or lines.

- An equation represents the set of *all* points (x, y) that satisfy the equation.
- To find the equation of a straight line we use the known coordinates of two given points and the unknown coordinates of a third variable point (x, y) which lies on the line.
- And we think about the solutions of simultaneous equations as the point, or points, where two or more lines or curves intersect.

So pupils need to learn to work with several points at once. The gulf between understanding ideas or methods *in isolation* (one-piece jigsaws) and being able to handle two or more simple ideas at once is indicated by the following item for Year 9 pupils in TIMSS 2011.

> **2.7.2A** $(0, -1)$, $(1, 3)$ Which equation is satisfied by **both** of these pairs of numbers (x, y)?
>
> A $x + y = -1$ B $2x + y = 5$ C $3x - y = 0$ D $4x - y = 1$

> **2.7.2A** Russia 53%, USA 38%, Hungary 29%, England 24%, Australia 22%

So before pupils begin to work with equations, basic work with coordinates should include learning to think about the "relative position" of *groups of points*. For example:

- One may give the coordinates of three vertices of a square, and require them to be located, and the coordinates of the fourth (unspecified) vertex to be found and the vertex marked.

- One may specify the coordinates of two *neighbouring* vertices of a square (for example, $(-4,2)$ and $(-3,-3)$), and ask for the possible coordinates of the other two vertices.

- One may specify the coordinates of two *opposite* vertices of a square and require that the other two vertices be marked and their coordinates found.

That is, pupils need lots of work which not only establishes the underlying conventions, but which teaches them to "see", and to think about, *groups* of points (and lines) that are related to each other in some way.

2.7.3 After sufficient experience imagining, and locating individual points and groups of points in all four quadrants, pupils will be well-placed to think about what links a given set of points (preferably given as a list, rather than as a table) such as:

$$(-6,-3),(-4,-2),(-2,-1),(0,0),(2,1),(4,2),(6,3),(8,4).$$

Plotting points should convey the idea that they appear to lie on a line, and that

> each time the x-coordinate increases by 2, the y-coordinate increases by 1 ("along 2, up 1").

One can then ask for the coordinates of *intermediate* points that lie on the same line, both to establish the possibility of fractional values (such as $\left(1,\frac{1}{2}\right)$, or $(3,\frac{3}{2})$, or $\left(-1,-\frac{1}{2}\right)$), and to extract

> the **unit** step: "along 1, up $\frac{1}{2}$".

Pupils can go further and then find $\left(\frac{1}{2},\frac{1}{4}\right)$ ("along $\frac{1}{2}$, up $\frac{1}{4}$"), and $\left(\frac{1}{3},\frac{1}{6}\right)$ ("along $\frac{1}{3}$, up $\frac{1}{6}$"), etc.. They should also be challenged to identify points on the same line with much more distant coordinates (such as $(100,50)$, or $(-200,-100)$).

Once these ideas (that the line extends indefinitely, and that it includes points that are as close together was we choose) have been firmly established, one can

- look for ways of relating x- and y-coordinates of points which lie on the line,
- obtain the usual *equation* "$y = \frac{1}{2}x$", and
- check that every point on the line satisfies this equation, and that every point whose coordinates satisfy the equation must lie on the line.

It may be necessary to repeatedly reinforce the idea that

- the collection of points on the line, and
- the collection of points whose coordinates (x, y) satisfy the equation $y = \frac{1}{2}x$

are the same (i.e. that points lie on the line *precisely when* their coordinates satisfy the equation): that is, that the equation provides an *algebraic* way of reasoning about, and calculating with, the *geometrical* line.

This whole sequence can then be repeated for a new set of points

$$(-6, -2), (-4, -1), (-2, 0), (0, 1), (2, 2), (4, 3), (6, 4), (8, 5).$$

Again, plotting points will indicate that the points lie on a line, that whenever the x-coordinate increases by 2, the y-coordinate increases by 1 ("along 2, up 1"), and that this line can never meet the first line (since the first line goes through $(-6, -3)$ and follows the rule "along 2, up 1", whereas the second line follows the *same* rule "along 2, up 1", but goes through a point $(-6, -2)$ *which does not lie on the first line*). Again one can ask pupils to find the coordinates of *intermediate* points on the line, and for points on the line with much more distant coordinates (such as $(100, 51)$, or $(-200, -99)$), and can then obtain the usual *equation* $y = \frac{1}{2}x + 1$. The significance of the parameters $m = \frac{1}{2}$, and of $c = 1$ can be established. And everything can be reinforced by considering the new set of points

$$(-6, -5), (-4, -4), (-2, -3), (0, -2), (2, -1), (4, 0), (6, 1), (8, 2).$$

In making sense of the linear equation $y = mx + c$, pupils need to internalise the significance

- of c (as the y-coordinate of the point where the line crosses the y-axis).

They also need sufficient experience to establish a clear mental image of how the parameter m affects the visual impression of the represented line (assuming that equal scales are used on both axes), so that they distinguish:

- lines in which $m = 1$ (rising to the right at 45°),
- lines with $0 < m < 1$ (rising to the right less steeply than $m = 1$)
- lines with $m > 1$ (rising to the right more steeply than $m = 1$), and
- lines with $m < 0$ (falling as one moves to the right).

Schools will need to decide for themselves how much of what follows is best handled at Key Stage 3 and how much fits more naturally within Key Stage 4. But at some point, once the basic ideas have been grasped, pupils need to do lots of work in the opposite direction:

- starting with linear equations given in a variety of forms (including with terms in "x" and in "y" on both sides of the equation, and where the y-terms may have any positive or negative coefficient),
- reducing the given equation to the "standard form $y = mx + c$" (or "$x = a$")
- and then sketching the line.

Pupils eventually need to be able to find the equation of a line which satisfies certain conditions, such as:

(a) passing through a given point with a given gradient m,

(b) with a given y-intercept $(0, c)$ and passing through a given point,

(c) with a given gradient m and a given x-intercept $(a, 0)$,

(d) with a given x-intercept and passing through a given point,

(e) passing through two given points.

2.7.4 Once the basic language of straight line graphs and linear equations has been established, pupils are ready to explore the wealth of problems whose natural representation is in terms of linear equations and straight line graphs.

We have already seen how this arises whenever two quantities are related in such a way as to be "in proportion", so that doubling the first quantity (such as the number of hours worked) leads to a doubling of the second quantity (the pay that is earned: see Section 1.9.2 above and Part II, Section 2.2.1). This is clearly relevant to the last requirement listed at the start of Section 2.7. If two different quantities vary "in proportion", and we know two corresponding numerical values—one of the first kind (a), and one of the second kind (c),

$$a \longrightarrow c$$

then any two corresponding *unknown* amounts x and y (one of the first kind and the other of the second kind) provide the third and fourth vertices of our "rectangular template"

$$x \longrightarrow y$$

and the proportion

$$x : a = y : c$$

translates into an equality of ratios, or fractions

$$\frac{x}{a} = \frac{y}{c}$$

which in turn gives rise to the linear equation

$$y = \left(\frac{c}{a}\right) x$$

with "constant of proportionality", or gradient, $\frac{c}{a}$.

Such examples also arise whenever one changes units. If the units belong to the same system, then the constant of proportionality will be exact, and relatively simple. For example, when changing from centimetres to metres, M metres becomes $C = 100M$ centimetres. But if the units come from *different* systems, then we usually simplify by using a convenient approximation to the "constant of proportionality". For example, when changing from miles into kilometres, M miles is generally taken to be

$K = \frac{8}{5}M$km, where we use 1.6 as the approximate scale factor in place of the messy actual value of "1.609344 to 6 decimal places".

However, just as most straight line graphs $y = mx + c$ do not have $c = 0$, so we must expect most linear relations to occur with a built-in "offset" $c \neq 0$. This offset can be interpreted as saying that the two scales we are comparing need to be "re-aligned". For example, the equation which relates the temperature F in Fahrenheit with the temperature C in Centigrade, or Celsius, is

$$F = \frac{9}{5}C + 32.$$

Here the "+32" arises because there is no obvious "zero" for measuring temperature; the Celsius scale uses the freezing point of water as 0°C, whereas the Fahrenheit scale locates this at 32°F. (In this instance, although the units arise from different systems, the scale factor "$\frac{9}{5}$" is *exact*, because the Celsius scale from 0°C to 100°C matches up uniformly with the Fahrenheit scale from 32°F to 212°F, so that each 1°C corresponds to *exactly* 1.8°F.)

A straight line graph tells us that there is a "linear relation" between x and y even if the line does not go through the origin. Most instances where there is some hidden proportion occur with an "offset" (that is, with $c \neq 0$). A good example is the graph which underlies example 2.5B:

> **2.5B** A taxi company has a basic charge of 25 zeds and a charge of 0.2 zeds for each kilometre the taxi is driven. Which of these represents the cost in zeds to hire a taxi for a trip of n kilometres?
>
> A $25 + 0.2n$ B $25 \times 0.2n$ C $0.2 \times (25 + n)$ D $0.2 \times 25 + n$

Here the cost of a journey is directly proportional to the distance travelled—except for the addition of a "basic charge of 25 zeds"; hence the charge "y zeds" for a journey of length x km (priced in "zeds"—the universal currency in TIMSS problems) is given by

$$y = 0.2x + 25$$

which is better written without decimals as

$$y = \frac{1}{5}x + 25.$$

Mathematics teachers need to remember that scientists, engineers and others will go to almost any lengths to reduce more complicated relationships to ones that give rise to straight line graphs—because empirical laws are easiest to discern, or to confirm, if the approximate data can be plotted to *look as though it fits on a straight line.* For example, if a scientist believes the data should satisfy an equation of the form $y = kx^2$ for some positive constant value k, then rather than plotting x against y and having to identify a parabola, they might well

- plot values of x^2 against values of y and hope to see a straight line with gradient k, or
- plot $\log(x)$ against $\log(y)$ and expect to see a straight line with gradient 2 and with y-intercept $c = \log(k)$.

2.7.5 Such connections and applications should be part of any treatment of linear equations at Key Stage 3 and Key Stage 4, and this presumably covers at least part of what is meant by the fifth requirement listed at the start of Section 2.7 ("model situations ..."), and also the sixth requirement ("interpret mathematical relationships ...").

2.7.6 The third and fourth requirements at the start of Section 2.7 mention *quadratic functions* and *quadratic graphs.* These references need to be interpreted with care.

The new GCSE specification (and hence the programmes of study for Key Stage 3 and 4) deliberately downplay premature reference to abstract "functions", and to function notation—such as $f(x)$. Instead, the programmes of study would appear to be designed to emphasise the *use* of such ideas *in concrete form* before abstractions such as $f(x)$ are introduced in Year 12 (though there is nothing to prevent a school from doing both prior to GCSE).

So when the word "function" appears in the context of linear and quadratic functions, *it is being used informally*, indicating that the curriculum should prepare the ground for a more abstract formulation in Year 12. In particular, work at Key Stage 3 should take account of the fact that GCSE will **no longer** expect pupils to use the abstract notation $f(x)$. Nor will pupils be expected to make sense of *general* transformations of coordinates

- moving the y-axis by rewriting the given expression for the function in the form $f(x \pm a)$, or
- moving the x-axis by rewriting the given expression for the function in the form $f(x) \pm a$, or
- moving both axes at once by rewriting the given expression for the function in the form $f(x \pm a) \pm b$.

Instead, by the end of Key Stage 4, pupils who expect to take Higher tier GCSE need to be able to implement such transformations **in the contexts of specific linear, or quadratic, or trig functions**. Pupils will therefore work with particular functions f and with particular numerical values of the parameters a and b. But for convenience we summarise these specific numerical examples by giving them in general symbolic form.

- The general *linear* equation $y = mx + c$ can be seen to be essentially the same as $Y = mX$ in two obvious ways:
  - by moving the origin to $(0, c)$, and setting $Y = y - c$, and $X = x$, and also
  - by moving the origin to $\left(-\frac{c}{m}, 0\right)$, and setting $Y = y$, and $X = x + \frac{c}{m}$.

- Pupils need exercises that lead them to recognise that any given quadratic equation behaves essentially just like $y = x^2$ or $y = -x^2$.
  - The first step is to understand the prototype of all quadratics, namely $y = x^2$,
    * to appreciate its symmetry about the y-axis (giving the same y value for $\pm x$)
    * to recognise how it "sits on" (or is tangent to) the x-axis
    * how this relates to the fact that squaring values of x between -1 and 1 produces a *smaller* output x^2 , while squaring values of x which are greater than 1 or less than -1 gives rise to *larger and larger* outputs x^2.
  - This analysis can then be extended to graphs whose equation has the form $y = x^2 + c$, where c may be either positive or negative, and where

moving the origin to $(0, c)$ corresponds to a change of coordinates: $Y = y - c$, $X = x$, so that the original equation $y = x^2 + c$ becomes $Y = X^2$.

- The same idea extends to equations of the form $y = (x - a)^2$, and to those of the form $y = (x - a)^2 + c$.
- And one can show (via particular numerical examples) how any given quadratic equation $y = x^2 + bx + c$ can be rewritten in such a form by "completing the square"

$$y = \left(x + \frac{b}{2}\right)^2 + \left(c - \left[\frac{b}{2}\right]^2\right),$$

so that the original equation becomes $Y = X^2$, where

$$X = x + \frac{b}{2},$$

and

$$Y = y - C = y - \left(c - \left[\frac{b}{2}\right]^2\right).$$

- Later (perhaps in Year 12) those who enjoy algebra can discover how the general quadratic $y = ax^2 + bx + c$ can be rewritten as

$$ay = (ax)^2 + b(ax) + ac = a^2\left(x + \frac{b}{2a}\right)^2 + \frac{1}{4}\left[4ac - b^2\right]$$

which turns into $Y = X^2$ after shifting the origin and dividing both x and y by "a". Hence, although some quadratics appear tall and skinny, while others appear short and fat, all parabolas are in fact *similar*, just as all circles, or all squares are similar.

2.7.7 The requirement to work with "given graphs of a variety of functions, including piece-wise linear, exponential and reciprocal graphs" needs to be interpreted carefully, in the spirit of 2.7.6. Given the apparent ruling about "functions" in general at GCSE, this stated requirement would seem to have limited relevance at Key Stage 3. Even at Key Stage 4 it may mean little more than that pupils

- should ideally be familiar with the graph of $y = \frac{1}{x}$ and its obvious variants (such as $y = \frac{k}{x}$, or possibly $y = \frac{1}{x-a}$);
- should have some experience of such graphs as $y = (1.05)^x$, that arise when exploring how an investment, or a debt of £1 would grow in x years at 5% per annum; and
- should be prepared to make sense of natural problems where the given data happen to give rise in some way to a graph that is (for example) piece-wise linear.

2.7.8 The fourth requirement listed at the start of Section 2.7 states that

- "pupils should be taught to use linear and quadratic graphs to estimate values of y for given values of x and vice versa, and to find approximate solutions of simultaneous linear equations."

The seventh listed requirement at the start of Section 2.7 also mentions finding "approximate solutions".

These two requirements appear to confuse two quite different things—each of which is valuable, but whose combination here is potentially confusing.

It is important for pupils to learn to "read a graph". By this we mean:

- that pupils be confronted with a graph whose equation is unknown,
- that they be given a value a of x, and have to trace the corresponding *abscissa* $x = a$ to see where it hits the graph, and then to trace the corresponding *ordinate* from that point to the y-axis to estimate the value of y corresponding to $x = a$ (using their eyes, or their fingers, or a carefully positioned—preferably transparent—ruler), and
- that they be given a value b of y, and have to trace the corresponding *ordinate* $y = b$ to find all the points where it hits the graph, and then to trace the corresponding *abscissas* from these points on the graph to the x-axis to estimate all the values of x corresponding to $y = b$.

An entirely separate (and equally important) requirement is, given a formula or equation relating x and y, to substitute values for x, so that expressions involving x become numerical expressions, and so to use arithmetic to discover what this says about the corresponding value of y (see Section 2.4.2 above). Note however, that in this process the calculations are **exact**, not estimates.

The listed requirement appears to confound these two very different, and entirely admirable, activities, by suggesting that pupils should engage in such "estimation" with "linear and quadratic graphs". But if we know that we are working with a "linear graph" or a "quadratic graph", then we must know its equation—so substitution becomes an exact calculation, rather than a matter of *estimation*—**with one exception**.

- If the equation is linear, then given a value of x, pupils should calculate an **exact** value of y; and given a value of y, one can equally demand that they calculate an **exact** value of x.
- If the equation is quadratic, then given a value of x, pupils should calculate an **exact** value of y.
- Hence, the only obvious scope for "estimating values" would seem to arise in asking, for a given quadratic graph or equation,

  – "Which possible values of x give rise to a given value of y?"

  This is an excellent requirement (namely to draw the relevant *ordinate* parallel to the x-axis, to estimate where it cuts the graph, and to infer the approximate values (if any) of x—which one can then check by substituting the estimated values in the known equation).

The final part of the fourth requirement

> "to find **approximate** solutions of **simultaneous linear equations**"

might be fine if it was stated at a point where pupils could see how it links up with

> finding the **exact** solution (by eliminating a variable).

But there is no mention of this requirement at Key Stage 3, so the requirement to address the significant challenge of working with *simultaneous* equations purely in order to find approximate solutions seems seriously premature.

At Key Stage 4, Higher tier candidates are expected to find the intersection points of a line and a circle, so it makes sense to consider how to prepare the ground for such pupils at Key Stage 3. In general one would eventually like all pupils to understand that

- the solutions of simultaneous equations

correspond to

- the coordinates of points where two lines or curves meet.

This is an important idea, provided it is not misrepresented as an alternative to "solving the equations algebraically". So at the point where simultaneous linear equations are to be solved exactly, pupils need to understand

- that the two linear equations correspond to two straight lines in the plane,

and

- that the output from the solving process is precisely the coordinates of the point where the two lines cross.

So as and when a class is ready to handle "elimination of a variable" in order to find the exact solution, it makes sense for them

- to draw the two lines,
- to recognise that the solution (x,y) that they seek corresponds to the coordinates of the point where the two lines cross, and
- to *estimate* the solution that is being sought (as a guide for what they should expect to emerge from the subsequent algebraic exact calculation).

They would then be in a good position to confront the algebraic challenge of "how to eliminate a variable", and to use this new-found skill to tackle lots of lovely problems. But there is something wrong with a programme that requires pupils to find "approximate" solutions while not revealing the fact that one can find the **exact** solution.

One would also like pupils to tackle problems where this geometrical interpretation is an essential part of the problem (for example, where they are given the coordinates of three vertices of a triangle, and are required to find the coordinates of the point where two medians meet). However, such problems are rather hard precisely because they require pupils to coordinate several steps (find the coordinates of the midpoints of the sides; find the equations of the two medians; solve these two simultaneous equations; extract the coordinates of the point where they cross).

2.8. [Subject content: *Algebra* p. 7]

- **generate terms of a sequence from either a term-to-term rule or a position-to-term rule**
- **recognise arithmetic sequences and find the nth term**
- **recognise geometric sequences and appreciate other sequences that arise.**

Work with sequences provides valuable opportunities:

- to revise and to strengthen arithmetic
- to cultivate the ability to notice basic patterns (constant, linear, powers, exponentials)
- to discover how geometrical and combinatorial sequences often give rise to familiar integer sequences
- to express numerical patterns algebraically
- to link discrete sequences with work on functions and graphs.

For example,

- if a *formula* is given for the nth term, then finding the succession of terms is an exercise in substituting easy numerical (integer) values into an expression;
- if the first few terms of a sequence are given (whether $2, 4, 6, 8, \ldots$, or $4, 7, 10, 13, \ldots$, or $0, 3, 8, 15, \ldots$, or $1, 3, 7, 15, \ldots$, or $2, 5, 13, 35, \ldots$), then it is an excellent exercise to think of the *simplest* algebraic expression that could generate the given sequence.

A **sequence**

$$x_1, x_2, x_3, x_4, x_5, \ldots$$

is a way of presenting an endless amount of information in a single list. There are two quite different ways of specifying the terms of such a *sequence*.

The first, and most primitive, way is to give the first few terms and then to specify a *term-to-term* rule (or "recurrence relation") that tells you how to work out the next term from the ones you already know. For example,

- $x_1 = 3$, $x_{n+1} = 2x_n$ defines the sequence $3, 6, 12, 24, 48, \ldots$;
- $x_1 = x_2 = 1$, $x_{n+1} = x_n + x_{n-1}$ defines the sequence $1, 1, 2, 3, 5, 8, 13, \ldots$
- $x_1 = 2$, $x_{n+1} = 3x_n - 2^n$ defines the sequence $2, 4, 8, 16, 32, \ldots$.

This first approach allows you to continue the sequence as far as you like, and determines the 10th, the 100th, and the 1000th terms uniquely. However, in order to find the 1000th term we first have to calculate the 1st, the 2nd, the $3^{\text{rd}}, \ldots$, **and** the 999th terms. In other words, we can generate terms of the sequence, but it may not be easy to obtain a proven closed formula giving the nth term of the sequence as a formula in terms of n. We may think we can guess how the sequence is behaving, but we are unlikely to be able to prove anything about *the sequence as a whole*.

- In the first of our three examples above, we can see that:

  the first term $x_1 = 3$ is doubled $n - 1$ times to get the nth term,
  so $x_n = 3 \times 2^{n-1}$.

- In the second example, it is easy to generate more and more terms, but it is quite unclear how to write the nth term as a *closed formula* in terms of n.

- In the third example, it is easy to guess that the *closed formula* for the nth term looks as though it "has to be" $x_n = 2^n$, but it is not at all clear how to prove that this is correct.

In short, a term-to-term rule is easy to use, but it is inefficient; and it gives us no way of reasoning in general about the nth *term*.

The second (and generally more powerful) way to specify a sequence is by a *position-to-term* rule, which tells you how the nth term can be calculated directly in terms of n. That is, the sequence of terms

$$x_1, x_2, x_3, x_4, x_5, \ldots, x_n, \ldots$$

is simply a listing of the outputs for a single rule, or *function* f, by listing

$$f(1), f(2), f(3), f(4), f(5), \ldots, f(n), \ldots.$$

A position-to-term rule may be given explicitly by a *formula*—as with

- the sequence of squares, where $x_n = n^2$, or
- the sequence of powers of 2, where $x_n = 2^n$.

But a position-to-term rule may also define a sequence **intrinsically**, with the nth term being defined to be a number which can be calculated from some algebraic procedure, or from some geometrical configuration. For example:

- Let the nth term t_n of a sequence be defined to be equal to the sum of the first n positive integers. Then

$$\begin{aligned} t_1 &= 1, \\ t_2 &= 1+2=3, \\ t_3 &= 1+2+3=6, \\ &\vdots \\ t_n &= 1+2+3+\cdots+n. \end{aligned}$$

- Let the nth term c_n of a sequence be defined to be the number of chords that can be created by joining pairs of points chosen from n points marked on a circle. Then

  1 point on a circle gives rise to $c_1 = 0$ chords;
  2 points on a circle give rise to exactly $c_2 = 1$ chord;
  3 points on a circle give rise to $c_3 = 3$ chords; etc..

- Let the nth term f_n of a sequence be defined to be equal to the number of positive factors of n. Then

  $f_1 = 1$, $f_2 = 2$ (factors 1 and 2); $f_3 = 2$ (factors 1 and 3), $f_4 = 3$ (factors 1, 2, and 4); ....

In these three examples, the position-to-term rule tells us exactly how to find each term; but the underlying function, or rule, is given as a *process* or a *recipe*, rather than as a formula. This makes it possible to generate

- the first sequence, whose n^{th} term is sum of the first n positive integers, by simply working out any term we need:

  1, 1+2 = 3, 1+2+3 = 6, 1+2+3+4 = 10, 1+2+3+4+5 = 15, 1+2+3+4+5+6 = 21, ...

- the second example, whose n^{th} term is equal to the number of chords created by n points on a circle:

$$0, 1, 3, 6, 10, 15, \ldots$$

- the third sequence, whose n^{th} term is equal to the number of positive factors of n:

$$1, 2, 2, 3, 2, 4, 2, 4, 3, 4, 2, \ldots.$$

Each sequence is well-defined, but we are not given either a term-to-term rule or a *closed formula* for any of the sequences. So any claims we might wish to make about how each sequence behaves must be deduced from the given algebraic or geometrical definition.

An *arithmetic sequence*

$$c, c+m, c+2m, c+3m, c+4m, \ldots$$

is one that goes up in constant steps: that is, where the term-to-term rule for the sequence is simply

"add m" for some fixed constant m.

The nth term is determined by the first term c and the $n-1$ steps of size m that take us from the 1st term to the nth term:

$\therefore$ the nth term is equal to "$c+(n-1)m$".

The prototype of every *arithmetic sequence* is the familiar counting sequence

$$0,1,2,3,4,5,6,7,8,9,10,\ldots.$$

The *general arithmetic sequence* arises from the counting sequence

- by first multiplying the whole sequence by m (to get

  "$0, m, 2m, 3m, 4m, \ldots, (n-1)m, \ldots$")

- then adding c to every term (to get

  "$c, c+m, c+2m, c+3m, c+4m, \ldots, c+(n--1)m, \ldots$")

If we think of the nth term "$c+(n-1)m$" as a function of $x=n-1$, then we see that the sequence lists the values of "$y=mx+c$ " for integer values of x. So the sequence corresponds to the sequence of points for $x=0$, $x=1$, $x=2$, etc. on the straight line $y=mx+c$; hence another name for an "*arithmetic* sequence" is a "**linear** sequence".

In general, once we have a closed formula for the nth term of a sequence, we can treat $n=x$ as the dependent variable and "plot the graph of the sequence" as a "point graph", with one graph point for each positive integer value of $x=n$. The "common difference" m is then the "gradient" of this point graph (for every unit step to the right in the positive $n=x$ direction, the point graph jumps up distance m in the y direction), and the initial value c is the point at which the point graph hits the y-axis. The tradition of using "a" for the first term in place of "c", and using "d" for the common difference in place of "m" makes it much less likely that pupils will appreciate this important connection.

A *geometric sequence*

$$c, cr, cr^2, cr^3, cr^4, cr^5, \ldots$$

is one for which the term-to-term rule for the sequence is simply

"multiply by r" for some fixed constant r.

Hence the nth term is completely determined:

- by the first term c, and
- by the $n-1$ steps "multiply by r" that take us from the 1st term c to the nth term.
- $\therefore$ the nth term is equal to "cr^{n-1}".

If we think of the nth term "cr^{n-1}" as a function of $x = n-1$, then we see that the sequence is specified by the two constants c and r, and lists the values of $y = c \cdot r^x$ for integer values of x (starting at $x = 0$). Because the term number "n" appears as an exponent, a *geometric* sequence is also called an **exponential** sequence.

In the third requirement listed at the start of Section 2.9 it is unclear what exactly is meant by

"and appreciate other sequences that arise".

However, these "other sequences" should certainly include:

- *linear* sequences (or arithmetic sequences)
- *quadratic* sequences, like the sequence of squares:

$$1^2,\ 2^2,\ 3^2,\ 4^2,\ 5^2, \ldots n^2, \ldots$$

- the sequence of *triangular* numbers

$$0,\ 1,\ 3,\ 6,\ 10,\ 15,\ 21, \ldots$$

- the sequence of *cubes*:

$$1,\ 8,\ 27,\ 64,\ 125,\ 216,\ 343,\ \ldots$$

- the *Fibonacci* sequence:

$$1,\ 1,\ 2,\ 3,\ 5,\ 8,\ 13,\ 21,\ 34,\ \ldots.$$

School mathematics often gives the impression that all sequences are *polynomial* sequences—that is, sequences where the nth term is a polynomial function of n, as with

- *linear* sequences (or arithmetic sequences)
- *quadratic* sequences, like the sequence of squares

$$1^2,\ 2^2,\ 3^2, \ldots, n^2, \ldots$$

or the sequence of *triangular* numbers

$$1,\ 1+2,\ 1+2+3,\ \ldots, 1+2+3+\cdots+n = \frac{n(n+1)}{2}, \ldots$$

- the sequence of *cubes*

$$1^3,\ 2^3,\ 3^3,\ \ldots, n^3,\ \ldots.$$

However, nature (and mathematics) often prefers geometric or exponential sequences, such as
the powers of 2:

$$2,\ 4,\ 8,\ 16,\ 32,\ 64,\ 128,\ \ldots,$$

or the *Fibonacci* sequence:

$$1,\ 1,\ 2,\ 3,\ 5,\ 8,\ 13,\ 21,\ 34,\ \ldots.$$

One key distinction between the two types of sequences becomes apparent if we compare what happens when we look at the sequence of "term-to-term differences" for each type of sequence.

(a) The sequence of "term-to-term differences" for a *linear* sequence, such as

$$2,\ 4,\ 6,\ 8,\ 10,\ 12,\ \ldots,$$

gives rise to a *constant* sequence of differences

$$2,\ 2,\ 2,\ 2,\ 2,\ \ldots.$$

The sequence of "term-to-term differences" for a *quadratic* sequence, such as

$$1, 4, 9, 16, 25, 36, \ldots$$

gives rise to a *linear* sequence of differences

$$3, 5, 7, 9, 11, \ldots,$$

whose own sequence of differences (or "second differences") is then *constant*

$$2, 2, 2, 2, \ldots.$$

The sequence of "term-to-term differences" for the quadratic sequence of triangular numbers

$$0, 1, 3, 6, 10, 15, 21, \ldots$$

gives rise to a *linear* sequence of differences

$$1, 2, 3, 4, 5, 6, \ldots,$$

whose own sequence of differences is then *constant*

$$1, 1, 1, 1, 1, \ldots.$$

(b) The sequence of "term-to-term differences" for a geometric sequence behaves quite differently. If we consider the geometric sequence of powers of 2:

$$2, 4, 8, 16, 32, 64, 128, \ldots$$

then the sequence of "term-to-term differences" gives rise to

$$2, 4, 8, 16, 32, 64.\ldots$$

which is the same as the original sequence, so taking second and third differences will never lead to anything simpler.

If we consider the Fibonacci sequence:

$$1, 1, 2, 3, 5, 8, 13, 21, 34, \ldots$$

Then taking differences gives rise to

$$0, 1, 1, 2, 3, 5, 8, 13, \ldots$$

which is essentially the same sequence again. Hence taking second and third differences will never lead to anything simpler.

In short, taking differences repeatedly for a polynomial sequence seems to lead eventually to a **constant** sequence, whereas the sequence of differences for a geometric (or exponential) sequence leads only to something closely related to the original sequence (from which it never escapes).

3. Geometry and measures

3.1. Background

Geometry should be one of the highlights of mathematics teaching in lower secondary school.

- The subject matter is intuitively appealing and practical.
- It offers extensive scope for drawing intriguing figures, for implementing unexpected constructions, and for making pleasing—even beautiful—models.
- The tools and principles which allow us to analyse this wonderful world *exactly* are surprisingly simple and accessible.
- All pupils can calculate some surprising things, can solve some interesting problems, and can **prove** some strikingly useful results; and more confident pupils can **prove** a wide range of remarkable and unexpected facts.

- Applications to the world around us are immediate, convincing, and impressive.
- The material of school geometry captures the spirit of mathematics better than almost any other part of elementary mathematics.

One would be hard-pressed to discern these strengths in the published programme of study. In particular, there is little emphasis on drawing and making, no clear indication of the intended deductive structure for geometry, and there is no mention of applications to the world around us. But the Good News is that the official programme is compatible with an approach based on the above bullet points—provided schools do not simply mimic the printed sequence of official requirements.

There is considerable confusion over geometry in many apparently authoritative pronouncements—including the requirements listed in the official Key Stage 3 programme of study. To understand why, teachers need to know how we got where we are. So we begin with a thumbnail sketch of some of the relevant historical and pedagogical roots of the current approach to school geometry in England.

School work with number and algebra tends to be relatively "one dimensional". Typical problems look fairly familiar, and can usually be solved by implementing some well-rehearsed "linear" procedure.

- One is told what is to be calculated (the goal).
- It is usually fairly clear where to begin.
- And with sufficient practice, one can more-or-less follow one's nose to get from the start to what is required.

Real mathematics is not like this, and is more like what secondary school geometry ought to be.

- We are given some information about a two- or three-dimensional configuration or shape.
- We are asked to calculate something, or to prove some fact.
- We have to draw and edit a diagram as a guide.

- Then we are left to find for ourselves
  (i) a suitable feature of the figure that might serve as a starting point, and
  (ii) a sequence of steps from this (elusive) start to what is required.
- Because figures and diagrams are in **two** dimensions, there is often no clear starting point, and no obvious route from start to finish.

For pupils (and teachers) who have come to see school mathematics as a collection of predictable, one-dimensional procedures, this experience is unsettling. The given figure may appear elementary; and one may understand what is wanted. But one often has **no idea where to begin, or how to proceed**. As we noted in Section 2.3 of Part II (*Solving problems*), in such a setting it does not take much for a routine *exercise* to become a frustratingly elusive *problem*. Geometry reveals this distinction more strongly than most other parts of elementary mathematics.

Most mathematics educators in England are aware of "a difficulty" with geometry; but there has been very little attempt to analyse it in detail, or to explore effective ways of overcoming it. Rather than attempt some easy explanation, our concern here is to draw attention to this neglect, in the hope that once it is recognised, teachers will be more willing to question the conventional wisdoms about school geometry which often take the place of serious analysis. For example, our ambivalence towards geometry has often been mixed up with attitudes towards "proof"— because historically geometry came to be seen as the main vehicle for conveying ideas of proof in school mathematics. This has led to a view that serious geometry and proof are "only for the few". Yet, as we have tried to illustrate, "proof" (whether used to derive new methods and results on the basis of what we already know, or to make sense of standard procedures) should be an integral part of school mathematics from the earliest years, and geometry should enrich everyone's experience of school mathematics.

Proposals for major change in secondary school "geometry for all" arose in the early 1900s, with John Perry's moves to advocate measurement, drawing, trigonometry, the solution of triangles, calculation of areas and volumes, coordinate geometry, and "technical drawing". Perry's ideas met with some success—possibly more so in the USA. In England the need for change was recognised, but the traditional influence of Oxford and Cambridge on secondary school curricula resulted in a very English compromise, which lasted in some sense until the 1950s.

The reorganisation of schooling after the Second World War re-opened the question of "geometry for all". However this liberal concern was overtaken by the "modernising" reforms which gained momentum in the late 1950s and early 1960s in the wake of the Soviet Union's launch of *Sputnik*. The official shock among western governments at being "left behind in the space race" strengthened the hand of those who wanted to "sweep away the old" and replace it by something more "up to date". In the USA the preferred "modern" approach was "axiomatic synthetic geometry". In the UK we tried to replace the uneasy compromise of classical and coordinate geometry (and technical drawing) by "transformations and matrices". In France there was a strong lobby in favour of linear algebra and affine geometry. All these approaches had some advantages for the very best pupils. But all approaches proved too ambitious—even wholly inappropriate—for most pupils, and failed. The British approach through transformations had some attractive features, and some strong advocates, which seems to have made it more difficult for us to admit that it had failed, and to engage in a serious review of what was actually needed. As a result, certain themes (e.g. nets of polyhedra, and selected transformations) continue to feature, even though they no longer deliver any significant *mathematical* pay-off. In place of a considered, if overambitious, progression from naïve symmetry, through transformation geometry, to matrices and affine transformations, we are left with a residual rump of bits and pieces.

In short, since the early 1980s, geometry teaching in England has increasingly served up a mish-mash. We abandoned the grand vision of the reforms of the 1960s and 70s, while retaining some of its language and content. And in the 1990s we revived a half-hearted version of traditional Euclidean geometry without ever really sorting out what was needed. (The new curriculum illustrates our current plight. There we are exhorted to "derive and illustrate properties of triangles, quadrilaterals, [...] and other plane figures", without any recognition of the central position of *isosceles triangles*—which are never mentioned; and without any hint that the most important "quadrilaterals" of all are *parallelograms*—which are only mentioned once, in the context of "formulae to calculate area" (p. 8).)

During the same period, university mathematics departments recognised that their students lacked the geometrical background that was assumed in many courses. But universities neither got involved at school level, nor did they develop an effective university level "introduction to geometry". Hence **most of those who now teach school mathematics have never experienced a systematic study of elementary geometry**—either in school, or at university. We have therefore erred on the side of including here more than is needed for most pupils, in order to provide teachers with a brief exposition of what they have been missing. In particular, we have included many details that belong more naturally in Key Stage 4—and then sometimes only for appropriate groups of pupils. We hope this will encourage schools to consider what is genuinely accessible at this level, to experiment, and to decide for themselves what to teach, to whom, and at which level.

To cut a long story short, it is our contention (though rarely admitted explicitly):

- that secondary school *geometry* is potentially attractive, but inevitably "hard" (e.g. because it cannot be reduced to a series of well-rehearsed, one-dimensional routines);

- that no one is well-served by the present confused mish-mash;

- that, although *translations* relate to work on vectors, and although there may be unstated aesthetic reasons for introducing the language of symmetry, patterns, rotations, reflections, translations, and enlargements (and the missing isometries, the *glide reflections*), these ideas **can never** constitute an effective mathematical way of analysing geometrical figures at this level;

- that all groups would benefit from a coherent initial approach to secondary geometry in Key Stages 1–3—even if not all follow through to the same endpoint at Key Stage 4;

- that the three basic principles (*congruence, parallels, similarity*) can be appreciated by everyone, and can be used on different levels in drawing, constructing, and analysing interesting configurations in 2D and 3D; and hence

- that we need to develop an effective approach to secondary geometry, which would be potentially accessible and appealing to most pupils, which is founded upon the *congruence criterion*, the *criterion for parallels*, and the *similarity criterion*, and which combines
  (a) drawing, measuring, and calculating (lengths, areas, volumes, angles, trigonometry),
  (b) analysing figures and configurations in terms of *points, lines, line segments, angles, triangles, parallelograms, circles*, etc.,
  (c) using a mix of deduction of key results with lots of lovely problems, and
  (d) linking with algebra and a suitable dose of coordinate geometry at Key Stage 4.

To create an internal scheme of work that reflects this, schools must be willing

(i) to interpret the official requirements intelligently,

(ii) to discriminate between what is important for their pupils' mathematical development and what is not,

(iii) "to join up the (sometimes invisible) dots" into a coherent scheme of work, and then

(iv) to review and refine the details in the light of experience.

We provide an initial supporting map by grouping most of the official requirements under three main headings:

3.2 *Drawing, measuring, and terminology*

3.3 *Perimeter, area, and volume*

3.4 *Constructions, conventions, and derivations*

Although it is left unsaid, we assume that under each heading, pupils will be expected to tackle a rich variety of suitable problems.

The remaining official requirements are then discussed in Section 3.5.

3.2. Drawing, measuring, and terminology

> - **draw and measure line segments and angles in geometric figures [...]**
> - **describe, sketch and draw using conventional terms and notations: points, lines, parallel lines, perpendicular lines, right angles, regular polygons, and other polygons that are reflectively [and/or] rotationally symmetric**
> - **[...] illustrate properties of triangles, quadrilaterals, circles and other plane figures [for example, equal lengths and angles] using appropriate language and technologies**
> - **identify properties of, and describe the results of, translations, rotations and reflections applied to given figures**
> - **draw and measure line segments and angles in geometric figures, including interpreting scale drawings**
> - **identify and construct congruent triangles, and similar shapes by enlargement, with and without coordinate grids**

Despite the emphasis here on "doing", the language remains vague. Teachers will need to be creative, and to identify those themes that deserve to be included but are here passed over in silence. In particular, there is no obvious mention of "applications": angles are to be drawn and measured, and scale drawings (presumably including maps) are specifically included, but there is no hint that one should include practical activities involving "bearings", or "angles of elevation"—so that these ideas will have some meaning when they arise in later paper exercises. So there is much to be "filled in".

However, if we leave aside the many ingredients which are omitted, one way to think about these six requirements is that:

- the **first two** involve basic opportunities to draw, to measure, and to describe;
- the **next two** involve more reflective preliminary analysis ("illustrating" and "identifying"—and one hopes *talking about*, and familiarising pupils with— "properties", as opposed to *deriving* them as some pupils should do later);
- in the **last two** requirements, pupils begin to grapple with the three basic principles of Euclidean 2D geometry: *congruence* and *similarity* are mentioned explicitly, while the characteristic property of *parallel lines* is implicit in the whole idea of "enlargement" and scale drawings.

Thus this first group of six requirements serves as a bridge—launching out from the familiar territory of "geometry as experience" at Key Stage 2 towards the pre-formal, more analytical world of constructions and deductions at secondary school (see Section 3.4).

3.2.1 Drawing, measuring, and describing One would like to see initial "measuring and drawing" tasks

(a) that check on, and strengthen skills from Key Stage 2;

(b) that develop pupils' facility and precision in working with ruler, protractor, and compasses;

(c) that use and establish the correct notation for line segments and for angles in *labelled* diagrams, and

(d) that give rise to slightly unexpected results, which can then be talked through in class.

The neglect (not just in England) of

(i) basic work on drawing and measuring, and

(ii) the cultivation of spatial common sense through learning to think through one's hands, fingers, and eyes,

is indicated by the following very basic Year 9 items from TIMSS 2011.

3.2.1A Points A, B, and C lie in a line and B is between A and C. If $AB = 10$cm and $BC = 5.2$cm, what is the distance between the midpoints of AB and BC?

A 2.4cm B 2.6cm C 5.0cm D 7.6cm

3.2.1A Russia 60%, Hungary 41%, Australia 40%, England 38%, USA 29%

3.2.1B [An 8 × 8 square grid is shown] The length of side of each of the small squares represents 1cm. Draw an isosceles triangle with a base of 4cm and a height of 5cm.

3.2.1B Russia 75%, Hungary 68%, Australia 41%, England 40%, USA 27%

The responses clearly suggest that pupils are never expected to construct the simplest diagrams for themselves. So we must be prepared to begin Year 7 with lots of drawing exercises that might once have been assumed from Key Stage 2, but which have fallen out of favour—perhaps because they cannot easily be assessed. This seems to hold for even the simplest traditional primary school activities, such as using compasses:

> "Draw a circle with centre O and with radius OA;
>
> then draw the circle with centre A passing through O, and meeting the original circle again at B and F;
>
> then draw the circles with centres at B and F and passing through O, to meet the original circle again at C and E;
>
> finally draw the circles with centres at C and E and passing through O, and notice that these circles meet the original circle at **the same point D**."

And then colour the resulting hexagonal pattern of flower petals!

To illustrate the kind of additional tasks that one might use we offer the following examples.

- Given a drawn rectangle $ABCD$ measuring 3cm by 4cm, require that the two diagonals AC, BD be measured, along with the angles $\angle BAC$ and $\angle DCA$.
- Given a square $ABCD$ with sides of length 10cm, require that the two diagonals AC, BD be measured, along with the four angles $\angle BAC$, $\angle BCA$, $\angle DCA$, $\angle DAC$.
- Given a regular hexagon $ABCDEF$, measure the edge length AB and the length of a "long diagonal" FC, and the angles $\angle BAC$, $\angle CAD$, $\angle DAE$, $\angle EAF$.
- Given a regular pentagon $ABCDE$ with sides of length 10cm, measure the length of the diagonals AD, BD, and the angles $\angle EAD$, $\angle ADB$, $\angle BDC$, $\angle DBA$, $\angle DAB$.

Such drawing and measuring exercises are intended to feed into subsequent class discussion, for which the initial practical activity serves as the directly relevant prior experience. The above tasks provide opportunities to consider:

- Whether the two diagonals AC, BD of the rectangle $ABCD$ really are equal?
- Whether the four angles $\angle BAC$, $\angle BCA$, $\angle DCA$, $\angle DAC$ in the square $ABCD$ really are equal, whether they are all equal to 45°, and whether something else seems to be true about the two diagonals AC and BD?
- Whether the diagonal FC in the regular hexagon $ABCDEF$ really is twice as long as the side AB, whether anything else seems to be true of the lines AB, FC, ED, and whether the angles $\angle BAC$, $\angle CAD$, $\angle DAE$, $\angle EAF$ really are all equal to 30°?
- Whether in the regular pentagon $ABCDE$ there is anything else that seems to be true about the side EA and the diagonal DB, or about the diagonal AD and the side BC, whether the angles $\angle EAD$, $\angle ADB$, $\angle BDC$ really are all equal (to 36°), whether the angles $\angle DBA$ and $\angle DAB$ are equal to each other and twice the size of the previous group?

Some of the equalities and relationships that emerge from such an exercise can be justified at this level. But others should be treated as genuine "surprises", which demand explanation *later*. In particular, teachers should hesitate before giving the impression that plausible-sounding catch-all "reasons" (e.g. in terms of the presumed "symmetry" of a regular n-gon) are acceptable as explanations of what is observed.

In primary school the approach to geometry is largely rooted in experience, with properties being observed and used. But in secondary school the approach should be more analytical, and should distinguish between the (minimal) definition of an object, and any derived properties. In particular, the definition of a regular n-gon says nothing about its symmetry. A *regular n-gon* is **defined** very simply to be

> a polygon in which the n sides are all equal and the n angles are all equal.

It is not at all obvious—though not difficult to **prove** later—that a regular polygon always has a "centre", can be inscribed in a circle with that centre, and has n-fold rotational symmetry and n lines of reflection symmetry. But at secondary level it is **wrong** to convey the impression that these additional properties are part of what we "know" *a priori* about a regular polygon. Hence the reference in the second listed requirement to

> "regular polygons, and other polygons that are reflectively [and/or] rotationally symmetric"

is thoroughly misleading. At the very least *the word "other" should be deleted.*

3.2.2 Establishing a basic repertoire: "illustrating, identifying and describing" The next two requirements in the list at the start of Section 3.2 ("to illustrate properties ... " and "to identify properties ... and describe ... ") are best not taken too literally, but should be interpreted as an

> "invitation to revise and to extend pupils' repertoire of language and observed facts in geometry".

In particular, schools will need to clarify for themselves

- how to interpret the indiscriminate word "quadrilaterals", by sorting out **which** quadrilaterals are most important (namely **parallelograms** including rectangles);
- what to make of the reference to "other plane figures" (which as far as one can tell should probably mean (a) properly defined "regular polygons", and (b) composite figures made from rectangles and arcs of circles which will be needed in Section 3.3);
- what is meant by the curious bracket

  "[for example, equal lengths and angles]",

  which we take to be an unedited cryptic allusion to

  - **isosceles triangles** (which receive no mention of any kind elsewhere), and to
  - the two basic results

    (i) if $AB = AC$ (i.e. triangle ABC is isosceles with base BC), then $\angle ABC = \angle ACB$;

    (ii) if $\angle ABC = \angle ACB$, then $AB = AC$ (so the triangle ABC is isosceles with base BC);
- whether the single isolated reference to "appropriate technologies" was included for a good reason in the only appropriate place, or whether this comment should be taken as a prompt to consider carefully the potential advantages, and dangers, of technology throughout the teaching of *Geometry and measures* at this level.

On the latter point, we merely note that active drawing exercises clearly help to cultivate pupils' geometrical thinking, whereas the passive enjoyment of ready-made enhanced graphics seems to convey no similar mental benefit.

3.2.3 Towards congruence (and similarity) The last two listed requirements ("draw and measure ..." and "identify and construct ...") are no longer merely elaborating what pupils bring with them from Key Stage 2.

- Making and "interpreting scale drawings" is a valuable common sense exercise, which can later be related to enlargement, proportion and similarity. But at this stage, the focus should be on interpreting lengths, distances, and perhaps areas.

  (Understanding that *angles are preserved* in such scale drawings should be appreciated informally at this stage. The proof may be best left until similarity is addressed later—at which point one can explain that:

  - If two lines AB and AC meet at A, and if the points A, B, C are represented by the points A', B', C' on a scale drawing, then

$$AB : A'B' = AC : A'C' = BC : B'C'.$$

  - Hence by the *similarity criterion* (Part II, Section 2.2.2.3 and Section 3.4.7 below), it follows that

$$\angle BAC = \angle B'A'C' :$$

    that is, the angle between the two original lines AB and AC is the same as the angle between the lines $A'B'$ and $A'C'$ in the scale drawing. **QED**)

- "Identify and construct congruent triangles" is best tackled separately from—and long before—"similar shapes by enlargement". The goal here should be to convey
  - the central importance of triangles;
  - the idea that a triangle ABC is an *ordered* triple;
  - that such a triangle ABC gives rise to **six** pieces of data: the three sides AB, BC, CA and the three angles $\angle CAB$, $\angle ABC$, $\angle BCA$;
  - that two (*ordered*) triangles ABC and DEF are congruent precisely when their vertices match up in order

$$A \longleftrightarrow D, \qquad B \longleftrightarrow E, \qquad C \longleftrightarrow F$$

so that the three pairs of sides in the two triangles match up exactly, with $AB = DE$, $BC = EF$, $CA = FD$, and the three pairs of angles also match up exactly, with $\angle CAB = \angle FDE$, $\angle ABC = \angle DEF$, $\angle BCA = \angle EFD$;

- but that in reality we can be sure that two triangles are congruent **without** having to check that all **six pairs** (i.e. three sides and three angles) match up: for to determine a triangle uniquely (up to congruence) we only need to know certain triples of information—namely:

  SSS: AB, BC, and CA; or
  SAS: AB, $\angle ABC$, and BC; or
  ASA: $\angle ABC$, BC, and $\angle BCA$.

To achieve this understanding, pupils need to be given specified lengths and angles and then be required to use ruler and protractor, or ruler and compasses, to construct the triangle, and hence to internalise a sense of how this limited information determines the final triangle. They should also be given lots of examples where the triangle is not determined by the given information, such as:

  AAA: given $\angle ABC$, $\angle BCA$, and $\angle CAB$ only; or
  ASS: given $\angle ABC$, BC, and CA only (e.g. $\angle ABC = 30^\circ$, $BC = \sqrt{3}$, and $CA = 1$).

As explained in Part II, Section 2.2.2.3, RHS congruence is a *consequence* of SSS and *Pythagoras' Theorem*, so RHS is not part of the basic *congruence criterion*. Hence it should be introduced, proved, and used somewhat later.

The reference to "similar shapes" here is clearly informal (the full notion of similarity is more subtle, and may be best postponed until later in Key Stage 3—see Part II, the end of Section 2.2.2.3, and Section 3.4.7 below). The emphasis should at first be practical: constructing "enlargements" initially in the spirit of the exercises in Section T8 of *Extension mathematics, Book Beta* by Tony Gardiner (Oxford University Press 2007), and later more formally in the spirit of section C26 in the same book. Work with "scale drawings" should be similarly practical—interpreting scale drawings and maps and using the scale factor to estimate actual distances, areas and angles, then constructing scale drawings of familiar locations. (Note that "scale factors" also feature in the requirements addressed in Section 1.9.)

3.3. Perimeter, area, and volume

- **derive and apply formulae to calculate and solve problems involving: perimeter and area of triangles, parallelograms, trapezia, volume of cuboids (including cubes) and other prisms (including cylinders)**
- **calculate and solve problems involving: perimeters of 2D shapes (including circles), areas of circles and composite shapes**

At first sight these two requirements may seem relatively straightforward. However, there is more here than may be apparent at first sight.

3.3.1 Trapezia: an example The mention of "trapezia" illustrates a general danger. Mathematical methods are too often taught by training pupils to use formulae which they do not understand, rather than by first helping them to achieve a basic understanding, and encouraging them to use their common sense. Once pupils achieve a clear understanding, that understanding may be suitably summarised in terms of a formula—provided this is never used as a substitute for thinking what they are doing.

The first listed requirement in Section 3.3 tries to compress too many ideas into one bullet point. Whenever the official programme of study tries to compress distinct topics into a single requirement in this way, the result is to distort the message—especially at the two ends of the spectrum of difficulty.

- It is unfortunate that the first requirement in Section 3.3 seems to suggest that a formula be used to calculate the "**perimeter of triangles**". There is no "formula". Common sense is all that is needed.

- At the other end of the difficulty scale, the apparent requirement that all pupils should

  > "derive and apply formulae to calculate [...the] area of [...] trapezia"

  cannot mean what it appears to say. For in the GCSE *Subject criteria* we are told (p. 15) that the formula for the area of a trapezium "is not specified in the content". So knowing and using the formula **cannot be intended for everyone** as part of the Key Stage 3 programme of study.

It is clearly more appropriate at Key Stage 3 for pupils to know

- that a quadrilateral $PQRS$ with two parallel sides PQ and SR is called a *trapezium*, and

- that, if the parallel sides have lengths $PQ = a$ and $SR = b$, and the perpendicular height is h, then the area of the shape can be found by dropping two perpendiculars, from P meeting SR at X and from Q meeting SR at Y, to produce a rectangle $PQYX$ and two right angled triangles PXS and QYR, whose areas can be combined (using addition or subtraction— depending on the shape of the trapezium) to find the area of $PQRS$.

This primitive method can later lead to a proof of the well-known formula—at least in the simplest cases.

Claim Suppose X and Y are "internal" to the line segment SR. Then

$$\text{area}(PQRS) = \frac{1}{2}(a+b) \times h.$$

Proof Since $PQYX$ is a rectangle, we know that: $XY = PQ = a$, and $PX = QY = h$, and that $SX + YR = SR - XY = b - a$.

$$\begin{aligned}
\therefore \quad \text{area}(PQRS) &= \text{area}(PQYX) + \text{area}(\triangle PXS) + \text{area}(\triangle QYR) \\
&= a \times h + \frac{1}{2}(SX \times h) + \frac{1}{2}(YR \times h) \\
&= a \times h + \frac{1}{2}((b-a) \times h) \\
&= \frac{1}{2}(a+b) \times h. \quad \textbf{QED}
\end{aligned}$$

3.3.2 "Composite shapes" The simple-minded approach to trapezia (by reducing the problem of finding the area of the trapezium to that of a rectangle and two right angled triangles) illustrates the reference to "composite shapes" in the second requirement. The kinds of combinations that are relevant here are very restricted, but they lie at the heart of all work with length, area, and volume.

- We calculate more complicated **lengths** (such as the perimeter of a polygon) by breaking them up into, or approximating them in terms of, combinations of *line segments* (or "one dimensional rectangles").
- We calculate the **area** of more complicated shapes in 2D by breaking them up into, or approximating them in terms of, combinations of *rectangles*.
- We calculate the **volume** of more complicated shapes in 3D by breaking them into, or approximating them in terms of, combinations of *cuboids* (or "three-dimensional rectangles").

In one dimension one may fudge the idea of "length" for the circumference of a circle by imagining a string wrapped round the circle, which is then "straightened out and measured". This is fine—both as a way of conveying what we mean by the "circumference", and to obtain a physical approximation. But it is not a *mathematical* method: the string is a *physical* object; the result is *approximate*—with no control over the error; and there is no way to be sure that the string does not change its length as one "straightens it out". However, the most serious objection is that **the idea does not extend to 2D and 3D**. For example, one cannot take a curved 2D shape like a circular disc, cut it up and rearrange the pieces exactly to find its exact area; and one cannot take a curved surface, like the surface of an orange and "straighten it out, or lay it flat" to find its surface area. The idea that can be made to work in all dimensions is to concentrate on **approximating more complicated shapes by "rectangles"** (line segments, 2D rectangles, cuboids, etc.).

It is true that in two dimensions we often dissect polygons and other shapes into triangles rather than rectangles. But this trick has to be interpreted carefully. When we move from 2D to 3D, there is no way to extend the idea of a "triangle" as a way of making sense of "calculating volumes": for there is no elementary way of finding the volume of a pyramid or tetrahedron. So we are free to use triangles in 2D, but we should think of each triangle as "**half a rectangle**" (on the same base, and with the same height), since the idea that works in all dimensions is to approximate shapes in terms of "n-dimensional rectangles". That is,

- the basic building blocks for length are *line segments* (one dimensional rectangles);
- the basic building blocks for area are *rectangles* (two dimensional rectangles);
- the basic building blocks for volume are *cuboids* (three dimensional rectangles).

We also use composite shapes to *approximate* more awkward figures.

- The circumference of a circle is approximated by the perimeter of an inscribed or a circumscribed regular n-gon.
- The area of a circle is approximated from below by counting the number of unit squares inside it, and from above by counting the number of unit squares needed to just cover it.

3.3.3 Understanding first, formulae second We repeat: pupils should be discouraged from using formulae *ab initio*. Instead they should be encouraged to imagine each "perimeter" as a sequence of separate line segments, and each "area" as being made up from, or approximated by, rectangles, or triangles (or a combination of both). In particular, they should use their common sense in working from the very beginning with composite shapes made from line segments, or from rectangles (or triangles), or from cuboids (or "wedges" as "half cuboids"). This helps to strengthen pupils' basic understanding, since such composite shapes admit no general formula.

The extent to which pupils do not at present use their common sense in such matters is indicated by the following Year 9 items from TIMSS 2011.

> **3.3.3A** The perimeter of a square is 36cm. What is the area of the square?

A 81cm^2 B 36cm^2 C 24cm^2 D 18cm^2

3.3.3B The area of a square is 144cm^2. What is the perimeter of the square?

A 12cm B 48cm C 288cm D 576cm

These are multiple choice items—so pupils were **not** required to calculate the answers. The false options here are either hard to obtain, or reflect severe mental sloppiness. So the results should provide serious food for thought (and not only in England).

3.3.3A Russia 62%, Hungary 55%, Australia 54%, USA 53%, England 51%

3.3.3B Russia 62%, Hungary 49%, Australia 48%, England 47%, USA 46%

3.3.4 Length There is more to Section 3.3.2 than may appear: in simple language, it incorporates a *definition* of what we mean by "length", of what we mean by "area", and of what we mean by "volume".

Pupils should understand the "perimeter of a *rectangle*" not via a formula, but using the common sense fact that it is made up of *four line segments*, whose lengths add up to give the perimeter (see examples 3.3.3A and 3.3.3B). The same idea applies to any polygon—where the perimeter is made up of a finite number of line segments, whose lengths can be added to give the perimeter of the polygon.

However, at first it is completely unclear how to extend this idea to measure the lengths of *curves*—such as the circumference of a circle of radius r. The *physical* idea of "the circumference of a circular, or cylindrical, lamp post" may be adequately captured by a piece of string that can be wound round the post and then straightened out and measured. But mathematics cannot depend on string. To capture the "length of a circular arc" *mathematically* we need

- to approximate it by a succession of line segments (such as the perimeter of a regular n-gon inscribed in, or circumscribed around, the circle), and

- then to realise that, as the number n of sides increases, the perimeter of the polygon gets closer and closer to the circle itself.

The cases which can be calculated easily, exactly, and instructively, without using trigonometry are:

$n = 3$: *Pythagoras' Theorem* gives

$$\text{"perimeter of inscribed regular 3-gon"} = 3r\sqrt{3}.$$

$n = 4$: *Pythagoras' Theorem* gives

$$\text{"perimeter of inscribed regular 4-gon"} = 4r\sqrt{2}.$$

$n = 6$: simple geometry gives

$$\text{"perimeter of inscribed regular 6-gon"} = 6r.$$

$n = 8$: *Pythagoras' Theorem* gives

$$\text{"perimeter of inscribed regular 8-gon"} = 8r\sqrt{2-\sqrt{2}}.$$

An inscribed regular octagon is still a long way from the circle itself, but we can see that the circumference of a circle of radius r is approximated ever more closely from below by the sequence

$$r \cdot 3\sqrt{3} < r \cdot 4\sqrt{2} < r \cdot 6 < r \cdot [8\sqrt{2-\sqrt{2}}] < \ldots$$
$$\cdots < \text{"circumference } C \text{ of circle of radius } r\text{"}.$$

The required circumference C of a circle would seem to be "some multiple of the radius r", and the mysterious multiplier "$\frac{C}{r}$" satisfies

$$5.1961\cdots < 5.6568\cdots < 6 < 6.1229\cdots < \cdots < \frac{C}{r}.$$

The multiplier "$\frac{C}{r}$" can also be bounded from above by considering circumscribed regular n-gons:

$n = 3$: *Pythagoras' Theorem* gives

$$\text{"perimeter of circumscribed regular 3-gon"} = 6r\sqrt{3}.$$

$n = 4$: *Pythagoras' Theorem* gives

"perimeter of circumscribed regular 4-gon" $= 8r$.

$n = 6$: simple geometry gives

"perimeter of circumscribed regular 6-gon" $= 4r\sqrt{3}$.

$n = 8$: *Pythagoras' Theorem* gives

"perimeter of circumscribed regular 8-gon" $= 16r(\sqrt{2} - 1)$.

Hence

$$5.1961\cdots < 5.6568\cdots < 6 < 6.1229\cdots < \cdots < \tfrac{C}{r} < \ldots$$

$$\cdots < 6.6274\cdots < 6.9282\cdots < 8 < 10.3922\,.$$

The mysterious multiplier "$\frac{C}{r}$" is clearly somewhere around 6.3. Once we give it a name "2π", and declare its actual value, we have the formula "$C = 2\pi r$" for the full circumference of a circle of radius r. We can then extend this to find the length of a semi-circle of radius r (πr), or of a quadrant ($\frac{\pi r}{2}$), or of the length of a circular arc of radius r with angle θ at the centre.

One can then pose lots of moderately challenging problems to find the perimeters of composite shapes which are made entirely of rectangles (such as staircase-shaped figures), or which combine rectangles and circular arcs (such as a "running track", or shapes made of rectangles and quadrants—both protruding and indented).

3.3.5 Area We make sense of "area" in much the same way.

- If we take the area of a unit square as "1", an m by n rectangle is made up of $m \times n$ unit squares, and so has area mn (square units)

- We can break up the sides of the unit square into unit fractions, and conclude that mn copies of a $\frac{1}{m}$ by $\frac{1}{n}$ rectangle have total area 1, so that each has area
$$\frac{1}{m} \times \frac{1}{n} = \frac{1}{mn}.$$

- A $\frac{p}{m}$ by $\frac{q}{n}$ rectangle can then be split into $p \times q$ rectangles each of which is $\frac{1}{m}$ by $\frac{1}{n}$, and so has area

$$pq \times \frac{1}{mn} = \frac{pq}{mn} = \frac{p}{m} \times \frac{q}{n}.$$

In short, the area of a rectangle with sides of lengths a units and b units can be shown to be equal to $a \times b$ square units for all possible values of a and b.

When we later come to consider "scaling" and "similarity", the two facts:

- that the area of any rectangle is equal to "length × breadth", and
- that the area of any more general shape is defined in terms of approximating the shape by combinations of rectangles

have an important hidden consequence. Whatever the area of a given shape may be, if we enlarge it (or "en-small" it) by multiplying all lengths by the same scale factor "r", then the area of each and every approximating rectangle is multiplied by r^2, so **the area of the shape** being approximated **is multiplied by r^2**. So if one square has sides that are three times as long as another, then its area is nine times as large; and a circle of radius 4 has area 16 times as large as a circle of radius 1.

Long before we attempt a formal treatment of enlargement, or similarity, we need to build up the repertoire of basic results involving measures (as listed in the official requirements at the start of Section 3.3) using congruence. In particular, we need to connect the area of other plane figures to our fundamental shape—namely rectangles. And the most important of these "other figures" are parallelograms and triangles.

Suppose a parallelogram $ABCD$ has longest diagonal AC. Let the perpendicular from A meet the line CD (extended) at X, and the perpendicular from C meet the line AB (extended) at Y. Then the parallelogram $ABCD$ is completely enclosed in the rectangle $AXCY$, and the excess is formed by the two right angled triangles AXD and CYB—which fit together to make a smaller rectangle. Hence $ABCD$ is equal to the *difference* between the large rectangle (with base XC and height XA) and the excess rectangle (with base XD and height XA)—whence:

Claim Area(parallelogram $ABCD$) = "base DC × height XA".

Given any triangle ABC with "base AB", we can draw the line through C parallel to the base AB, and the line through A parallel to the side BC. If these two lines meet at D, then $ABCD$ is a parallelogram.

Claim $\triangle ABC$ is congruent to $\triangle CDA$

Proof $\angle BAC = \angle DCA$ (alternate angles—see Part II, section 2.2.2.3)
$AC = CA$ (same side)
$\angle BCA = \angle DAC$ (alternate angles)
$\therefore \triangle ABC$ is congruent to $\triangle CDA$ by the ASA congruence criterion. **QED**

Corollary Area($\triangle ABC$) $= \frac{1}{2} \times$ area(parallelogram $ABCD$)
$= \frac{1}{2}$(base $AB \times$ height).

Pupils may think they already "know" the Corollary. What is new at Key Stage 3 is the idea that one can organise the vast lit of "known facts" in a way that identifies which are the "most basic" (namely *congruence* and the area of a rectangle), and how everything else can be derived from these basic results. Hence, one would like as many pupils as possible to appreciate

- that the result for the area of a triangle follows from

  (i) congruence and
  (ii) the result for the area of a parallelogram, and

- that the result for the area of a parallelogram follows from that for a rectangle.

In other words, we first highlight the *congruence criterion*, and then use it to reduce every question about the areas of other shapes (first parallelograms, then triangles, polygons, circles, etc.) to the basic question about the area of a rectangle. This is in some sense what we find in Book I of Euclid's *Elements* (c. 300BC), where he goes on to show (in Proposition 47) the remarkable fact that this is all that is needed to prove *Pythagoras' Theorem.*

Claim Let $\triangle ABC$ be a right angled triangle with a right angle at C. Then the square $ABPQ$ on the hypotenuse AB is equal to the sum of the squares $CARS$ on side AC and $BCTU$ on side BC.

Proof Let the perpendicular from C to AB meet AB at X and QP at Y.

It suffices to show that (half of) the square $CARS$ is equal to (half of) the rectangle $AXYQ$.

AR is parallel to BS.

$\therefore \triangle ARC$ and $\triangle ARB$ have the same base AR and the same height RS, so have the same area.

Also $\triangle ARB \equiv \triangle ACQ$ (by SAS), so $\triangle ARC$ and $\triangle ACQ$ have the same area.

AQ is parallel to XY.

$\therefore \triangle ACQ$ and $\triangle AXQ$ have the same base AQ and the same height AX, so have the same area.

Hence $\triangle ARC$ and $\triangle AXQ$ have equal area. **QED**

The proof needs to be acted out and expanded, but it has several advantages over most other proofs:

- It is very basic, in that it only uses congruence and the area of a triangle.
- It explains *why* the "square on the hypotenuse AB" is equal to a **sum** in a way that most proofs do not.
- The construction used is entirely natural: indeed, given a right angled triangle ABC with a right angle at C, the line CXY is the only way of splitting the "square on AB" into two parts that could possibly produce one part equal to the square on CA and the other equal to the square on CB.

In John Aubrey's *Brief lives* (1694) we read of the philosopher Thomas Hobbes, that:

> He was 40 years old before he looked on Geometry; which happened accidentally. Being in a Gentleman's Library, Euclid's **Elements** lay open, and 'twas the *[Proposition] 47 [Book I]*. He read the Proposition. By God, sayd he (he would now and then swear an emphaticall Oath by way of emphasis) this is impossible! So he reads the Demonstration of it, which

> referred him back to such a Proposition; which proposition he read. That referred him back to another, which he also read. *[Continuing in this way, checking one thing after another]* at last he was demonstratively convinced of that trueth. This made him in love with Geometry.

It is worth pondering on Hobbes' scepticism and astonishment. *Pythagoras' Theorem* is a completely unexpected result—and yet one that heralds much that lies ahead (from the Cosine rule, to scalar products, vector analysis, linear algebra, quadratic forms, and much, much more). One would like all pupils to recognise something of Hobbes' surprise: Who would think of squaring lengths before adding?

Meantime, once we know how to calculate the area of a triangle, we can use this as required to calculate the area of any polygon by breaking it up into triangles and rectangles. For example, we saw in Section 3.3.1 that:

- if a trapezium $ABCD$ has AB parallel to DC, then we can drop perpendiculars to break up the problem of finding the area of $ABCD$ into that of finding the area of a rectangle and two right angled triangles;
- by cutting a regular n-gon into n congruent isosceles triangles we show later in the section that

$$\textbf{area(regular } n\textbf{-gon with incircle of radius } r\textbf{)} = \tfrac{1}{2}\textbf{(perimeter} \times \textbf{radius } r\textbf{)}$$

The area enclosed by any shape (including *curved* shapes such as a circular disc), is a measure of the "size" of the enclosed region. For a circle of radius r the exact value may prove elusive, but it can be approximated internally and externally to provide lower and upper bounds. For example, if we draw a circle of radius 5 centred at the origin $(0,0)$ on a square grid, the circle passes through the twelve grid points $(\pm5,0)$, $(0,\pm5)$, $(\pm3,\pm4)$, $(\pm4,\pm3)$. Counting unit squares inside the circle and those which just surround it then leads to the crude estimate

$$60 < \text{area of circle of radius } 5 < 88.$$

If we divide each unit in two and use squares of side $\frac{1}{2}$, the circle with centre $(0,0)$ passes through $(\pm5,0)$, $(0,\pm5)$, $(\pm3,\pm4)$, $(\pm4,\pm3)$, with the points

$(\pm\frac{7}{2},0)$, $(0,\pm\frac{7}{2})$ just inside the circle. Counting squares of size $\frac{1}{2} \times \frac{1}{2}$ leads to the slightly better estimate

$$69 < \text{area of circle of radius } 5 < 86.$$

However, merely counting smaller and smaller squares does not in itself suggest the crucial fact that the desired area is equal to **a constant multiple of r^2**. For that we need something more systematic. There are two natural approaches to this: one is highly suggestive, but mathematically less precise; one is more precise and initially less suggestive (though ultimately suggestive in a different way).

The less precise (but more intuitive) approach is to cut the circular disc into $2n$ equal *sectors*, or "cake slices", and arrange the pieces alternately pointing up and down, to form an "almost rectangle" with slightly sloping ends (each of length r—the radius) and slightly bumpy top and bottom edges (each of length equal to exactly half the perimeter of the circle—which we now know to be πr from Section 3.3.4). For larger and larger values of n—that is, for sectors with smaller and smaller angle $\left(\frac{180}{n}\right)^\circ$ at the centre—the rearranged shape is more and more like a rectangle. This suggests that the total area of the circular disc is very close to that of an r by πr rectangle—namely $r \times \pi r = \pi r^2$.

The more precise approach is to consider regular n-gons inscribed in, and circumscribed around, a circle of radius r. One should start by carrying out the exact calculations for $n = 4$ and $n = 6$ as a concrete preliminary to the beautiful, and highly suggestive, general argument for regular n-gons that follows:

$$\text{if } n = 4: \quad \text{area(inscribed square)} = 2r^2 < \text{area(circle radius } r) < 4r^2 = \text{area(circumscribed square)};$$

$$\text{if } n = 6: \quad \text{area(inscribed hexagon)} = \frac{3\sqrt{3}}{2} \cdot r^2 < \text{area(circle)} < 2\sqrt{3} \cdot r^2 = \text{area(circumscribed hexagon)}.$$

These calculations suggest that the area A of a circle of radius r is some "constant" multiple of r^2, and that the mysterious *constant* satisfies

$$2 < \frac{3\sqrt{3}}{2} = 2.598\cdots < \textit{constant} < 3.464\cdots = 2\sqrt{3} < 4.$$

In general, if a regular polygon $ABCDEFG\ldots$ has an inscribed circle with centre O and radius r, then joining all vertices to the centre breaks up the polygon into n congruent isosceles triangles ABO, BCO, CDO, ... We know that

$$AB = BC = CD = \ldots,$$

that the area of each triangle such as ABO is equal to

$$\frac{1}{2}(\text{base } AB \times \text{height } r),$$

and that the regular n-gon is equal to the sum of exactly n such triangles. Hence

$$\begin{aligned}\text{area}(ABCD\ldots) &= \frac{1}{2}(\text{base } AB \times \text{radius } r) + \frac{1}{2}(\text{base } BC \times \text{radius } r) \\ &\quad + \frac{1}{2}(\text{base } CD \times \text{radius } r) + \ldots \\ &= \frac{1}{2}([AB + BC + CD + \ldots] \times \text{radius } r) \\ &= \frac{1}{2}(\text{perimeter of regular } n\text{-gon } ABCD\cdots \times \text{radius } r).\end{aligned}$$

As the number n of sides increases, the regular n-gon approximates the circle more and more accurately and its area approaches the area of the circular disc.

$$\begin{aligned}\therefore \text{area}(\text{circle of radius } r) &= \frac{1}{2}(\text{circumference of circle} \times \text{radius } r) \\ &= \pi r \times r = \pi r^2.\end{aligned}$$

This links what we know about the **circumference** of a circle of radius r with the **area** of a circular disc of radius r, and shows that the mysterious "constant multiplier" is *exactly* π (that is, "half of the constant multiplier" 2π for the circumference of a circle).

Once the area of a circle of radius r is determined, one can pin down the area of a semicircle of radius r, of a quarter of a circle, and the area of a circular sector of radius r with angle θ at the centre. Pupils can then be asked to find the areas of all sorts of lovely composite shapes made from rectangles, triangles, and, circular sectors (both protruding and indented).

3.3.6 Volume In one dimension there is really only one possible "shape", namely a *line segment*. And the basic unit for "area" in 2D (namely the *rectangle*) is obtained by moving this 1D shape "perpendicular to itself in 2D". Hence in 2D there is only one possible shape that results from moving a 1D figure (a line segment) perpendicular to itself—namely a rectangle. Our whole approach to area started by assuming that we know how to find the area of a rectangle. And the step from 1D to 2D was so short and sweet that we hardly noticed it.

But in 2D there are many different shapes, each of which can be moved "perpendicular to itself in 3D" to obtain a right prism with the given shape as base.

- Our basic unit of volume, the cuboid, is obtained by moving a rectangle perpendicular to itself in 3D to create a right prism with a rectangular base.
- We could just as easily start with a *triangular* base and move that perpendicular to itself.
- Or we could start with a *regular polygon* as base.
- Or we could start with a *circle* as base.

So there is much more initial work to be done before we begin to worry about how to find the volume of curved shapes— such as cones and spheres.

The first move is to establish the formula for the volume of a general cuboid. A cuboid with integer length sides can be built up by taking an integer number of unit cubes in each of the three directions. The formula can be extended to cuboids with fractional length sides in the same way that we extended the formula for the area of a rectangle. It follows that the volume of a general cuboid with sides of lengths a units, b units, and c units can be shown to be equal to $a \times b \times c$ (cubic units) for all possible values of a, b and c giving the familiar formula:

$$\text{volume(cuboid)} = \text{length} \times \text{breadth} \times \text{height}.$$

Once this has result been established, the following sequence of steps allows us to calculate the volume of many other 3D shapes.

- First consider the cuboid as a *right prism*, (that is, as a three dimensional shape formed by moving the base rectangle at "right" angles to its plane) and interpret the formula for its volume as being

  volume(right rectangular prism) = (area of base rectangle) × height .

- Then cut the base rectangle into two congruent right angled triangles, and so extend this formula to give the volume of a right prism with a right angled triangle as base (a "right triangular wedge") as

  volume(right prism with right triangular base)

  = (area of base) × height.

- Then extend this formula to give the volume of any right prism with a *parallelogram* as base (surround the parallelogram by a rectangle, and hence surround the prism by a cuboid; then, just as in two dimensions, obtain the volume of the right prism by subtracting two "right triangular wedges" from the surrounding cuboid) to get:

  volume(right prism with parallelogram base)

  = (area of base parallelogram) × height.

- Then use the fact that any right triangular prism is half of a right prism with a parallelogram as base to show that its volume is given once more by:

  volume(right prism with triangle as base)

  = (area of base triangle) × height.

- We can then extend this same formula to any right prism with a polygon as base (by cutting up the base into triangles, and then adding up the volumes of the right triangular prisms):

  volume of any right prism = (area of base figure) × height.

- Finally we extend this formula once more to a *right circular cylinder* (by approximating the base circle by regular polygons).

All these formulae can be explained and understood—and can then be used to find the volumes of an interesting variety of compound shapes. The formulae for the volumes of more complicated shapes (such as pyramids, cones, spheres) are more subtle, and are best delayed until Key Stage 4.

When we come to consider "scaling" and "similarity", the two facts:

- that the volume of any cuboid is equal to

  "(area of base) × height",

  or

  "length × breadth × height",

and

- that the volume of any more general shape in 3D is defined in terms of approximating them by combinations of cuboids (including "half cuboids", or triangular wedges)

have a hidden consequence. Whatever the volume of a given shape may be, if we enlarge it (or "en-small" it) by multiplying all lengths by the same scale factor "r", then the volume of each and every approximating cuboid **is also multiplied by r^3**, so the volume of the shape being approximated is multiplied by r^3. If one cube has sides that are three times as long as another, then its volume is 27 times as large; and a sphere of radius 4 has volume 64 times as large as a sphere of radius 1.

3.4. Constructions, conventions, and derivations

> – **use the standard conventions for labelling the sides and angles of triangle *ABC*, and know and use the criteria for congruence of triangles**
>
> – **derive and use the standard ruler and compass constructions (perpendicular bisector of a line segment, constructing a perpendicular from/at a given point,**

bisecting an angle); recognise and use the perpendicular distance from a point to a line as the shortest distance to the line

- **apply the properties of angles at a point, angles at a point on a straight line, vertically opposite angles**
- **apply [...] triangle congruence [...] to derive results about angles and sides [...], and use known results to obtain simple proofs**
- **derive and illustrate properties of triangles, quadrilaterals, circles and other plane figures [for example, equal lengths and angles] using appropriate language and technologies**
- **understand and use the relationship between parallel lines and alternate and corresponding angles**
- **derive and use the sum of angles in a triangle and use it to deduce the angle sum in any polygon, and to derive properties of regular polygons**
- **apply angle facts, triangle congruence, similarity and properties of quadrilaterals to derive results about angles and sides, including *Pythagoras' Theorem*, and use known results to obtain simple proofs**

Congruence has already been introduced and used; and parallels have also featured (e.g. in parallelograms and trapezia). So this group of requirements, taken together, amounts to a relatively systematic "Euclidean" reorganisation of pupils' geometrical knowledge and methods. But this "reorganisation" is not an end in itself. Once the three basic principles (congruence, parallels, similarity) have been clarified, once the backbone sequence of basic results has been established, and once the idea of only using previously proved results has been grasped, pupils gain access to what should be the main educational content of secondary school geometry—namely the **wonderful world of accessible, yet elusive**

problems. To keep things relatively short, the exposition here focuses mainly on the underlying framework of basic results and methods which is needed to support this pupil activity. However, it is essential for teachers not only to grasp the underlying framework, but also to engage with the kinds of problems this framework opens up for pupils (and teachers) to enjoy. For a systematic development of deductive problems for mid-late Key Stage 3, we recommend the book *Crossing the Bridge* by G. Leversha (UKMT Publications 2008). Dedicated sets of problems can also be found in the series *Extension Mathematics* by Tony Gardiner (Oxford University Press 2007):

- *Book Alpha*: T5 (perimeters); T9, E2 (angles); T11, C7 (drawing conclusions); C17 (triangles); C19, E14 (areas and volumes)
- *Book Beta*: T11, T15 (drawing conclusions); C4, C7, C15 (congruence); T17, C11, E4 (angles); T20 (triangles); T26, C18 (areas and perimeters); C2 (parallel lines); C5 (ruler and compass constructions); C27 (volumes)
- *Book Gamma*: T10 (parallel lines); T17, C35 (Pythagoras' Theorem); T24 (loci); T8, C8 (circles); C10 (angles in regular polygons); C15 (volumes and prisms); C3, C39 (miscellaneous problems).

After a brief general introduction (Section 3.4.1) we address the very first listed requirement in two parts (Sections 3.4.2 and 3.4.3). We then discuss the role of the standard "ruler and compass constructions" in Section 3.4.4, before focusing on angles, and deriving the simplest consequences of the congruence criteria (relating to isosceles triangles and regular polygons) in Section 3.4.5. Section 3.4.6 examines the consequences of the parallel criterion—in particular the sum of angles in a triangle and results relating to parallelograms. Finally Section 3.4.7 comments briefly on the requirements relating to similarity. (The two remaining official requirements under the heading of *Geometry and measures* are discussed briefly in Section 3.5.)

3.4.1 Towards formal geometry As with all aspects of elementary mathematics, there is no "royal road" to success in geometry. The approaches adopted in England since the 1960s introduced all manner of delights, which one may hesitate to discard. *But they have singularly failed to produce school leavers able to analyse configurations in two- and three-dimensions.*

During this period a number of teachers and authors have continued to insist, and to demonstrate, that the most effective framework within which ordinary students can apprehend and 'calculate exactly' with geometrical information is that which analyses more complicated figures in terms of *triangles*. This is the thrust of the **Euclidean** framework illustrated by the sequence of official requirements listed at the start of Section 3.4.

Informal work at Key Stage 1 and Key Stage 2 to make sense of shapes and patterns in 2D and 3D prepares the ground for the 'more formal' treatment later in Key Stage 3 and at Key Stage 4. We have already stressed the need for structured work at Key Stage 2 and in early Key Stage 3 to include drawing and measuring (Section 3.2.1), calculating angles (described briefly in Part II, Section 2.3.5), and work with lengths, areas and volumes (Section 3.3.1). Such work develops the ideas and language that are needed when we begin to reorganise our approach to **Euclidean geometry** during Key Stage 3 (in terms of congruence, parallels, and similarity). The sequence of requirements listed at the start of Section 3.4 should be seen as ushering in this semi-formal phase.

The full thrust of formal Euclidean geometry only takes root late in Key Stage 3. And though the foundations are laid in Years 7 and 8, it is not surprising that most of the released Year 9 items from TIMSS 2011 focus on *calculation* and *construction*, rather than on *deduction*. However, one item is perhaps relevant.

> **3.4.1A** [A convex pentagon labelled $ABCDE$ is shown, including diagonals AC and AD.] What is the sum of all the interior angles of pentagon $ABCDE$? Show your work.

The dissection of the pentagon in the accompanying diagram into three triangles ABC, CAD, and DEA invites (but does not force) pupils to use the "known fact" that the angles in any triangle add to 180°. Since most Year 9 pupils have known this "fact" for several years, it seems reasonable to hope that significant numbers might manage to produce the answer of 540°, with an acceptable justification—even if expressed rather crudely as:

$$\triangle ABC + \triangle ACD + \triangle ADE = 180 + 180 + 180 = 540,$$

or

$$\square ABCD + \triangle ADE = 360 + 180 = 540.$$

The reported results therefore underline the challenge of trying to get pupils to "reason geometrically". The mark scheme awarded 2 points for an acceptable solution (*including* a justification), with 1 point for the numerically correct answer, but with an incorrect reason (and maybe for an acceptable reason, with an incorrect answer). We give the percentage of pupils scoring 2 points (with the percentage scoring at least 1 point in brackets):

3.4.1A Hungary 22% (29); Russia 19% (35);
England 17% (20); Australia 13% (19); USA 12% (16)

It is probably worth noting three additional results from the Far East. The Japanese scores of 72% (and 81%) show that it is possible to do considerably better than we do at present. At the same time the Singapore scores of 55% (and 60%), and the Hong Kong scores of 38% (and 51%), suggest that it would be rash to expect too much, too soon, from too many pupils.

3.4.2 Conventions The details relating to the first half of the first listed requirement were explored at length in Part II, Section 2.2.2.3, namely for pupils to learn

- **to use the standard conventions for labelling the sides and angles of triangle *ABC*.**

These conventions establish the language and grammar of all "geometrical calculation".

Mathematics in general succeeds by translating sense impressions, and language or sounds, into **symbols** which allow *exact calculation*. For example, we replace "words for numbers" by *numerals* and *place value*, which then makes it possible to develop exact methods for "numerical calculation". Similarly, it is only when general relations are expressed as *algebraic expressions* that we have a chance of making deductions we might otherwise overlook. For example, as long as the problem

"Find a prime number that is one less than a square"

is presented in non-mathematical language, its analysis remains elusive. But as soon as it we translate this into the appropriate mathematical language:

"When is $n^2 - 1$ prime?"

we immediately have the chance of seeing how to proceed by engaging in "algebraic calculation", since "$n^2 - 1$" should trigger the well-known factorisation

$$n^2 - 1 = (n - 1)(n + 1),$$

so $n^2 - 1$ can only be prime if $n - 1 = 1$.

In the same spirit, the English words "triangle" or "quadrilateral" conjure up a visual impression, or imagined shape. But one cannot calculate with such a visual impression. If we wish to refer to, and to calculate with, a particular triangle or quadrilateral, we need to **give it a name** in accordance with certain conventions.

The labelling conventions are chosen to communicate reliably between individuals, and to reflect the geometric structure of the object being labelled. Points are routinely denoted by capital letters (preferably *italic*). Two points A, B determine a **line** AB. But in England we use *the same notation* for the line **segment** which starts at A, runs to B, and then stops. And we use *the same notation* again for the **length** of the line segment! In other countries, these three different ideas are given different notations. It is unclear who has the power to change this confusion. But it is completely clear that, as long as we continue to use "AB" to denote all three ideas, it is essential for teachers to make sure that the *associated language* used in the classroom and in pupils' written solutions always makes it clear which meaning is intended.

A polygon is a "broken" (or bent) **sequence** of line segments. Hence, when labelling a polygon, the **sequence** in which the vertices are named matters. A quadrilateral $ABCD$ has to be labelled **in cyclic order**, where the edges are the successive line segments, or edges, that make up the quadrilateral: with edges AB and BC (meeting at the vertex B), BC and CD (meeting at vertex C), CD and DA (meeting at vertex D), and DA and AB (meeting at vertex A).

The whole of geometry in 2D and in 3D rests on the discovery that **triangles** hold the key to the construction and analysis of more complicated shapes. When we label the vertices of a triangle $\triangle ABC$, the cyclic order is not a problem: because there are only three vertices, the only choice is to list the vertices in *clockwise*, or in *anticlockwise* order. Each of the three vertices gives rise to an (internal) *angle*:

> $\angle ABC$ (often abbreviated as "$\angle B$", or just "B"), $\angle BCA$ (abbreviated as "$\angle C$", or "C"), and $\angle CAB$ (abbreviated as "$\angle A$", or "A").

And the *length of each side* of the triangle is conventionally labelled with the lower case version of the opposite vertex:

> side AB (opposite vertex C) has length c, side BC has length a, side CA has length b.

More awkward is the fact that whenever push comes to shove, a 'triangle' is not just a three-cornered shape: it is a *labelled*, or *ordered*, *triple* ABC, where **the order matters**. If one only knows the three vertices, but not the order, then this corresponds to several *different* triangles: the triangles $\triangle ABC, \triangle BCA, \triangle CAB, \triangle BAC, \ldots$ are in some sense *different* (as becomes clear when aligning triangles to demonstrate congruence—see Section 3.4.3). Even if we choose not to insist on such precision all the time, whenever we come to do some kind of calculation with a triangle, or a quadrilateral, we find that the **order** matters.

In a similar spirit, Key Stage 3 should witness a marked shift in how geometric objects are **defined**.

- In primary school, an object is pinned down (or "apprehended") by accumulating an ever-increasing list of "properties" (so that a "rectangle" is understood through *all* its properties: opposite pairs of sides equal and parallel, four right angles, equal diagonals which bisect each other, and so on).
- In Key Stage 3 this "encyclopedic" approach to the question "What is a rectangle?" should be replaced by the idea of a *definition* as a **minimal specification**. Hence

- a "rectangle" is defined to be "a parallelogram with one right angle";
- a "parallelogram" is defined to be "a quadrilateral with opposite pairs of sides parallel"; and
- a "right angle" is defined to be "half a straight angle".

This not only makes it clear what exactly we mean by a "rectangle", it also makes it much easier to check that a given quadrilateral is in fact a rectangle (since we only have to check (a) that it is a parallelogram, and (b) that it has at least one right angle). Once we have done this, we know that every other property of a rectangle comes for free—without the need to check.

3.4.3 Congruence The second half of the first listed requirement, namely

> **– to know and use the criteria for congruence of triangles**

was explored in Section 3.2.3 above and in Part II, Section 2.2.2.3. Further consequences arise in Section 3.4.4, 3.4.5, and 3.4.6 below.

Two (ordered) triangles $\triangle ABC$ and $\triangle DEF$ are *congruent* if the (ordered) correspondence

$$A \longleftrightarrow D, \qquad B \longleftrightarrow E, \qquad C \longleftrightarrow F$$

matches up each of the six ingredients of triangle $\triangle ABC$ with those of triangle $\triangle DEF$ in such a way that

- all three *corresponding* pairs of line segments are equal:

$$AB = DE,\ BC = EF,\ CA = FD,$$

and

- all three *corresponding* pairs of angles are equal:

$$\angle A = \angle D,\ \angle B = \angle E,\ \angle C = \angle F.$$

We write this as: $\triangle ABC \equiv \triangle DEF$ (which we read as "triangle ABC is *congruent* to triangle DEF").

"Congruence of triangles" only makes sense between **ordered** triangles. And it can help pupils to see more clearly which vertex of the first triangle corresponds to which in the second triangle, and which side of the first triangle corresponds to which in the second triangle if pupils initially write

$$\begin{aligned} &\triangle ABC \\ \equiv\ &\triangle DEF \end{aligned}$$

lining up corresponding vertices and edges vertically over each other (as with column arithmetic):

- with vertex A directly above vertex D, B directly above E, C directly above F, and
- with edge AB directly above edge DE, BC directly above EF, CA directly above FD.

The three basic *congruence criteria* (SSS, SAS, and ASA) arise naturally from drawing and construction exercises, and the SSS-congruence criterion plays a significant role in the next Section 3.4.4 to show that the standard ruler and compass constructions do what they claim:

> triangles $\triangle ABC$ and $\triangle DEF$ are congruent (by SSS) if $AB = DE$, $BC = EF$, and $CA = FD$;
>
> triangles $\triangle ABC$ and $\triangle DEF$ are congruent (by SAS) if $AB = DE$, $\angle BAC = \angle EDF$, and $AC = DF$;
>
> triangles $\triangle ABC$ and $\triangle DEF$ are congruent (by ASA) if $\angle BAC = \angle EDF$, $AB = DE$, and $\angle ABC = \angle DEF$.

The RHS congruence criterion is not part of this basic congruence criterion, so does not really belong at this stage. It arises as the degenerate instance of the failed ASS criterion (where the angle "A" in "ASS" is a right angle, and so is neither acute nor obtuse). The fact that RHS guarantees congruence depends on *Pythagoras' Theorem*, since knowing two sides and a right angle then determines the third side. So RHS is a special case of SSS.

3.4.4 Congruence and ruler and compass constructions "Construction" at Key Stage 3 takes on a slightly different meaning, moving

- **from measuring work with rulers and protractors at Key Stage 2 and early Key Stage 3**
- **to a simple, hands-on, geometrical framework using "ruler and compasses",** ***which avoids measuring altogether,*** **in which the familiar "measuring ruler" becomes a** ***straightedge*** **(that is, a mere straight-line-drawer), and the focus switches from measuring lengths to "equality" of line segments (e.g. as radii of a given circle, created by a pair of compasses).**

We stick to the tradition of referring to these latter constructions as **ruler and compass constructions**—even though the ruler is being used as an "ideal" *mental straightedge* (and its crude, approximate markings play no role).

- Given two points A and B, the "ruler" is simply a way of physically capturing the idea that one can imagine the *line or line segment "AB"* determined by these two points; and
- given a point O (as centre) and another point P, the "compasses" are a way of physically capturing the "ideal" construction of the circle with centre O and passing through P.

That is, the two instruments are in some sense not being used to perform actual constructions, but to illustrate *imagined ideal constructions* (performed with 'heavenly' straightedge and compasses).

Ruler and compass constructions offer a natural psycho-kinetic embodiment of the simplest parts of *formal* geometry (for example, allowing pupils to experience SSS-congruence directly). The constructions themselves are experienced directly; and the *proofs* that the basic constructions do what they claim constitute an introduction to the subsequent transition from physical to *formal* geometry. Hence ruler and compass constructions embody four rather different aspects of secondary mathematics.

- The first is the clean simplicity of the basic moves:
  - to construct the line AB through two known points A and B,
  - to construct the circle with known centre A passing through a known point B, and

  - to obtain "new known points" as the points of intersection of two constructed lines, or of a constructed line and a circle, or of two constructed circles.

- The second aspect is the act of drawing itself (which may at first be ungainly, but which benefits hugely from practice, which exploits the links between hand, eye, and brain, gives physical substance to geometrical ideas, and leads ultimately to quiet satisfaction after a well-implemented construction).

- The third aspect is to *imagine* the act of drawing without first carrying out each construction, so that one can begin to combine standard constructions as basic moves in a chain that achieves some more complicated goal: (for example, we can imagine how one might use ruler and compasses to construct an equilateral triangle—or a square, or a regular pentagon, or a regular hexagon, or a regular octagon—inscribed in a circle with centre at O and passing through the point A).

- The fourth aspect is the simple *deductive structure*, based mainly on the SSS-congruence criterion, that shows how "equal lengths" (which is all one can create using compasses, where two radii of the same circle are necessarily equal) leads to congruence, and hence forces certain *angles* to be equal.

The idea that mathematical objects need to be "constructed", rather than "postulated" or plucked out of thin air, lay at the heart of ancient Greek mathematics. The assumptions which underlie ruler and compass constructions were declared as the first three of their five "axioms" or principles:

- to construct a line segment AB joining two known points A, B;

- to extend this line segment as far as one wishes in either direction;

- to construct the circle with known centre O and passing through a known point A.

Many of the results they proved were presented as *constructions*. For example, the very first Proposition in Book I of *Euclid*'s *Elements*:

> "On a given finite straight line [segment AB] to construct an equilateral triangle [ABC]."
>
> **Construction:** Draw the circle with centre A passing through B, and the circle with centre B passing through A. Let these two circles meet at C and at D.
>
> $\therefore AB = AC$ (radii of the same circle) and $BA = BC$ (radii of the same circle).
>
> $\therefore \triangle ABC$ is equilateral. **QEF**

Genuine *proofs* ended with a statement (in Greek)

> "which is that which was to be *proved*".

This is rendered in Latin as "*Quod Erat Demonstrandum*" and abbreviated as "QED". In contrast, *constructions* like the one above ended with the statement

> "being what it was required to *do*",

which is rendered in Latin as "*Quod Erat Faciendum*" and abbreviated as "QEF".

This may all seem to have little to do with school mathematics. But it is worth reflecting on the links between this "constructive" approach to mathematical concepts and the *psychology of the learner*. As mathematics became more abstruse in the eighteenth, nineteenth, and early twentieth centuries, its ideas and methods were increasingly postulated abstractly. This approach proved exceedingly powerful; but it also made the subject less accessible, and led to philosophical difficulties. The advent of computers has reminded us afresh of the need to be able to construct the ideas about which we reason in mathematics: knowing that a curve crosses the x-axis and so has a "root" is one thing; but we also need effective methods for **finding** that root. Something analogous applies to learners, where a constructive approach often allows a more meaningful kind of engagement than a purely logical analysis. (This observation also seems to have been behind John Perry's proposed reforms in the early 1900s.)

The official requirement that pupils should

> – **derive and use the standard ruler and compass constructions (perpendicular bisector of a line segment, constructing a perpendicular from/at a given point, bisecting an angle); recognise and use the perpendicular distance from a point to a line as the shortest distance to the line**

encourages this kind of healthy, constructive engagement, and does so using "ruler and compasses" in a way that is consistent with the Euclidean reworking of geometry. It is therefore to be welcomed (though, as we shall see, the final reference to "shortest distance to the line" is slightly out of place).

The first "standard construction" is implicit in *Euclid*'s Proposition 1.

To construct the perpendicular bisector of a given line segment AB.

Construction: Draw the circle with centre A passing through B, and the circle with centre B passing through A. Let these two circles meet at C and at D.

We may not yet know how to *construct* the midpoint of the line segment AB; but the midpoint certainly exists, so let us "imagine" it (somewhere between A and B) and give it a name, M.

We claim that $\triangle CMA \equiv \triangle CMB$ (by SSS).

$\therefore \angle CMA = \angle CMB$, so each angle is half a straight angle, and CM is perpendicular to AB.

Similarly, DM is perpendicular to AB.

$\therefore$ CMD is a straight line, so the line CD crosses AB at its midpoint M.

$\therefore$ CD is the required perpendicular bisector. **QEF**

The second standard construction uses the same idea.

Given a line segment AB and a point P, to construct the perpendicular from P to AB.

Construction:

(i) Suppose first that P lies on the line AB.

Clearly P cannot be the same point as both A and B. So we may suppose that $P \neq B$.

Draw the circle with centre P passing through B, and let it meet the line AB (= BP) again at C.

Then P is the midpoint of BC.

Use the first standard construction to find the perpendicular bisector of BC, and this will be the perpendicular to AB at the point P.

(ii) Suppose next that P does not lie on the line AB.

By drawing the circles with centre P passing through A and through B we can choose the point *furthest* from P—which we may suppose is B.

Draw the circle with centre P passing through B, and let it meet the **line** AB again at C. (The point C lies on the line AB, but is not internal to the line segment AB.)

Use the first standard construction to find the midpoint M of BC.

$\therefore \triangle PMB \equiv \triangle PMC$ (by SSS)

$\therefore \angle PMB = \angle PMC$, so each is half a straight angle.

$\therefore PM$ is the perpendicular from P to AB. **QEF**

The third standard construction is slightly different. Because ruler and compasses can only make *lengths* equal, it again uses SSS-congruence—this time to conclude that two angles are equal.

Given two lines BA and BC meeting at the point B, to construct the bisector of $\angle ABC$.

Construction: Draw the circle with centre B passing through C and let this circle meet the segment BA (extended if necessary beyond the point A) at D.

$\therefore BC = BD$ (radii of same circle)

Draw the circle with centre C passing through B, and the circle with centre D passing through B, and let these two circles meet at B and again at E.

$\therefore CB = CE$ (radii of same circle) and $DB = DE$ (radii of same circle).

$\therefore \triangle CBE \equiv \triangle DBE$ (by SSS)

$\therefore \angle CBE = \angle DBE$, so the line BE bisects $\angle ABC$. **QEF**

There are lots of lovely problems which exploit these three basic constructions. Once we are in a position to use "equal alternate (or corresponding) angles" as a criterion for two lines to be parallel, we can extend the second standard construction to obtain the line through P parallel to AB.

Given a line AB and a point P not on AB, to construct the line through P parallel to AB.

Construction: Construct the perpendicular from P to AB, meeting AB at the point X.

Then construct the perpendicular PY to PX at the point P.

The fact that $\angle AXP$ and $\angle XPY$ are right angles, then implies that PY is parallel to AB. **QEF**

We can also explore the question of constructing regular polygons. The flower petal construction described in Section 3.2.1 shows how to construct a **regular hexagon** $ABCDEF$ inscribed in a given circle with centre O and passing through A. By taking every second vertex, we obtain a way of constructing an **equilateral triangle** ACE inscribed in the circle with centre O.

The question as to which other regular polygons can be constructed in this way was addressed (and answered completely) by *Carl Friedrich Gauss* in his late teens in the mid-late 1790s, and published in his famous book *Disquisitiones arithmeticae*, 1801 (at the time, Latin was still the main international language for communicating scientific results). To construct a **square**, let AO meet the circle again at C, construct the perpendicular bisector of the line segment AC, and let this meet the circle at B and at D; then one can prove that $ABCD$ is a square. One can also find relatively simple ways of constructing a **regular pentagon** in the circle with centre O (though proving that they really work may have to wait until Key Stage 4). And once we know how to construct a regular 4-gon $ACEG$ in the circle with centre O passing through A, we can use the first standard construction to construct the perpendicular bisector of each side and so find the points B, D, F, H where these perpendicular bisectors cut the circle—thus constructing a **regular 8-gon** $ABCDEFGH$. Similarly, once we know how to construct a regular 5-gon, we can construct a **regular 10-gon**. But it is **impossible** to construct a regular 7-gon, or a regular 9-gon, or a regular 11-gon with ruler and compasses.

The final requirement for pupils to:

> **recognise and use the perpendicular distance from a point to a line as the shortest distance to the line**

is slightly out of place here. We saw how to construct the perpendicular from a point P to meet AB at the point X. But it is not obvious that PX is the *shortest* distance from P to AB. (The easiest way to see this is to consider any other point Y on the line AB and then to apply *Pythagoras' Theorem* to the right angled triangle PXY to see that PY is greater than PX.)

3.4.5 The basic consequences of congruence The simplest geometrical result of all is that "vertically opposite angles are always equal" as required by

> – **apply the properties of angles at a point, angles at a point on a straight line, vertically opposite angles.**

Claim Whenever two lines cross at a point P, any pair of vertically opposite angles A and A' at P are necessarily equal.

Proof: Let B be the angle "between" the two vertically opposite angles A and A' at P.
Then $A + B$ is the straight angle on one line, and $B + A'$ is the straight angle on the other line.
$\therefore A + B = B + A'$, so $A = A'$. **QED**

In general the size of an angle is defined in terms of fractions of a "straight angle" (the "angle" at a point P on a straight line). For example, if we *bisect* a straight angle, then each half is a *right angle*. Thanks to the ancient Babylonians, we still measure angles in *degrees*, with each straight angle equal to $180°$, so each right angle is equal to $90°$. We are not sure why they chose $360°$ for a full turn. However, it may be related in some way

(a) to their use of the sexagesimal numeral system (base 60), and

(b) to their use of angles in astronomy, and the connection between the apparent movement of the observed stars and what they took to be the number of days in a year.

The rest of this section focuses on the SSS, SAS, and ASA congruence criteria. These are in many ways more fundamental than the criterion for two lines to be parallel (which we address in Section 3.4.6), in that they apply to geometries where the parallel criterion fails—allowing us to show that certain angles, or line segments, are equal (as in Section 3.4.4, where we dropped perpendiculars, and where we bisected any given angle). The miracle of Euclidean geometry is how much more one can prove by *combining* these two principles.

We start by developing the "backbone" of results that depend only on congruence. This obliges us to interpret the two slightly confused official requirements:

- **apply [...] triangle congruence [...] to derive results about angles and sides [...], and use known results to obtain simple proofs**

– **derive and illustrate properties of triangles, quadrilaterals, circles and other plane figures [for example, equal lengths and angles] using appropriate language and technologies**

The problem here is that the wording in the full requirement (including the parts which have here been omitted) confuses

- the experiential Key Stage 2 approach to geometry (where one "collects and uses facts" without any definitions or proofs) and
- the Key Stage 3 approach, which begins to organise geometrical knowledge through *minimal definitions*, respecting conventions, emphasising the three basic *principles* (the congruence criterion, the parallel criterion, and the similarity criterion), and **deriving** those "facts", or "properties", which are most useful.

If we disentangle this confusion, and focus on what should be the distinctive Key Stage 3 approach, then the first move has to be to prove the basic facts about isosceles triangles. A triangle ABC in which $AB = AC$ is called *isosceles*, with *base* BC and with *apex* A. ("Iso" means "same" in Greek; and "sceles" means "legs", or sides.)

Claim if $AB = AC$, then $\angle ABC = \angle ACB$ ("the base angles of any isosceles triangle are equal"). Moreover, the line AM joining the apex A to the midpoint M of the base BC (the "median") is also the perpendicular bisector of the base BC, and the bisector of the apex angle $\angle BAC$.

Proof Construct the midpoint M of the base BC.

Then $\triangle ABM \equiv \triangle ACM$ (by SSS).

$\therefore \angle ABM = \angle ACM$, so the two base angles $\angle ABC$ and $\angle ACB$ are equal.

Also $\angle AMB = \angle AMC$, so each is equal to half a straight angle—that is, a right angle.

And $\angle BAM = \angle CAM$, so AM bisects the angle $\angle BAC$. **QED**

Claim If $\angle ABC = \angle ACB$, then $AB = AC$ ("if the base angles are equal, the triangle is isosceles").

Proof $\triangle ABC \equiv \triangle ACB$ (by ASA).

$\therefore AB = AC$. **QED**

Claim (a) If M is the midpoint of BC, and MX is perpendicular to BC, then $XB = XC$. That is, each point on the perpendicular bisector of BC is equidistant from B and from C.

(b) Conversely, if Y is equidistant from B and from C, then Y lies on the perpendicular bisector of BC.

Hence the perpendicular bisector of a line segment BC is precisely the *locus* of all points that are equidistant from B and from C.

Proof (a) $\triangle XMB \equiv \triangle XMC$ (by SAS, since $XM = XM$, $\angle XMB = \angle XMC$, $MB = MC$).

$\therefore XB = XC$.

(b) Join YM. Then $\triangle YMB \equiv \triangle YMC$ (by SSS).

$\therefore \angle YMB = \angle YMC$, so each is half of a straight angle. **QED**

Isosceles triangles arise naturally when working with circles: if A and B lie on the circle with centre O, then $OA = OB$, so $\triangle OAB$ is isosceles. Hence the perpendicular from O to AB bisects the base AB and also bisects the angle $\angle AOB$. Isosceles triangles also feature in the following useful result.

Claim A regular n-gon $ABCDEF\ldots$ has a centre O, and is inscribed in a circle with centre O.

Proof Let the perpendicular bisector of AB meet the perpendicular bisector of BC at O. By a previous result, $OA = OB$, and $OB = OC$. Hence $OA = OC$ and the circle with centre O passing through A, also passes through B and C. We show that this circle necessarily passes through the vertex D, and hence through all vertices of the regular polygon.

$\therefore \triangle OAB$ is isosceles, so $\angle OAB = \angle OBA$, and $\triangle OBC$ is isosceles, so $\angle OBC = \angle OCB$.

Moreover $\triangle OAB \equiv \triangle OBC$ (by SSS: since $OA = OB$, $OB = OC$, and $AB = BC$).

$\therefore \angle OAB = \angle OBC$, so

$$\angle OAB = \angle OBA = \angle OBC = \angle OCB = \frac{1}{2}(\angle ABC).$$

$\therefore \angle OCD = \angle BCD - \angle OCB = \frac{1}{2}(\angle ABC) = \angle OBC.$

$\therefore \triangle OBC \equiv \triangle OCD$ (by SAS: $OB = OC, \angle OBC = \angle OCD, BC = CD$).

$\therefore OC$ (in $\triangle OBC$) $= OD$ (in $\triangle OCD$) so the circle with centre O passing through A also passes through D.

Continuing in this way shows that the circle passes through every vertex of the regular polygon. **QED**

3.4.6 The parallel criterion and angles in a triangle To prove more interesting results—such as to

> – **derive and use the sum of angles in a triangle and use it to deduce the angle sum in any polygon**

we need more than just the congruence criterion. In particular, we need to

> – **understand and use the relationship between parallel lines and alternate and corresponding angles.**

This is the second organising principle in geometry—namely the criterion for two lines in the plane to be *parallel*. Given any two lines in the plane, a *transversal* is a third line that cuts both of the two given lines. The *parallel criterion* declares that:

- two lines are *parallel* precisely when the *alternate angles* (or the *corresponding angles*) created by a transversal are equal.

This is a rather subtle criterion, but one which can be made thoroughly plausible.

The formal proof that the three angles in any triangle ABC add to a straight angle echoes the primary school activity of tearing off the three corners and fitting the pieces together crudely against a ruler. But here we use "God's ruler" (namely the line through C parallel to AB), and we fit the three angles together *perfectly* and in a very particular order ($\angle A + \angle C + \angle B$).

Claim The three angles in any triangle $\triangle ABC$ add to a straight angle.

Proof Construct the line XCY through C parallel to AB (with X on the same side of CB as A).

Then $\angle XCA = \angle BAC = \angle A$ (alternate angles)

and $\angle YCB = \angle ABC = \angle B$ (alternate angles).

$\therefore \angle A + \angle C + \angle B = \angle XCA + \angle ACB + \angle YCB$. **QED**

A quadrilateral $ABCD$ can be split into **two** triangles (by drawing one of the diagonals AC, BD), so the sum of the four angles in any quadrilateral is "$2 \times 180°$". The same idea shows that the angles in any polygon with n sides have sum $(n-2) \times 180°$. These simple observations open the door to hundreds of wonderful (non-obvious, multi-step) problems involving *angle chasing* (see, for example, *Extension mathematics*, Tony Gardiner: *Book Alpha*, Sections T9, E2; and *Book Beta*, Sections T17, C11, E4).

The last seven words of the requirement

> – **derive and use the sum of angles in a triangle and use it to deduce the angle sum in any polygon, and to derive properties of regular polygons**

are slightly out of place here. A *regular polygon* is defined to be a polygon whose sides are all equal and whose angles are all equal. It should be a major focus of secondary geometry to explore the geometry of regular polygons—at least including regular 3-gons, regular 4-gons, regular 5-gons, regular 6-gons, and regular 8-gons. And whilst it follows from the above that each angle in a regular n-gon is equal to

$$\left(1 - \frac{2}{n}\right) \times 180°,$$

almost anything else one might prove about regular polygons depends on the congruence criteria (in particular, properties of "isosceles triangles").

This observation even applies to proving that certain diagonals and sides are parallel.

Claim Let $ABCDE$ be a regular pentagon. Then each diagonal is parallel to the opposite side.

Proof We show that AC is parallel to ED.

$\angle ABC = \left(1 - \frac{2}{5}\right) \times 180^\circ = 108^\circ$.

$BA = BC$, so $\triangle BAC$ is isosceles. Hence $\angle BAC = \angle BCA = 36^\circ$.

$\therefore \angle CAE = 72^\circ$, so $\angle CAE + \angle DEA = 180^\circ$ whence AC is parallel to ED. **QED**

The most important application of the basic property of parallel lines is to derive results about parallelograms. A *parallelogram* is a quadrilateral $ABCD$ in which opposite pairs of sides AB, DC and BC, AD are parallel. Most results relating to parallelograms depend on the congruence criteria. But two results depend only on the basic property of parallel lines.

Claim If $ABCD$ is a parallelogram, then opposite angles are equal: $\angle A = \angle C$, $\angle B = \angle D$.

Conversely, if $ABCD$ is a quadrilateral with $\angle A = \angle C$, $\angle B = \angle D$, then $ABCD$ is a parallelogram.

Proof Suppose $ABCD$ is a parallelogram. Then AB is parallel to DC, so $\angle A + \angle D = 180^\circ$.

And AD is parallel to BC, so $\angle D + \angle C = 180^\circ$.

$\therefore \angle A = \angle C$, and $\angle B = 180^\circ - \angle A = 180^\circ - \angle C = \angle D$.

Conversely, suppose $ABCD$ is any quadrilateral in which opposite angles are equal in pairs: $\angle A = \angle C$, $\angle B = \angle D$. Since

$$\angle A + \angle B + \angle C + \angle D = 360^\circ,$$

it follows that $\angle A + \angle B = 180^\circ$, so AD is parallel to BC. Similarly $\angle B + \angle C = 180^\circ$, so AB is parallel to DC. **QED**

A *rectangle* is defined to be "a parallelogram with (at least one) right angle". If the rectangle is $ABCD$, and if the right angle is at A, then from the above result it follows that $\angle C$ is also a right angle. Hence $\angle B + \angle D = 180°$; since $\angle B = \angle D$, it follows that $\angle B$ and $\angle D$ are also right angles. However, there is no simple way to conclude that "opposite sides of a rectangle are equal" other than by proving the result for parallelograms in general (using ASA-congruence).

Claim If $ABCD$ is a parallelogram, then opposite sides are equal in pairs: $AB = DC$ and $BC = AD$.

Proof Draw the diagonal AC.

$\therefore \angle BAC = \angle DCA$ (alternate angles)

$AC = CA$

$\angle BCA = \angle DAC$ (alternate angles)

$\therefore \triangle BAC \equiv \triangle DCA$ (by ASA)

$\therefore BA = DC$ and $BC = DA$. **QED**

Claim If $ABCD$ is a rectangle, then $AC = BD$.

Proof We claim that $\triangle ABC \equiv \triangle BAD$ (by SAS: since $AB = BA$, $\angle ABC = \angle BAD = 90°$, and $BC = AD$ (opposite sides of parallelogram)).

$\therefore AC = BD$. **QED**

Each result one can prove for parallelograms has a converse which (if true) should also be proved, since it allows us to identify a parallelogram on the basis of other characteristic properties.

Claim If $ABCD$ is a quadrilateral in which $AB = DC$ and $BC = AD$, then $ABCD$ is a parallelogram.

Proof Draw the diagonal AC.

$\therefore \triangle BAC \equiv \triangle DCA$ (by SSS).

$\therefore \angle BAC = \angle DCA$, so AB is parallel to DC (alternate angles equal), and $\angle BCA = \angle DAC$, so BC is parallel to AD (alternate angles equal). **QED**

Claim If $ABCD$ is a parallelogram, then the diagonals AC and BD bisect each other.

Conversely, any quadrilateral $ABCD$ whose diagonals bisect each other is a parallelogram.

Proof Let the two diagonals meet at X.

$\therefore \angle ADX = \angle CBX$ (alternate angles)

$DA = BC$ (opposite sides of a parallelogram)

$\angle DAX = \angle BCX$ (alternate angles).

$\therefore \triangle ADX \equiv \triangle CBX$ (by ASA)

$\therefore DX = BX$ and $AX = CX$, so the diagonals bisect each other.

Now let $ABCD$ be any quadrilateral whose diagonals AC, BD bisect each other at X.

Then $AX = CX$ and $DX = BX$, and $\angle AXD = \angle CXB$ (vertically opposite angles).

$\therefore \triangle ADX \equiv \triangle CBX$ (by SAS).

$\therefore \angle DAX = \angle BCX$, so DA is parallel to CB (alternate angles equal), and

Similarly we can show that $\triangle ABX \equiv \triangle CDX$ (by SAS).

Hence $\angle BAX = \angle DCX$, so AB is parallel to DC (alternate angles equal). **QED**

A *rhombus* is a parallelogram $ABCD$ with adjacent sides equal; $AB = AD$. And a *square* is a rhombus which is also a rectangle.

Claim The two diagonals of a rhombus $ABCD$ are perpendicular.

Proof Let the two diagonals meet at X. Then $DX = BX$ so $\triangle AXD \equiv \triangle AXB$ (by SSS).

$\therefore \angle AXD = \angle AXB$. **QED**

In a rhombus $ABCD$, each diagonal splits the rhombus into two *isosceles triangles*. Hence other properties of a rhombus (and their converses) tend to exploit the basic property of isosceles triangles (and its converse).

3.4.7 Similarity (from 3.2)

> - **identify and construct congruent triangles, and similar shapes by enlargement, with and without coordinate grids**
> - **apply angle facts, triangle congruence, similarity and properties of quadrilaterals to derive results about angles and sides, including *Pythagoras' Theorem*, and use known results to obtain simple proofs**
> - **use *Pythagoras' Theorem* and trigonometric ratios in similar triangles to solve problems involving right angled triangles**

The first two requirements have both been addressed elsewhere (in Section 3.2 and 3.2.3, and in Section 3.4.5 respectively). They are linked here because both mention "similar shapes" or "similarity", and this idea has to be addressed to prepare the way for simple trigonometry (as in the third listed requirement).

We noted in Section 3.2 that the reference to "similar shapes" in the first of the above requirements is largely "informal", and that the initial emphasis here should be practical. The formal notion of *similarity* should emerge from pupils' own experience. For example, they should construct "enlargements" in the spirit of the exercises in sections T8 and C26 of *Extension mathematics, Book Beta* by Tony Gardiner (Oxford University Press 2007). And their understanding and interpretation of "scale drawings", and the effect of scale factors on lengths, areas and volumes, should also be rooted in practical work and calculation (see, for example, sections T21, C41 in *Extension mathematics Book Gamma*).

However, pupils need more than this in preparation for simple trigonometry (see Section 3.5). So once sufficient foundations-in-experience have been laid (as indicated below), it is certainly worth explaining clearly what it means for two figures to be similar: namely that two polygons $ABCD\ldots$ and $A'B'C'D'\ldots$ are **similar** if

- corresponding *angles* are *equal*:

$$\angle A = \angle A', \angle B = \angle B', \angle C = \angle C', \angle D = \angle D', \ldots$$

and

- corresponding *sides* are *proportional*:

$$AB : A'B' = BC : B'C' = CD : C'D' = \ldots.$$

Pupils need to recognise that these two conditions seem to capture what we mean when we say that "two polygons have the same shape".

A square (or *regular* 4-*gon*) is defined as "a quadrilateral having all sides equal and all angles equal". Two different squares $ABCD$ and $A'B'C'D'$ have all angles equal to 90°; hence they automatically satisfy the first bullet point. And the four sides of each square are equal: if the first square has sides of length a and the second has sides of length b; then each ratio in the second bullet point is equal to $a : b$, so the second bullet point is satisfied. Hence any two squares are mathematically *similar*. They are also "physically similar-looking", in that a large square that is some distance away leaves the same image on the retina as a nearby smaller square.

To establish that **both** bullet points are needed, pupils should think of examples

- of two rectangles whose angles clearly match up in pairs, but whose sides are **definitely not** proportional (such as a 1 by 1 square and a 2 by 1 rectangle), or
- of two parallelograms whose sides are in proportion, but whose angles are not equal in pairs (such as a 1 by 1 square and a 60° rhombus with sides of length 1).

It should then be clear that our idea of "same shape" requires **both** conditions.

However, there is a remarkable difference between polygons with more than three sides (such as quadrilaterals), and polygons with exactly three sides (i.e. triangles). Any two *equilateral* triangles of different sizes are similar—and for much the same reason as any two squares are similar: (i) all angles are equal to 60°, so are certainly "equal in pairs", and (ii) all three sides of one triangle have equal length (say a), and all three sides of the other triangle have equal length (b say), so the ratios of corresponding sides are all equal to $a : b$. But, unlike the case of squares (where both conditions are needed), one of these conditions for equilateral triangles comes for free. As the name implies, for $\triangle ABC$ to be equilateral, all we need is

> "that the three sides are all equal: $AB = BC = CA$".

The fact that the three angles are all equal to 60° then comes for free—thanks to the SSS congruence criterion (since $\triangle ABC \equiv \triangle BCA$, so $\angle ABC = \angle BCA$ and $\angle BCA = \angle CAB$). Hence, to check the claim that any two equilateral triangles are similar, it is enough to observe that the second bullet point is satisfied (and the first then comes for free).

The same is true whenever we apply the idea of "similarity" to triangles in general. Officially two (ordered) triangles $\triangle ABC$ and $\triangle DEF$ are *similar* (which we write as $\triangle ABC \sim \triangle DEF$) if

- corresponding *angles* are equal: $\angle A = \angle D$, $\angle B = \angle E$, $\angle C = \angle F$,

and

- corresponding *sides* are proportional: $AB : DE = BC : EF = CA : FD$.

Yet the challenge, to think of

- two triangles whose angles match up in pairs, but whose sides are **not** proportional, or
- two triangles whose sides are proportional but whose angles are **not** equal in pairs,

leads to a surprise.

- If $\triangle ABC$ and $\triangle DEF$ have angles equal in pairs, the three pairs of corresponding sides always turn out to be proportional; and
- if $\triangle ABC$ and $\triangle DEF$ have corresponding sides proportional, then corresponding angles are automatically equal.

This fact is unlikely to make sense if simply stated in the way we have stated it here. So pupils need prior experience of drawing and measuring that makes this important statement meaningful and plausible: the *similarity criterion* states that, **for triangles**, each of the above bullet points implies the other. (See, for example, "Problem 0" in Section T13 of *Extension mathematics Book Gamma*.)

Initially pupils need the idea of similar triangles for simple trigonometry: i.e. only for *right-angled* triangles. We can even restrict to right angled triangles $\triangle OBC$, with a right angle at B, and $\triangle OB'C'$ with a right angle at B', sharing a common vertex O (which we may take to be the origin), with B and B' lying on the positive x-axis. If we fix the angle at O $\angle BOC = \theta$, and choose C' to lie on the line OC, then the angles of the two triangles $\triangle OBC$ and $\triangle OB'C'$ are equal in pairs (namely to θ, 90°, and $90^\circ - \theta$); and we can establish as a fact of experience (by drawing and measuring; or partly of deduction—first for $k = 2$ or $k = \frac{1}{2}$, then for any integer or unit fraction, and finally for any fraction) that

> if $OB' = k \cdot OB$ (so to get from O to B' we go "k times as far **along**" as we did to get to B)
>
> then $B'C' = k \cdot BC$ (so to get to B' from C' we go "k times as far **up**" as we did to get from B to C)

It follows (by *Pythagoras' Theorem*) that $OC' : OC = k$. So the first bullet point implies the second. Hence if $\angle BOC = \angle B'OC' = \theta$ (and $\angle OBC = \angle OB'C' = 90^\circ$), then corresponding sides are in proportion:

$$OB' : OB = OC' : OC = B'C' : BC.$$

Cross-multiplying shows that

$$B'C' : OB' = BC : OB,$$

so the quotient "$\frac{\text{opposite}}{\text{adjacent}}$" depends only on the angle $\angle BOC = \theta$, and not on the choice of triangle. Hence we can safely write it as "$\tan\theta$"—that is as a *function* that only depends on the angle θ. (See Section C20 in *Extension mathematics Book Gamma*.)

Similarly $B'C' : OC' = BC : OC$, so the quotient "$\frac{\text{opposite}}{\text{hypotenuse}}$" depends only on the angle $\angle BOC = \theta$ and not on the choice of triangle, so we can safely write it as "$\sin\theta$"—that is, as a function of θ. And the ratio $OB' : OC' = OB : OC$, so the quotient "$\frac{\text{adjacent}}{\text{hypotenuse}}$" depends only on the angle $\angle BOC = \theta$ and not on the choice of triangle, so we can safely write it as "$\cos\theta$". (See Section C33 in *Extension mathematics Book Gamma*.)

The congruence criterion and the parallel criterion allow one to transfer *exact* relations (such as *equality* of line segments or of angles) from one place to another. The *similarity criterion* goes beyond this world of *exact equality* to allow one to deal with ratios, scaling, and enlargement. Hence this criterion is probably best delayed until the basic consequences of congruence and parallelism have been sufficiently explored, and until pupils are sufficiently confident in working with ratio. (The *similarity criterion* may be thought of as a substitute for the evidently false "AAA congruence criterion". The criterion can also be re-formulated as SAS-similarity: (see Section C13 of *Extension mathematics Book Gamma*).

As hinted above, special cases of the similarity criterion can actually be proved using the congruence criterion and the parallel criterion—namely where the ratio between corresponding sides in the second bullet point is a fraction. The most important example occurs when this ratio is equal to 2 (or to $\frac{1}{2}$) and is called the *Midpoint Theorem*, which says that:

> if in $\triangle ABC$, M is the midpoint of AB and N is the midpoint of AC,
>
> then MN is parallel to BC and $BC : MN = 2 : 1$.

That is $\triangle ABC \sim \triangle AMN$, with the corresponding scale factor

$$AB : AM = AC : AN = BC : MN = 2 : 1$$

(see section T13, Problem 6 in *Extension mathematics Book Gamma*).

The third requirement listed at the start of Section 3.4.7 concerns applications of these ideas. Once we know *Pythagoras' Theorem* we can use it to find lengths exactly (in surd form). An equilateral triangle of side 2 has height equal to $\sqrt{3}$. A square $ABCD$ of side 1 has diagonal AC of length $\sqrt{2}$. A regular pentagon $ABCDE$ of side length 1 has diagonal AC

of length $\frac{1+\sqrt{5}}{2}$. A regular hexagon $ABCDEF$ with sides of length 1 has two different length diagonals—a diameter AD of length exactly 2, and a shorter diagonal AC of length exactly $\sqrt{3}$. The square of side 1 allows one to write down the exact values for $\tan 45° = 1$, and for

$$\sin 45° = \frac{1}{\sqrt{2}} = \frac{\sqrt{2}}{2} = \cos 45°.$$

In the equilateral triangle of side 2, the perpendicular from the apex to the base bisects the apex angle into two angles of 30°, and meets the base at its midpoint. Hence we can write down the exact value for

$$\sin 30° = \frac{1}{2} = \cos 60°,$$

for

$$\sin 60° = \frac{\sqrt{3}}{2} = \cos 30°,$$

for $\tan 30° = \frac{1}{\sqrt{3}}$, and for $\tan 60° = \sqrt{3}$. One can also use *Pythagoras' Theorem* to find the distance between any two points whose coordinates are given (in 2D or in 3D).

Wherever right angled triangles appear, one can use sin, cos and tan (or similar triangles) to find missing angles or lengths. Classical applications include

- "angles of elevation (or depression)", where we might know that "from the top of a vertical cliff 40m high, we can see a buoy whose angle of depression (from our position on top of the cliff) is 35°. How far is the buoy from the base of the cliff?", or
- the traditional exercise of "calculating the height of a tree without measuring directly", where we line up our eye (at ground level), the top of a pupil's head and the top of a tree, and then measure
  - (i) the pupil's height and
  - (ii) the distances from our eye to the pupil's feet, and to the base of the tree.

One would also like to see other applications of angles which do not involve right angled triangles directly (e.g. angle problems involving bearings).

3.5. The remaining requirements

- **use the properties of faces, surfaces, edges and vertices of cubes, cuboids, prisms, cylinders, pyramids, cones and spheres to solve problems in 3D**
- **interpret mathematical relationships both algebraically and geometrically**

These two final requirements look very much like a collection of "remnants". Both seem to relate to rather late in Key Stage 3 or even to Key Stage 4.

Pythagoras' Theorem and similarity (or trig) feature in solving problems relating to regular polygons or familiar figures in 3D—whether calculating the lengths of ladders leaning against walls, or the height of some point above the ground or table, or surface areas and volumes. However, the examples listed seem better suited to Key Stage 4 than to Key Stage 3. Nevertheless one would love to see problems at some stage that involve finding and using the slant height of a cone, or the height of a pyramid, or the distance between two opposite corners of a cube, or the angles between lines in 3D figures, or the angle between a slanting face and the base of a pyramid.

The final requirement is admirable as a general idea. But it is also rather too vague for us to try to interpret it reliably here.

4. Probability and Statistics

The requirements under these headings leave many questions unanswered. It is not always clear how to interpret them as they stand, so we have tried to suggest "alternative readings". We have also taken the opportunity to discuss some of the background which needs to be borne in mind when devising a scheme of work.

4.1. Probability

4.1.1 Introduction

> **– record, describe and analyse the frequency of outcomes of simple probability experiments involving randomness, fairness, equally and unequally likely outcomes, using appropriate language and the 0–1 probability scale**

Our understanding of how to teach probability is less well developed than our understanding of how to teach geometry. So it is difficult to know exactly where the problems lie. But there would seem to be considerable potential for confusion here between

> the language of messy "experiments" in the real world,

and

> language that belongs to a pristine mathematical universe (namely *probability*).

This confusion is especially awkward given the explicit mention of "using appropriate language".

Of course the mathematical universe often has its roots in the real world, so terms and expressions may at times inhabit both worlds. Nevertheless it may be easier to interpret the above official requirement if one imagines added quotation marks (and the extra word "eventually") roughly as follows:

- record, describe and analyse the frequency of outcomes of simple "probability experiments" involving "randomness", "fairness", "equally and unequally likely outcomes", using appropriate language and [eventually] the 0–1 probability scale.

"Record, describe and analyse the frequency of outcomes of simple [...] experiments" is an excellent requirement: pupils need such experience in order to develop their ideas of variability, and to understand how these are ultimately captured by the universal model of a sample space (S, p), where p assigns values between 0 and 1 to subsets of S according to certain rules (e.g. for a single toss of a fair coin, $S = \{H, T\}$, with $p(H) = p(T) = \frac{1}{2}$). However, this step lies some way off—though it is alluded to vaguely in the next batch of requirements, where we read (see Section 4.1.2):

> "generate theoretical sample spaces for simple and combined events with equally likely, mutually exclusive outcomes".

The idea also features in the GCSE *Subject Criteria* using curious, non-standard language

> "construct theoretical *possibility* spaces for single and combined experiments with equally likely outcomes" [emphasis added].

In contrast, there is no hint of "sample spaces" in the Key Stage 4 programme of study.

However, given the explicit mention of "theoretical sample spaces" in the next official requirement (see Section 4.1.2), we assume that the "experiments" referred to in the first Key Stage 3 requirement are intended to open up *informal* consideration of questions involving "fairness", "randomness", and the crucial idea of "equally likely". And if these informal considerations are to lead (eventually!) to the idea of a sample space (S, p), we may need a shift of focus from arbitrary real-world experiments to more carefully chosen settings (such as coin tossing, or dice rolling, or equally divided spinners), where a theoretical analysis is possible.

Hence, if pupils' understanding of probability is to progress, we may need to distinguish three separate settings:

> experiments in the *real world* of messy data;
>
> experiments and analysis in the *in-between world* of controlled data (fair coins, dice, etc.);

and

> the *mathematical* world of theoretical probability.

We may choose to start in the real world of messy data: for example, with pupils examining the apparent likelihood of being born on each day of the week. The obvious "sample", or experiment, (namely, collecting all the results for pupils in the class) leads first to the need for them to use their known birthday and age to discover the day of the week when they were born; the class can then record numbers for each day of the week; and finally one can introduce the idea of using "relative frequencies" as a better measure than the raw numbers. The resulting distribution will inevitably raise the question of "fair sampling" and "randomness" (for it is almost bound to contradict pupils' gut feeling by deviating from the expectation that each day should be "equally likely"). More representative data—if it can be procured—is just as likely to challenge this understandable assumption.

The use of "relative frequencies" introduces the idea of a 0–1 scale (though not at this stage a "*probability* scale"). And one can emphasise the fact that the relative frequency of those born on a weekday (say) is obtained by adding the five separate relative frequencies for Monday-Friday.

But relative frequencies only tell us what **was** observed—**once**; and this would seem to tell us nothing about what *will* be observed *in the future*. This is the whole point of non-deterministic data. We may know that the recorded relative frequencies add up to 1; and that the relative frequency of a combined event is equal to the sum of the ingredient relative frequencies. But this only tells us *what happened last time*. We cannot calculate with observed relative frequencies to learn anything more general—as one can to some extent with probabilities. So it should soon become clear that this is not a mathematical world, where one can answer more interesting questions using exact calculation.

Classical science is deterministic, and reported results in classical science must be replicable: if you or I repeat a deterministic experiment as it was reported, we expect to replicate the stated results. And if we fail, then we have to question either the reported result or our own attempted replication. But with stochastic processes, the situation is completely different. When we repeat a "probability experiment", the observed outcomes vary considerably. Yet within the observed variations one can discern certain clear *trends*. This new science is no longer to be judged by, or analysed through, the outcomes of a single experiment, but through patterns in the variation of the outcomes of repetitions of the experiment. Single snapshots are of little relevance; instead we try to summarise the background reality that lies behind what we observe by integrating *all possible snapshots* into a single model of "probabilistic reality".

4.1.2 Theoretical probability

- **understand that the probabilities of all possible outcomes sum to 1**
- **enumerate sets and unions/intersections of sets systematically, using tables, grids and Venn diagrams**
- **generate theoretical sample spaces for single and combined events with equally likely, mutually exclusive outcomes and use these to calculate theoretical probabilities**

So there are strong reasons to move beyond messy real-world "experiments", and to focus on a more restricted (or more artificial) *mathematical* universe—such as coin tossing or dice rolling—where everything is much more clearly defined. Here one can perform *repeated* experiments relatively easily. And one can also analyse the background situation precisely—by counting.

Even in this restricted world, there are elephant traps to be identified and avoided. For example, when tossing two coins, time is needed to clarify the expected ratios of the three possible outcomes—"two Heads", "two Tails", and "one Head and one Tail". But unlike the messy real world, it is now natural to imagine an idealised version where one thinks of a "fair coin", with Head and Tail truly "equally likely" (or a "fair die", where each of the six outcomes is "equally likely"). Experiments show that the observed "relative frequencies" of Heads and Tails (or of the six possible outcomes for rolling a die), vary significantly. But they always add to 1, and can always be combined to find the relative frequencies of compound events (such as "rolling an odd number").

More importantly, experimental results can now be compared with what one would "expect" on the basis of the idealised model. This background "expectation", based on counting within the idealised model, is quite different from "the recorded results of experiments". And whereas the results from successive experiments will vary, the "expected" results stay the same. It is as though the calculated expected results are some kind of "ideal summary", and each experiment is only an approximation to, or a flickering shadow of this ideal summary. For example, within the model we can *count exactly*: there are 2^4 possible sequences of 4 tosses of the coin, and exactly 4 of these sequences have just one "Tail"—which seems to say that, if we record 100 such sequences of 4 tosses, then we should "expect" $\frac{4}{16}$ of them to have just one "Tail". The reality will of course usually be different; but pupils may gradually come to realise that the existence of the idealised model provides a *fixed reference point* with which we can compare the results of different experiments, and provides the key to making sense of their variability (as "deviations from the expected ideal").

There are many advantages in working within these carefully chosen, controlled settings. In particular, they clarify the difference between observed "relative frequencies" from a single experiment and the expected frequencies, or "theoretical probabilities". The theoretical model also allows us to see more clearly how the cumulative results of many experiments tend to "average out", and how this long-term average tends to approximate the theoretical probability ever more closely.

An experiment, and the associated set of observed frequencies, is like a single snapshot *of a ghost*, or *a shadow* of some hidden object. This is especially true if the experiment involves messy real world data. The snapshot gives one a record of vague outlines—hints of something substantial. Yet one cannot be sure of the precise outline or shape which gave rise to this impression; that is, one may at first have no knowledge of the "background reality" that caused the impression or shadow. The observed results (of say "days of birth") may suggest a surprising pattern, but it is only a hint: the actual reality that lies behind the observations remains elusive. Subsequent snapshots of apparently the same object may vary greatly from each other—and yet between them reveal patterns that suggest that there really is some "background reality" that lurks out of sight.

This is a classic instance of Plato's parable of *The Cave*. We can only discern shadows of some presumed "Platonic reality" ("theoretical probability" in this instance), and must somehow *infer* what we can about the hidden reality that is casting the shadow, or leaving a ghostly impression. And the test for any inferred "reality" is whether it explains the shadows that we do see, and *why we do* **not** *see the shadows that we do* **not** *see*. If the observed shadows were always the same shape (as would be the case if the object were a solid statue, and the light source remained constant), then the "Platonic reality" might be a classical numerical measurement from elementary mathematics (like "the height of Nelson's column").

Probability and statistics are different, in that the observed "facts" differ each time we look. Yet there is still something substantial behind the observation. A single experiment, or sample, and the associated set of "observed relative frequencies", is but a single shadow of an elusive, moving object. And our inferred "Platonic reality" must somehow combine all *conceivable* observations into a single idea, which somehow incorporates the observed variability, and explains how each snapshot arises as a single view, or aspect of it. That is the role played here by the idea of a **sample space**: a set of atomic outcomes, with a *probability* assigned to each, so that their sum is 1.

Elementary mathematics can be largely summarised as *the art of exact calculation* with numbers, symbols, geometrical entities, etc. If we wish to find "the height of Nelson's column", though we do not know the answer, it is natural to *assume it has a definite value*, and then use the methods of elementary mathematics to calculate this presumed "definite value" using other known facts (e.g. properties of similar triangles). That is, the objects to which this "art of exact calculation" applies—whether represented by numerals or letters—are usually assumed to have *definite* values (possibly unknown). The associated mathematical universe may be abstract; but its objects have specific values, which remain constant throughout any subsequent calculation. Such entities are relatively tame, and static; they can be imagined relatively easily.

However, the numerical data related to probability and statistics is more elusive than this—though the fact that it is clearly still numerical (in some sense), may tempt us to overlook its more elusive character. Consider, for example,

> the number of "Heads" obtained in a sequence of 4 coin tosses.

Each particular "instance" (toss a coin 4 times and keep track of the number of "Heads") gives rise to a *single value*—namely, the number of "Heads" obtained. So this "number of Heads in 4 tosses" is superficially *like* "the height of Nelson's column". However, the object of thought is not the individual value that we obtained on this one occasion, but

> the *totality* of all possible "numbers of Heads" that could be obtained if we repeated the experiment,

together with

> the way these "numbers of Heads" are *distributed* between 0 and 4.

This object of thought is multi-layered: there is a **sample space** S (the set of integers between 0 and 4), with each member having an attached *number* (the relative frequency with which this number of "Heads" occurs). If we shift from repeated experiments and observed "relative frequencies", we can use the idealised model of a "fair coin" with

$$p(H) = p(T) = \frac{1}{2}$$

to calculate exactly the expected frequency for each number of "Heads". This "expected frequency" varies with the number (though 0 "Heads" turns out to be exactly as likely, or as unlikely, as 4 "Heads", and 1 "Head" turns out to be exactly as likely as 3 "Heads"). We therefore get a new probability P for this sample space S, where

$$P(0) = P(4) = \frac{1}{16}, \quad P(1) = P(3) = \frac{4}{16}, \quad P(2) = \frac{6}{16}.$$

The nature of variability, and the difference between

(i) deterministic systems (such as classical science, where one expects to be able to replicate an experiment and observe the same results), and

(ii) stochastic data

can be explored in the messy real world. But at this level, the analysis of stochastic data is largely restricted to discussion and qualitative statistics. So one needs to move the field of play to the in-between world of controlled data (fair coins, dice, etc.). Here one can still do experiments; but one can also analyse things in a way that offers a bridge to *theoretical probability*. One can construct a natural God-given model, and can compare its predictions with the results of experiments to see just how variable things can be. In particular, it makes didactical sense to choose in-between examples with *finitely many* atomic outcomes, and to focus on examples where symmetry guarantees that the atomic outcomes are *equally likely*. **Everything then reduces to counting.** And one can compare the relative frequencies that arise in experiments with the "God-given" relative frequencies derived from counting (which form the model for our idea of a "sample space and probability").

With luck it may now be a bit clearer why we questioned the informal mix of words "probability experiment", "randomness", "fairness", "equally and unequally likely outcomes", "0–1 probability scale" in Subsection 4.1.1 and suggested there was a danger they might blur the distinction between

(i) the world of observed real-world data, and

(ii) the hidden Platonic reality, or the theoretical model.

The requirement in Subsection 4.1.1 used language that ultimately belongs to our inferred Platonic model, and imposed it upon the world of shadows, or observed data. Pupils should definitely "record, describe, and analyse the frequency of outcomes from simple [...] experiments", whose results are "non-deterministic" in that the data vary from one experiment to the next; but these are not really *probability* experiments. Repeated coin tossing, or dice rolling, or drawing pin tossing force us to address the underlying issue of "variable outcomes" and to nurture ideas of probability. But they can only be described as "probability experiments" in retrospect—once we have the background notion of an underlying sample space S and a probability function p. The language used in this official requirement is the language that should emerge as a result of a carefully chosen sequence of such experiments and analysis: it should not really be used "up front". Hence its use is best interpreted as a summary of what is needed—used informally for ease of communication between parties who are already "in the know".

We end this rather heavy digression on a lighter note. During a test in which all the questions required only a true/false response, a pupil was observed to be repeatedly tossing a coin until he had answered every question. When asked what he was doing, he replied: "I have no idea of what is going on in this course. So I flip the coin; if it turns up Heads, I choose true and if it turns up Tails I choose false." The invigilator tried to keep a straight face, and moved on. Later, the invigilator announced: "You have five minutes remaining" and was surprised to see the pupil madly tossing a coin once more. Puzzled, he asked: "What exactly are you doing now?", only to be told: "I'm checking my answers!"

4.2. Statistics

No-one should doubt the increasing importance of statistics in the modern world. But it is less clear how this fact should influence the school curriculum—and in particular, the school *mathematics* curriculum. The world is awash with data. But the information available to decision makers in government, in business, in management, in operating public utilities, etc. only tells part of the story. They may collect "random samples" to try to eliminate bias, but the result is still an incomplete "snapshot". What can one infer about the true situation from such a snapshot? And how much confidence can one place in the resulting inference? If one takes a second sample from a different source, or at a different time, it is bound to differ from the first. But when are the differences such as to suggest that "something has really changed"? These are the kinds of questions addressed by statistics. It is one thing to suggest (rightly) that the mathematics curriculum must think carefully about how to prepare pupils so that they have a chance of making sense of the way statistics is used at Key Stage 5 and beyond; it is quite another thing to suggest that significant chunks of elementary mathematics should be sidelined, or de-emphasised, in order to make room at Key Stage 1–3 for possibly premature, low grade statistical content.

The situation we face should sound familiar. No one disputed the realisation in the 1950s and 1960s of the increasing importance of a kind of "modern mathematics" that was very different from school mathematics as then taught. However, the inference that school mathematics should be re-formed into something closer to the said "modern mathematics" proved to be thoroughly misguided—and it took us two decades before we finally admitted this fact. In much the same way, no-one doubted the claim that the 1970s and 1980s witnessed the beginning of a revolution in computational technology, that led to a marked shift in the way mathematics was being used in the outside world; yet the assertion that primary school mathematics "therefore" needed to be radically re-formed to incorporate calculators proved once again to be misguided. Claims were made at the highest level that pupils no longer needed to "learn their tables"; and it again took twenty years for us to discover that "learning one's tables" is important **not** so that we can compete with a calculator, but because it is part of the way young minds internalise an understanding of *the way numbers work*—and so is essential if we are to help pupils prepare to make use of the new technology **later**.

Hence, while welcoming the commitment and enthusiasm of those with a special interest in statistics, it is important not to repeat the same mistake of unquestioningly accepting the claims of those who may have allowed their enthusiasm to run away with them. We would all like the next generation to be well-placed to use statistics intelligently in adult life. But the experience of the last 25 years should convince us that this is not likely to be achieved by neglecting parts of elementary mathematics that are needed for the subsequent effective analysis of statistical methods in favour of low-level qualitative methods of little lasting value. In particular, the basic framework for statistics depends on having a firm grasp of theoretical probability.

Given the ubiquity of statistical data, some understanding of the associated problems deserves attention. But it remains unclear how this experience should be embedded within the wider curriculum, and how much of it, and which aspects, are best treated in the time allocated to *mathematics* (and at what stage). The dilemmas were clearly indicated in the analysis and recommendations of the Smith report *Making mathematics count* (2004)—see para 0.28, paras 4.16–4.18 and **Recommendation 4.4.**[21]

Curricula since 1988 have allocated significant amounts of classroom time to *Handling data* many years before pupils master the mathematics that is needed for statistical calculation. As a result, the content listed under *Handling data* has been largely restricted to *descriptive statistics*. Whilst there is some value in using common sense to extract simple information from statistical data in all subjects, and to use this to draw pupils' attention to misconceptions, we need to consider carefully how much of the necessary time should be taken from that allocated for *mathematics*. There is a balance to be struck between on the one hand alerting pupils to the challenge presented by statistical data, and on the other developing the mathematical tools that will subsequently allow pupils to engage in some more significant analysis of problems—including statistical problems. If the necessary tools are not mastered, pupils are likely to be reduced to applying cookbook procedures which they cannot possibly understand. Moreover, this contradicts the declared *Aims* of the curriculum, and the idea that one should insist on *meaning* and *understanding*. So we should perhaps look for ways of treating this material at a later stage when pupils can make sense of it using mathematics that they understand.

4.2.1

- **describe, interpret and compare observed distributions of a single variable through: appropriate graphical representation involving discrete, continuous and grouped data; and appropriate measures of central tendency (mean, mode, median) and spread (range, consideration of outliers)**

[21] http://www.mathsinquiry.org.uk/report/MathsInquiryFinalReport.pdf

> – **construct and interpret appropriate tables, charts, and diagrams, including frequency tables, bar charts, pie charts, and pictograms for categorical data, and vertical line (or bar) charts for ungrouped and grouped numerical data**

The listed requirements have acquired a fairly standard interpretation in current textbooks and assessments. Yet it is worth asking how well this standard interpretation *prepares* pupils to understand the more serious statistics that is used in many subjects *beyond Key Stage 4*.

Most of the elementary mathematics we have covered so far can be summarised *as the art of exact calculation* with numbers, symbols, geometrical entities, etc. Suppose we wish to find "the height of the school building", or "the height of Nelson's column". Though we do not know the answer, we assume it has a definite value. We then use the methods of elementary mathematics to calculate this value. That is, the objects to which this "art of exact calculation" applies (whether represented by numerals or by letters) can be assumed to have *definite* values, which remain constant throughout any calculation. Such entities are static, and can be imagined relatively easily.

However, stochastic, or statistical data—though still numerical—is not quite like this. Consider, for example, "the height of a UK adult male in 2014". Each particular instance of such data ("choose one adult UK male, then measure and record his height") gives rise to a *single value*—the height of that particular individual. So one might think that "the height of a UK adult male in 2014" is like "the height of Nelson's column". But the object of thought here is not the single value obtained by choosing and measuring the height of one adult male: we are interested in the *totality of individual heights*, and the way these individual heights are distributed throughout the whole population of "UK adult males in 2014". This object of thought has several 'layers':

- there is a **population** S (the set of UK adult males in 2014);
- each member has an attached *number* (his height);

- this attached number varies as one varies the choice of individual, and does so in such a way as to give rise to a *distribution* of possible values, where each "height" occurs with its own *frequency*, or **probability**.

Later, these multi-layered objects will be formalised as *random variables*, and captured via *distributions*. No matter how they may eventually be formalised, all we need to notice here is that they are clearly more elusive than the numbers studied elsewhere in elementary mathematics.

And this is just the easy part of the story. The harder part is that we rarely know the underlying *distribution* precisely. So we try to draw inferences about the underlying distribution on the basis of some more-or-less representative *random* **sample**! (The word "random" deserves a whole mini-essay of its own; but it indicates that the sampling is done in a way that avoids giving a systematically false impression of the population being sampled.) Or we may want to decide whether the apparent differences between two different random samples can be explained by "natural variation", or whether the differences suggest that something significant has changed.

The specific (possibly unknown, but fixed) numbers of more familiar elementary mathematics have here been replaced by *distributions*, where a range of possible values can occur—each with its own frequency. The background *distribution* may be unknown—and instead all we know is information from one or more *samples*. And the goal is to decide what one can infer about the (unknown) background *distribution*, or whether the differences between two different samples are significant. This is an important art. But it is very different from (and conceptually much more demanding than) the mathematics of numbers, measures, symbols, or functions that is studied elsewhere in Key Stages 1–3.

4.2.2

> **– describe simple mathematical relationships between two variables (bivariate data) in observational and experimental contexts and illustrate using scatter graphs**

Any tabulation, or graphical representation, involves two variables! In Section 4.2.1 there was an initial imagined "single variable", whose *frequency* of occurrence was being recorded. So one was dealing with two linked variables: the original variable, and the counting numbers. But in some sense the counting numbers did not have an independent interest. In Section 4.2.2 we are concerned with two independently existing variables which may be related (such as height and weight among adult males), and where we wish to understand the possible linkage better.

An obvious trick is to plot linked pairs (x, y), with one variable along the x-axis, and the other variable along the y-axis. The resulting collection of points in 2D is called a *scatter graph*. This is not the graph of a function, since

(a) not all possible x-values occur, and

(b) those x-values that do occur may occur more than once (with different y-values).

The idea that there might be a "connection" between the two variables then translates into the idea that the scatter graph may reveal some structure.

The simplest imaginable structure would be for the plotted points to lie along some straight line, or to reflect some other functional dependency of one variable upon the other. A non-statistical example might plot the temperature in "degrees Fahrenheit" against the temperature in "degrees Centigrade": here because the relationship is deterministic and exact, the data sits along a perfect straight line $y = \frac{9}{5}x + 32$. But statistical data is never quite so well-behaved.

When trying to spot a hidden relationship with messy data it can help to impose an additional **constraint**. For example, we may consider whether there is some special point that should be forced to lie on any possible curve which links the two variables x and y. The data points themselves are all as reliable, or as unreliable, as each other. But examples can be used to support the idea that the point $(\text{Av}(x), \text{Av}(y))$, where $\text{Av}(x)$ is the average of all the x-values, $\text{Av}(y)$ is the average of all the y-values, serves as a kind of "representative centre" for the set of data points, and so should lie on any resulting curve. In particular, if we decide that the relationship is approximately linear, then requiring the line to pass through the point $(\mathrm{Av}(x), \mathrm{Av}(y))$ makes it much easier to choose the gradient "by eye" so that we get a line that seems to follow the data approximately, and which leaves deviant data points (x, y) in some sense "equally distributed" above and below the line. The whole thrust of this analysis is to try to see patterns in the data that might not be apparent from a mere list of numbers. However, the analysis remains at best weakly "mathematical": we are not yet sufficiently well-placed to engage in genuine calculations.

In the relatively tame world of elementary mathematics we have already highlighted the difference between *direct* calculation, where the answer can be ground out deterministically, and *inverse problems*, whose solution forces us to "work backwards" from some "output" in search of some direct calculation that might give rise to the given data (see Part II, Section 1.2.3, and Part III, Sections 1.2.2, 1.2.4). The art of analysing statistical data mathematically would seem to be an important instance—and a rather subtle instance—of such *inverse problems*. This art is therefore doubly challenging. Not only are the objects of the relevant *direct* statistical calculations more subtle than those we meet in the rest of elementary mathematics; but *handling data* is useful precisely because statistical problems are *inverse* problems—we typically know only selected information (from some presumed *random sample*), and we need to assess what we may infer from this *sampled* data about the unknown background *distribution* of the whole *population*—and what degree of confidence we may attach to such inferences.

Despite the difficulties, this material plays such an important role in modern society that it is natural for educators to try to find ways of introducing pupils to the underlying ideas. It is not easy to summarise the experience of the last 25 years; but it is probably fair to say that the rhetoric has been consistently ahead of the reality. Thus there are many outstanding issues which a programme of study, or a scheme of work, needs to weigh up and resolve. Three important questions concern

- the age, or prerequisite maturity, that is required before simple mathematical analysis of statistical material can be handled effectively;
- the technical prerequisites that pupils need to master before this analysis can make worthwhile progress;

- the time that is needed to make the engagement with statistical questions worthwhile at a given stage, the likely progress that might be made at that stage, and (crucially) *what other topics would have to be sidelined* in order to make that time available.

4

Curriculum Development

What follows stems from an attempt to consider what a "humane mathematician and educator" might expect to see included at each Key Stage of a National Curriculum—under the assumption that:

- one would like to see number, measures and calculation grasped (in some sense) at primary level, with
- further work on number, together with algebra, geometry, and trigonometry being mastered by age 16 to a level that would allow those who proceed to further studies, in whatever subjects, to be in a position to use the mathematics they have learned.

In particular, the sample curriculum tries to set realistic (rather than ambitious) goals for primary mathematics. It also tries to restrict the extent of abstraction at Key Stage 3, on the assumption that for a significant group of pupils this material may form the core of work at secondary level (age 11–16), along with consolidation of material from upper primary school. More abstract material has been delayed wherever possible until Key Stage 4, where it serves as a transition from elementary mathematics to higher mathematics for all pupils who intend to proceed to further academic studies beyond age 16 (in any subject). Hence teachers may choose to blur the boundary between Key Stages 3 and 4 for many pupils, taking much longer to cover the listed Key Stage 3 material for some, while others may treat Key Stage 3 material more abstractly than is suggested here in preparation for Key Stage 4.

Having produced a *Brief Version* (which was already fairly detailed—see Section 2 below), we then drafted two further versions:

- a *Fuller Version,* which unpacked in greater detail some of the cryptic references we were advised might not be immediately understood; and
- a *Very Brief Version* (see Section 1 below) which rashly tried to compress the essence of each Key Stage into a single page.

We have chosen to reproduce here (and to improve) the *Brief Version* and the *Very Brief Version,* to provide an easily accessible reference for the reader of Parts I, II, and III. Some words that appear in **bold type** have a technical meaning that will have been explained in detail in Part II or Part III. If some aspect remains unclear, we recommend that readers refer to the *Fuller Version,* which is freely available at The De Morgan Forum.[22]

1. Very Brief version

1.1 Key Stage 1

By the end of Year 2 pupils:

Counting, reading and recording number

- use the language for numbers and quantities in everyday settings
- count accurately; read, write and order numbers to at least 100; understand place value, know what each digit of any two-digit number represents, and know that the position of a digit determines its "value"

Recalling facts

- have instant recall of addition and subtraction facts for numbers to 10; have instant recall of ×2, ×5, ×10 multiplication tables, and derive corresponding division facts

[22] http://education.lms.ac.uk/wp-content/uploads/2012/02/KS_1-4_DMJ.pdf

Calculating

- use the language for simple calculations in everyday settings
- carry out mental and informal written calculations using the four operations of addition, subtraction, multiplication and division
- recognise and use effectively the fact that subtraction is the inverse of addition, and in simple cases that division is the inverse of multiplication
- handle confidently two-digit addition and subtraction in **standard written column format**

Describing shapes and measuring

- recognise, name, and describe properties of common 2D and 3D shapes
- measure and draw straight lines accurate to the nearest centimetre; estimate lengths and other quantities; tell the time to the nearest quarter of an hour, compare durations using standard units, and order events chronologically; use measuring instruments to measure length (cm, m), weight (kg), capacity (l), reading and interpreting scales to the nearest labelled division; use money

Solving problems, reasoning, and using language and symbols

- apply their understanding of number and arithmetic to work with measures and to solve **word problems**
- use mathematical language accurately; read and interpret text, diagrams, and symbols when solving problems; record their results clearly; explain their methods and reasoning

1.2 Key Stage 2

By the end of Year 6 pupils:

Place value

- handle place value to represent and order numbers to 10 000 and beyond; extend this to negative integers and decimals; work with decimals and measures involving tenths, hundredths and thousandths; multiply and divide integers and decimals by 10, 100, 1000

- round integers, decimals and measures to the nearest "ten", integer, or tenth

Recalling facts; correct use of language and symbols

- recall instantly addition and subtraction facts for numbers to 20; "know by heart" multiplication tables to 10×10 and corresponding division facts; factorise any two-digit integer; recognise primes and squares
- use mathematical language and notation correctly; understand that some statements are **exact** and can be clearly demonstrated

Structural arithmetic

- add and subtract positive and negative integers; multiply and divide positive integers; use place value and the structure of arithmetic to **simplify** calculations
- work flexibly with fractions and percentages; switch freely between equivalent fractions; add and subtract simple fractions
- understand the order of operations and the use of brackets

Calculating

- add and subtract any two two-digit integers mentally, and three-and four-digit integers using **standard written column format**
- multiply and divide mentally a two-digit integer by any one-digit integer; complete written short multiplication and division of three-digit and four-digit integers by numbers up to 12, and long multiplication of three-digit by two-digit integers

Geometry and measures

- copy simple figures; work with common 2D and 3D shapes; find unknown angles in simple figures; plot points with given coordinates
- measure and draw line segments accurate to the nearest millimetre and angles to the nearest degree; calculate reliably with standard measures; find the areas of rectangles and shapes made from rectangles, and the volumes of cuboids and shapes made from cuboids

- use and calculate with money; tell the time to the nearest minute; read scales—interpolating between marks; convert between related units

Solving problems

- tackle and solve **word problems** and simple **multi-step** problems involving numbers, measures, and shapes; make sensible estimates; make **connections** between topics; explain their reasoning

1.3 Key Stage 3

Key Stage 3 revisits important Key Stage 2 material—partly for revision, but mainly to reinterpret old material from a new "viewpoint" (extending the written algorithms to decimals, shifting the focus from bare hands mental methods to structural arithmetic and the simplification of expressions, etc.). By the end of Year 9 pupils:

Place value

- handle **place value** to represent and order integers and decimals with up to six digits; multiply and divide by 10, 100, 1000
- work with decimals and measures involving up to four decimal places; write terminating decimals as fractions and vice versa, and know that some fractions have decimals that recur
- round numbers and measures freely and flexibly

Calculating

- use multiplication tables freely to multiply and divide mentally in context;
- compute with integers and decimals using **standard column format**
- compare and compute with fractions; work flexibly with fractions, **ratios**, percentages

Structural arithmetic

- use **place value**, factorisation, and the algebraic structure of arithmetic to **simplify** and to evaluate numerical expressions and calculations—including with fractions and negatives

- test for divisibility by 2, 3, 4, 5, 10; find HCFs and LCMs; factorise integers as a product of primes; recognise squares and cubes; find or estimate square roots
- represent numbers as powers—including simple fractional powers; work with powers of 10
- use the algebraic equivalence of expressions to **simplify** calculations

Simplification of algebraic expressions; solving linear equations

- use unknowns and variables in context (formulae); substitute values in expressions; use algebraic rules to **simplify** expressions and calculations—collect like terms, expand and factorise simple expressions; work with simple sequences
- set up and solve a single linear equation in one unknown in complete generality; use the rules of algebra to "change the subject of", or to rearrange, equations and formulae; solve two simultaneous linear equations; solve linear inequalities in one unknown

Geometry and measures

- measure and draw accurately; read scales; change units; understand and use basic formulae; find lengths, areas, and volumes for common 2D or 3D shapes—including triangles, parallelograms, circles, cuboids, and prisms; calculate reliably with standard measures
- plot points in all four quadrants; find the midpoint of a line segment, and the distance between two given points; understand and work with linear equations and straight line graphs; interpret gradient as a **ratio** or rate; use trig ratios in right-angled triangles
- use basic **ruler and compass constructions**, parallels, angles in a triangle, **angle-chasing**, congruence; establish a preliminary basis for 2D **Euclidean geometry**; prove and use *Pythagoras' Theorem*

Solving problems

- tackle and solve **word problems** and simple **multi-step** and **inverse** problems involving numbers, measures, symbols and shapes

- use the **unitary method** to solve **proportion** problems involving rates and **ratios**
- make sensible **estimates**
- make **connections** between topics; explain their reasoning

1.4 Key Stage 4

Key stage 4 revisits important Key Stage 3 material—partly as revision, but also to interpret it afresh. For some pupils, this re-working and strengthening of Key Stage 3 material (together with consolidation of Key Stage 2 material) will be their main goal at Key Stage 4; other pupils may supplement revision of Key Stage 3 material with a programme that covers selected parts of what is summarised here. Those who expect to continue to further academic studies beyond Key Stage 4 should aim to cover everything summarised here.

By the end of Year 11 pupils who complete the Key Stage 1–4 programme:

Number and measures

- handle (positive and negative) large numbers and decimals, with and without units, possibly expressed using powers or standard form
- move freely between fractions and decimals
- use rounding and **exact** arithmetic to work with **approximations**
- calculate **probabilities** in standard models; analyse sampled data

Calculating and simplifying

- compute with fractions; work flexibly with fractions, **ratios**, percentages
- solve problems involving **proportion** (including **the unitary method**)
- use algebraic structure and multiplication facts to simplify numerical expressions—including those involving fractions and powers
- calculate with surds and mixed surd expressions (without evaluating)

Algebra (expressions, formulae, equations, identities) and graphs

- use algebraic equivalence (including the index laws) to **simplify** expressions
- know, use, and rearrange standard formulae
- work in all four quadrants; work with equations of straight lines in 2D
- solve any linear equation or inequality in one unknown; solve any pair of simultaneous linear equations or inequalities in two unknowns; interpret the solutions graphically
- know and use standard quadratic identities; solve any quadratic equation or inequality; solve easy simultaneous equations—one linear and one quadratic; interpret solutions graphically
- understand linear and quadratic expressions in one variable as functions; sketch and analyse linear and quadratic graphs

Geometry

- use *Pythagoras' Theorem* to solve problems in 2D and 3D; find lengths, surface areas, and volumes for common 2D and 3D shapes—including regular polygons
- use basic trigonometry and the Sine and Cosine rules to "solve triangles"
- understand and use basic **ruler and compass constructions**
- understand how congruence, parallels, and similarity provide a basis for **Euclidean geometry**; use these to derive results and to solve problems
- understand, prove, and use the basic properties of circles
- understand how scaling affects angles, lengths, areas, and volumes analyse standard 2D and 3D figures—including prisms, pyramids, cylinders, cones, spheres

Solving problems

- solve **word problems** and simple **multi-step** and **inverse** problems

- make **connections** between topics; write well-presented **proofs**; explain their reasoning
- calculate with standard and compound measures; work with "rates"

2. Brief version

2.1 Key Stage 1

Breadth of study

1. During the Key Stage pupils should be taught the required *Knowledge, Skills, and Understanding* through:

(a) practical activity, exploration and discussion

(b) linking the language of mathematics with spoken and written English

(c) **learning key facts by heart**; learning to store tens and units temporarily in the mind (including as intermediate outputs in a longer calculation) to support the development of mental calculation strategies

(d) using mathematical ideas in practical activities, then recording these ideas using objects, pictures, diagrams, tables, words, and numbers

(e) developing rich mental calculation strategies, and **standard written procedures** for addition and subtraction

(f) drawing, measuring and estimating in a range of practical contexts

Knowledge, Skills, and Understanding

Teaching should ensure that appropriate connections are made between the section *Number and measures* and the section *Shape, space, and measures.*

Ma1 Number and measures

1. ***Using and applying "Number and measures"***

Pupils should:

Solving problems

(a) explore, interpret, develop flexible approaches to, and persist with problems involving number and measures in a variety of forms

Communicating

(a) use correct language, symbols, and vocabulary associated with number and measures

(b) explain and record methods and results in spoken, pictorial, and written form

Reasoning

(a) present results in an organised way; sort and classify numbers according to given criteria

(b) understand that some statements are **exact** and can be clearly demonstrated

2. ***Numbers and the number system***

Pupils should: **Counting**

(a) count reliably at first up to 20 objects, later extending counting to 100 and beyond (to 120 say), remaining secure across "tens boundaries" [e.g. from 19 to 20, or from 99 to 100]; recognise the invariance of quantity

(b) estimate a number of objects that can be checked by counting; round two digit numbers to the nearest 10

The base 10 number system

(a) understand the groupings into units and 10s (and later into 100s) that underpin **place value**; know what each digit represents (including 0 as a number, and as a placeholder), and how the "value" represented by each digit is determined by its position

(b) read and write two-digit and three-digit numbers in figures and words

(c) order two-digit numbers and position them on a number line; use =, <, and > and the associated language

Number patterns and sequences

(a) create, describe, and explore basic number patterns and sequences—including odd and even numbers, multiples of 2, multiples of 5, and multiples of 10

3. *Calculation*

Pupils should:

Number operations and the relationship between them

(a) understand addition and use related vocabulary and notation; understand subtraction (as "take away" and as "difference") and use the related vocabulary and notation; recognise that subtraction is the inverse of addition

(b) identify and use the calculations needed to solve simple **word problems** and **inverse** problems [e.g. oral "I'm thinking of a number" problems]

(c) understand simple instances of multiplication as repeated addition, and division as "grouping", and as "sharing"; use the vocabulary and notation associated with multiplication and division; find one half, or one quarter of a familiar shape, or of a small set of objects

Mental, informal, and standard written methods

(a) develop instant recall of number facts; know addition and subtraction facts with totals less than 10, and use these to derive other facts; learn addition facts with totals up to 20

(b) know ×2, ×5, and ×10 multiplication tables, and derive the corresponding division facts; know the doubles of numbers to 20 and the corresponding halves

(c) use practical and informal written methods to add and subtract two-digit numbers

(d) develop mental methods which flexibly use known facts to calculate the answer to less familiar "sums" [e.g. working out 4×6 by doubling 2×6, or by doubling 4×3]; add 10 to any single digit number, then add and subtract a multiple of 10 to or from a two-digit number

(e) make sense of number sentences involving all four operations

(f) lay out and complete simple two-digit additions and subtractions in **standard column format**

(g) use practical and informal written methods and related vocabulary to support multiplication and division, including calculations with remainder

4. ***Solving numerical problems***

Pupils should:

(a) choose sensible calculation methods to solve simple **word problems** involving whole numbers—including problems involving money or measures, drawing on their understanding of arithmetical operations

5. ***Processing, representing, and interpreting data***

Pupils should:

(a) solve suitable problems using simple lists, tables, and charts to sort, classify, and organise information; discuss the methods they use and explain what they find

Ma2: Shape, space, and measures

1. ***Using and applying "Shape, space, and measures"***

Pupils should:

Solving problems

(a) follow instructions to construct simple 2D and 3D objects; represent 3D objects via 2D drawings

Communicating

(a) use correct language and vocabulary for shape, space, and measures

(b) measure objects using ad hoc informal as well as standard measures; record measurements in ordered tables

Reasoning

(a) recognise simple spatial patterns and relationships; sort and classify shapes according to given criteria

2. *Understanding properties of shapes, position, and movement*

Pupils should:

(a) describe relationships using the language "larger – smaller", "higher – lower", "longer – shorter", "above – below", "left of – right of"

(b) draw and describe properties of 2D and 3D shapes; recognise, name, and sort common 2D and 3D shapes—including triangles, rectangles (including squares), circles, cubes, cuboids, hexagons, pentagons, cylinders, pyramids, cones, and spheres

(c) recognise right angles; understand whole turns, and quarter- and half-turns (clockwise and anticlockwise)

3. *Understanding measures*

Pupils should:

(a) use direct comparison to order objects by size, using appropriate language; put familiar events in chronological order

(b) measure and draw straight lines accurate to the nearest centimetre

(c) estimate, compare, and measure lengths, weights, and capacities; choose and use standard units (m, cm, kg, litre); compare durations (using seconds, minutes, hours, days); read and interpret numbers on scales to the nearest labelled division, interpreting the divisions between them; identify time intervals, including those that cross the hour

2.2 Key stage 2

Breadth of Study

1. During the Key Stage pupils should be taught the required *Knowledge, Skills, and Understanding* through:

(a) extending **place value** to larger integers and to simple decimals

(b) extending their understanding of the number system to include integers, fractions, and decimals

(c) **learning key facts by heart**; learning to store hundreds, tens and units temporarily in the mind (including as intermediate outputs in a longer calculation) to support the development of mental calculation strategies

(d) extending **exact** arithmetic to the **standard written algorithms** for integers and simple decimals

(e) using **structural arithmetic** to calculate efficiently and to develop (pre-)algebraic thinking

(f) drawing and measuring; using **exact** arithmetic to make good **estimates** when solving problems; recording results using words, pictures, numbers, diagrams, and tables (and symbols where appropriate)

(g) linking the language of mathematics with spoken and written English using carefully crafted problems; solving **word problems**; establishing **connections** between number work, measures, geometry, and practical tasks; distinguishing between sensible and misleading uses of mathematics

Knowledge, Skills, and Understanding

Teaching should ensure that appropriate connections are made between the section *Number and measures* and the section *Geometry and measures.*

Ma1 Number and measures

1. ***Using and applying "Number and measures"***

Pupils should:

Solving problems

(a) extract numerical, geometrical, and logical information from simple problems expressed in words

(b) make **connections**; use integers, decimals, and fractions (and arithmetic) when solving problems involving measures, and in other settings

(c) solve **multi-step**, and simple **inverse** problems

(d) solve problems involving tables, lists, and information presented pictorially;

(e) use knowledge of **exact** arithmetic to make good mental **estimates**

Communicating

(a) use notation, terminology, symbols, and language correctly

(b) present results and solutions to problems clearly; explain reasoning, methods, and conclusions

(c) interpret tables, lists, and charts; construct and interpret frequency tables

Reasoning

(a) present results in an organised way; sort and classify numbers and shapes according to given criteria

(b) investigate apparent patterns; understand that some statements are **exact** and can be clearly explained

2. ***Numbers and the number system***

Pupils should:

Counting

(a) count reliably beyond 100, passing smoothly from any given set of "90s" onto the next hundred

(b) count on and back in steps of constant size, starting from any integer, extending to negative integers

The base 10 number system

(a) use **place value** in representing numbers first up to 1000, then up to 10 000 and beyond; extend to decimals with up to three decimal places

Number patterns and sequences

(a) recognise two- and three-digit multiples of 2, 5 and 10; find the factors of a given integer, and the common factors of two given integers; find the HCF and the LCM of two given integers; recognise prime numbers to 50, and square numbers to 10×10; find factor pairs and all the factors of any two-digit integer; double or halve any two-digit integer

Integers

(a) read, write (in figures and words), and order whole numbers to 10 000

(b) multiply, and divide, any integer by 10 or 100, and then by 1000; round integers to the nearest 10 or 100, and then 1000

(c) understand and use negative integers; order a given set of positive and negative integers

Integers and decimals

(a) use decimal notation for tenths, hundredths, and thousandths; order a set of numbers or measurements

(b) compare and order integers and decimals in different contexts; locate integers (positive and negative), fractions, and decimals on the number line; use correctly the symbols $=, \neq, <, \leqslant, >, \geqslant$

(c) multiply and divide, any integer or decimal by 10 or 100; round integers and decimals to the nearest integer, to the nearest ten, and to the nearest tenth

Fractions, percentages and ratio

(a) understand fractions; locate fractions on a number line; find fractional parts of shapes or quantities

(b) understand equivalent fractions; **simplify** by cancelling common factors

(c) order simple fractions

(d) understand percentage; use simple percentages for comparison; find fractions and percentages of whole number quantities, and express part of a given whole as a percentage; express one whole number quantity as a fraction of another

(e) divide a given quantity into two parts in a given **ratio** (both part-to-part and part-to-whole); compare quantities in a given (external) ratio; solve simple problems involving ratios

3. ***Calculation***

Pupils should:

Number operations and the relationship between them

(a) develop their understanding of the four number operations—including inverses, and operations with zero

(b) find remainders after division; express a quotient as a fraction or decimal; relate $\frac{p}{q}$ to $p \div q$

(c) know and use the conventions for the order of operations; understand and use **structural arithmetic** to **simplify** calculations; write numerical expressions involving brackets; group related terms in a sum and related factors in a product to simplify, and hence evaluate, numerical expressions

Mental methods

(a) achieve instant recall of all addition and subtraction facts for integers up to 20

(b) add or subtract any pair of two-digit integers; handle suitable three-digit and four-digit additions and subtractions presented in written form

(c) add and subtract positive and negative integers mentally

(d) achieve instant recall of (i.e. **know by heart**) multiplication tables to 10×10 and use them to derive division facts

(e) multiply and divide in the range 1 to 100, then for larger numbers

(f) derive multiplication and division facts involving decimals

(g) relate fractions to multiplication and division; work with simple quotients as fractions and as decimals; switch freely between equivalent fractions; add and subtract simple fractions by reducing to a common denominator

Written methods

(a) use the **standard written method** in column format to add and subtract three-digit positive integers, then four-digit positive integers; add and subtract numbers involving decimals

(b) use the *standard written method* in column format for short multiplication (of two- and three-digit integers by a single digit multiplier), then long multiplication of two-digit and three-digit integers by two-digit multipliers; extend to simple decimal multiplication

(c) use short division of two-digit and three-digit integers by numbers up to 12

(d) use **approximations** and other strategies to check that answers are reasonable

Measures

(a) calculate reliably with standard measures, money, and time; convert measures from one unit to a related unit

(b) relate distance, time, and speed in uniform rectilinear motion; work with other simple rates and compound measures

4. ***Solving numerical problems***

Pupils should:

(a) use the four number operations to solve **word problems** involving numbers, or money, or measures of length and area, mass, capacity, or time

(b) solve **multi-step** and **inverse** problems with confidence

(c) check that their results are reasonable; explain why their answers are correct

5. ***Processing, representing, and interpreting data***

Pupils should:

(a) solve suitable problems using simple lists, tables, and charts to sort, classify, and organise information, discuss the methods they use, interpret their results, and explain what they find

(b) explore the notions of "centre" and "spread" for numerical data sets

Ma2: Geometry and measures

1. ***Using and applying "Geometry and measures"***

Pupils should:

Solving problems

(a) recognise standard geometrical figures; use their properties to select and perform appropriate calculations; measure and draw accurately to construct 2D and 3D figures

(b) use standard units of measurement and simple compound measures; convert reliably between related units

Communicating

(a) use geometrical notation, terminology, and symbols correctly; interpret solutions to problems involving geometrical figures and measures; organise work and record findings clearly

Reasoning

(a) analyse standard 2D and 3D figures; calculate efficiently and make simple deductions with angles, lengths, areas, volumes, time, and other measures

2. ***Understanding properties of shape***

Pupils should:

(a) recognise right angles, perpendicular and parallel lines; know that angles at a point total 360°, that angles at a point on a straight line total 180°, and that angles in a triangle total 180°

(b) describe relationships using the language "larger – smaller", "higher – lower", "longer – shorter", "above – below", "left of – right of", "top – bottom", "in front of – behind", "closer – further away", "between"

(c) talk clearly about common 2D and 3D shapes; visualise 3D shapes from 2D drawings

(d) make and draw shapes with increasing accuracy, and analyse their geometrical properties

3. ***Understanding properties of position and movement***

Pupils should:

(a) read and plot coordinates—eventually in all four quadrants; draw, or locate, shapes with given properties in the coordinate plane

(b) visualise, predict, and represent the position of a shape following a rotation, reflection, translation, or glide reflection

4. ***Understanding measures***

Pupils should:

(a) draw and measure lines to the nearest millimetre; combine linear measurements to measure perimeters

(b) draw and measure acute and obtuse angles of a given size to the nearest degree; estimate the size of given angles and order them; draw angles reliably as parts of compound shapes

(c) read the time to the nearest minute; calculate time intervals from clocks, from timetables, and from calendars

(d) use standard units of length, area, volume, mass, and capacity; measure and weigh items; convert between related units

(e) find areas of rectangles and of shapes composed of rectangles

(f) measure and compare capacities; understand conservation of volume; find volumes of cuboids and of simple shapes composed of cuboids

(g) read scales with increasing accuracy; record measurements using decimal notation

2.3 Key stage 3

Breadth of Study

1. During the Key Stage pupils should be taught the required *Knowledge, Skills, and Understanding* through:

(a) extending **place value** to arbitrary integers and decimals

(b) extending their understanding of numbers to include integers (positive and negative), fractions, and decimals

(c) extending **exact** arithmetic to the **standard written algorithms** for integers and decimals, and the standard procedures for calculating with fractions

(d) using **structural arithmetic** for efficient numerical calculation, and for algebraic **simplification** of numerical, fractional, and symbolic expressions

(e) representing unknowns and variables by letters; using formulae; solving linear equations; representing and interpreting straight lines and linear equations

(f) engaging in tasks that develop short chains of deductive reasoning and that bring out the centrality of **proof** in number, algebra, and geometry

(g) drawing and measuring; using **ruler and compass constructions**; calculating areas and volumes; recording results using diagrams, words, numbers, and symbols; **angle-chasing** and analysing more complex figures in terms of triangles

(h) linking the language of mathematics with spoken and written English; building simple logical expressions such as "... and ...", "... or ...", "if ..., then ...", "not only ..., but also ..."; interpreting carefully crafted "realistic" problems; solving **word problems**; distinguishing between sensible and misleading uses of mathematics

(i) routinely tackling familiar and unfamiliar problems, including **multi-step** and **inverse** problems; recognising that mathematical operations often come in 'direct-inverse' pairs, and that the inverse operation depends on robust fluency in the direct operation

(j) practical work in which they draw inferences from a mathematical analysis of data, and consider how statistics can be used to inform decisions

Knowledge, Skills, and Understanding

Teaching should ensure that appropriate connections are made between the section on *Number and algebra* and the section on *Geometry and measures.*

Ma1 Number and algebra

1. *Using and applying "Number and algebra"*

Pupils should:

Solving problems

(a) use numerical, geometrical, and logical information in analysing data and in solving simple problems

(b) make connections; use the arithmetic of integers, decimals, and fractions when solving problems

(c) regularly solve **multi-step** problems and **inverse** problems

(d) solve problems involving measures, rates and compound measures, ratio and proportion; make and justify **estimates**

Communicating

(a) use spoken and written language, notation, diagrams, terminology, and symbols correctly

(b) recognise when information is presented in a misleading way

(c) present results and solutions to problems clearly, declare unknowns explicitly, and lay out solutions logically **line-by-line**

(d) interpret tables, lists, and information presented graphically; construct and interpret frequency tables; use precise measures of "centre" and "spread"

Reasoning

(a) understand that some statements can be clearly **proved**, and that other statements can be shown to be false

(b) use **place value** and **structural arithmetic** to **simplify** calculations and expressions; recognise and use the fact that mathematical operations often come in "direct-inverse" pairs

(c) use basic results and step-by-step deduction to draw conclusions; investigate apparent patterns and test the validity of statements—proving or disproving these statements conclusively where possible

2. ***Numbers, the number system, structural arithmetic, simplification, and algebra***

Pupils should:

Counting and numbers

(a) count reliably forwards and backwards across hundreds and thousands boundaries

(b) solve problems involving **counting** [e.g. How many pages from page 171 to 263?—inclusive and exclusive; How many dots are in a 5 by 7 rectangular array? How many chords are there joining 10 points on a circle?]

(c) use **place value** in representing integers to 1 000 000, and decimals with up to four decimal digits; express position as a "power of 10"; choose the power of 10 to transform a given decimal to an integer (by multiplying)

Sequences; powers and roots

(a) recognise multiples of 2, 4, 5, 10, 20, 25, 50, 100; factorise instantly any output from multiplication tables to 10×10; recognise (or test quickly) prime numbers to 100 and test possible primes up to 500; recognise square numbers to 20×20; find all the factors of a given integer

(b) recognise powers of 2, powers of 3, and powers of 5; recognise square and cube roots of familiar squares and cubes; understand and find, or estimate, the square root of any positive number; use index notation for small positive integer powers

(c) find specified terms of a sequence given a **term-to-term** or a **position-to-term** rule; guess the simplest position-to-term rule for the nth term given the first few terms of a sequence

Integers and decimals

(a) read, write (in figures and words), and order whole numbers and decimals with up to six digits; understand, use, and calculate freely with (positive and negative) integers; use correctly the symbols $=$, $\neq$, $<$, $\leqslant$, $>$, $\geqslant$ and the associated language; order a set of positive and negative integers and decimals, or measurements

(b) use correctly the terms factor, multiple, common factor, common multiple; find and use the HCF and LCM of two given integers; test for divisibility by 2, by 3, by 4, by 5, by 9, by 10

(c) multiply, and divide, any integer or decimal by 10, 100, 1000, or 10 000; know the multiplicative complements for 10 (2×5), for 100, and for 1000, and the corresponding decimals [e.g. $\frac{1}{2} = 0.5$, $\frac{1}{5} = 0.2$, $\frac{1}{8} = 0.125$]; recognise as alternative representations the decimal and fraction forms of simple fractions

(d) express any given large number as a number less than 10 times a power of 10, and a small number as a number greater than or equal to 1 times a power of 10

(e) compare measurements (in various contexts); round integers and decimals

Fractions, percentages and ratio

(a) understand general fractions in terms of **unit fractions**; switch freely between mixed numbers (with fractional part < 1) and standard fractional form $\frac{p}{q}$

(b) find fractional parts of shapes and quantities, and recognise the fractional part represented; solve simple **ratio** problems

(c) understand equivalent fractions; express two given fractions with a common denominator; simplify a given fraction; order a list of integers and fractions

(d) understand "percentage" as a fractional operator with denominator 100; find fractions and percentages of given quantities; express one quantity as a fraction of another; use the multiplicative character of percentage as an operator in calculations involving percentage increase and decrease; distinguish between absolute and relative increase and decrease

(e) reduce a *ratio* to its simplest form, and establish the connection with "fractional parts"; divide a given quantity into two parts in a given *ratio*; solve problems involving **ratio and proportion**

3. *Calculation*

Pupils should:

Number operations and mental methods

(a) extend existing mental calculation to include negative numbers, decimals and fractions

(b) calculate effectively in solving problems

Structural arithmetic

(a) use multiplication tables freely to simplify fractional expressions; convert fractions to decimals and terminating decimals to their simplified fraction equivalents

(b) obtain the prime-power factorisation of a given integer by successive division

(c) understand and use **place value,** inverse operations [e.g. cancellation], and **structural arithmetic** to **simplify** calculations; represent numbers and roots as powers, including fractional powers; work with powers of 10

(d) understand why $(-1) \times (-1) = 1$ and why $a - (-b) = a + b$; use these to simplify and to evaluate numerical expressions

(e) use the idea of choosing a suitable (common) denominator to add, subtract, multiply and divide fractions

(f) solve **word problems** involving rates and **ratios**, including the **unitary method**

(g) give both roots of simple quadratic equations; simplify numerical expressions involving simple surds [e.g. $\sqrt{8} = 2\sqrt{2}$ because both are positive and have the same square]

Algebraic simplification

(a) substitute numerical values into **formulae** and **expressions** and evaluate; multiply out brackets, collect like terms, identify and take out common factors to simplify expressions; recognise that different-looking expressions may be identical; prove simple algebraic **identities**, and explain why two given expressions are not identical

Written methods

(a) relate decimal arithmetic to integer arithmetic; use **standard written methods** in column format for addition and subtraction, short and long multiplication, short (and long) division of integers and decimals

Inequalities

(a) solve simple linear **inequalities** in one variable and represent solutions on a number line

Measures

(a) calculate and work with perimeters, areas, volumes, durations, capacities, and simple compound measures; use standard units of length, area, volume, mass, and capacity; read scales with appropriate rounding; record and order measurements using decimal notation; convert between related units

(b) estimate the size of any given angle; draw and measure angles reliably to the nearest degree

(c) calculate reliably with measures; extract and use information from tables and charts; solve **word problems** involving money, time, length, and compound measures (speed, rates)

4. ***Algebra: equations, formulae, identities, and functions***

Pupils should:

(a) set up and solve linear equations in complete generality [e.g.

$$2 - \frac{3}{4}x = \frac{2 - 4x}{5}];$$

reduce a linear equation in two variables to standard form ($ax + by = c$, or $y = mx + c$); eliminate a variable from two simultaneous linear equations in two unknowns; solve linear inequalities in one unknown

(b) change the subject of a formula; draw the graph of a linear function, identifying its gradient, and interpreting its position; construct linear functions arising from real problems, sketch and interpret their graphs; establish the link to **ratio and proportion**

(c) use letters in general expressions; use index notation for small positive integer powers; **simplify** given expressions

(d) use algebra to find the exact solution of two simultaneous linear equations in two unknowns by eliminating a variable

(e) sketch the graphs of simple quadratic functions; solve simple quadratic equations

5. ***Solving numerical problems***

Pupils should:

(a) solve arithmetical problems, **word problems**, and geometry problems involving numbers and measures; check that their results are reasonable

(b) solve **multi-step** and **inverse** problems with confidence

(c) use the **unitary method** to solve **proportion** problems and problems involving ratios and rates

(d) use algebraic formulae; set up and solve equations

6. *Processing, representing, and interpreting data*

Pupils should:

(a) solve problems involving lists, tables, charts, and graphs; sort, classify, and organise information; discuss the methods they use and explain what they find

(b) find the average (i.e. mean) and other measures of "centre", and measures of spread for small datasets; identify the modal class for grouped data; interpret frequency diagrams and histograms; use cumulative frequency

(c) use **counting** where each outcome is "equally likely" to calculate **probabilities**

Ma2: Geometry

1. *Using and applying "Geometry"*

Pupils should:

Solving problems

(a) solve geometrical problems involving standard geometrical figures in 2D and 3D, and angles, length, area, and volume

(b) measure and calculate accurately to construct and analyse 2D and 3D figures; use standard units in geometry

Communicating

(a) use geometrical language, notation, terminology, and symbols correctly

(b) work in all four quadrants of the coordinate plane

(c) lay out calculations, constructions, and **proofs line-by-line**

Reasoning

(a) use basic geometrical principles to justify each step in a calculation or deduction

(b) analyse 2D and 3D configurations in terms of triangles

2. ***Constructing and analysing geometrical configurations***

Pupils should:

Know and analyse

(a) recognise right angles, perpendicular and parallel lines, and use the associated language precisely; know that angles at a point total 360°, and that angles at a point on a straight line total 180°

(b) know that two lines are parallel precisely when alternate angles are equal (or, equivalently, when corresponding angles are equal); prove and use the usual consequences (including the angle-sum in any triangle)

(c) use known angles and angle properties to find unknown angles in given configurations (i.e. **angle-chasing**)

(d) motivate the formula for the circumference of the circle and estimate π; solve related problems

(e) talk about and work with common 2D and 3D shapes (including triangles [e.g. right angled, isosceles, and equilateral], quadrilaterals [e.g. parallelograms, rhombuses, rectangles, squares, and trapezia], cuboids, and prisms); correctly copy drawings from the board; make and draw shapes with increasing accuracy, and analyse their geometrical properties

Constructions and congruence

(a) use ruler and protractor to draw triangles with given data; extract and apply the basic congruence criteria (SAS, SSS, ASA; RHS) to prove standard results (including that the base angles in any isosceles triangle are equal, and the converse)

(b) draw specified figures using "ruler" (i.e. *straightedge*) and compasses only; use the basic **ruler and compass constructions** to complete other constructions

Area and Pythagoras

(a) find the area of rectangles and shapes made from rectangles; find the area of right angled triangles and of general triangles; find the area of a general parallelogram

(b) relate the formula for the area of a circle to the formula for the circumference; use the formula to solve related problems

(c) state, **prove**, and use *Pythagoras' Theorem*

Circles

(a) understand and use the terms centre, radius, chord, diameter, circumference, tangent, arc, sector, segment

(b) **prove** the basic properties of a circle [e.g. centre and any chord form an isosceles triangle; angle in a semicircle is a right angle; tangent is perpendicular to radius; tangents form an external point are equal]; apply these results to solve problems

Volume and 3D

(a) calculate volumes of cuboids and shapes made of cuboids; calculate volumes of a "wedge" (half a cuboid), polygonal right prisms, and cylinders

(b) find lengths and angles in simple 3D figures by considering 2D cross-sections

Scaling and enlargement

(a) draw figures to scale; interpret distances, angles, and areas on maps and other scale drawings

Loci

(a) interpret a circle as a locus; interpret the perpendicular bisector of a given line segment as a locus

3. ***Coordinates and graphs***

Pupils should:

(a) read and plot coordinates in all four quadrants

(b) use *Pythagoras' Theorem* to calculate the distance between two given points (simple cases); find the coordinates of the midpoint of a line segment (simple cases)

(c) establish the link between straight lines in the coordinate plane and linear equations in x and y; understand that parallel lines have the same gradient; find the intersection of two given straight lines

(d) sketch the graphs of simple quadratic functions

(e) explore and use coordinates in 3D

2.4 Key stage 4

Breadth of Study

1. During the Key Stage pupils should be taught the required *Knowledge, Skills, and Understanding* through:

(a) activities that revisit and extend material from Key Stage 3, moving on to achieve **fluency** and **automaticity** in using a wide range of procedures

(b) using language, terminology, and logic precisely and correctly; linking the language of mathematics with spoken and written English

(c) learning basic facts and techniques by heart; using them to tackle two-step and **multi-step** exercises and **problems** in different contexts, and in solving unfamiliar problems (including **word problems**)

(d) exploiting **connections** between superficially different topics; compressing ideas and techniques

(e) recognising that operations often come in "direct-inverse" pairs, that the **inverse** operation is often the more demanding one, and that its mastery depends on robust fluency in the direct operation

(f) using **calculators** intelligently where needed, whilst avoiding inappropriate dependence

(g) extending **exact** arithmetic (without calculators) to fractions, surds, and numerical and algebraic expressions involving powers; routinely using algebraic structure to **simplify** numerical, fractional, and symbolic expressions

(h) making intelligent **estimates** and **approximations** and handling the associated calculations reliably

(i) combining **congruence** and **ruler and compass constructions, parallels**, and **similarity** to establish a formal basis for elementary **Euclidean geometry**

(j) working with tables and information presented graphically; drawing inferences from a mathematical analysis of data drawn from a population with inherent variability; considering how statistics can be used to inform decisions

Knowledge, Skills, and Understanding

Teaching should ensure that appropriate connections are made between the section on *Number and algebra* and the section on *Geometry*.

Ma1 Number and algebra

1. *Using and applying "Number and algebra"*

Pupils should:

Solving problems

(a) use numerical, algebraic, geometrical, and logical information in tackling problems in *Number and algebra*, in solving **word problems**, and in analysing data

(b) use the structure of arithmetic and the laws of algebra when working with integers, decimals, fractions, surds, and algebraic expressions in solving problems

(c) regularly solve **multi-step** problems and **inverse** problems

(d) make use of relevant **connections** between topics

(e) solve problems involving measures, rates and compound measures, ratio and **proportion**

(f) make and justify **estimates**

Communicating

(a) use spoken and written language, notation, diagrams, terminology, and symbols correctly

(b) recognise when information is presented in a misleading way

(c) present results and solutions to problems clearly, declare unknowns explicitly, and lay out solutions and **proofs** logically **line-by-line**

(d) interpret tables, lists, and charts; present information graphically

(e) construct and interpret frequency tables; use precise measures of "centre" and of spread

Reasoning

(a) investigate apparent patterns; generate, interpret, test, and prove (or disprove) simple conjectures

(b) use **place value**, index laws, and **structural arithmetic** to **simplify** calculations and expressions, and to justify the extension of known conventions (including $(-1) \times (-1) = 1$, $2^0 = 1$, $\cos 120^\circ = -\frac{1}{2}$)

(c) use known results and step-by-step deduction to draw conclusions

2. ***From numbers to algebra (including calculation)***

Pupils should:

Numbers and arithmetic

(a) use **place value** in calculating with decimals; work effectively with very large numbers

(b) multiply, and divide, any integer or decimal by any power of 10; know the multiplicative complements for powers of 10 [e.g. $1000 = 8 \times 125$], and the corresponding decimals [e.g. $\frac{1}{8} = 0.125$]; recognise the decimal forms of simple fractions

(c) understand and use **divisibility tests**

(d) understand why $(-1) \times (-1) = 1$; work with integers, decimals, fractions, and surds, **simplifying** routinely

(e) solve problems involving **counting**; understand and use the **product rule** for counting

(f) consolidate and extend short and long division

Measures

(a) compare measurements; round integers and decimals appropriately

(b) calculate and work with perimeters, areas, volumes, durations, capacities; use standard units of length, area, volume, mass, capacity, and simple compound measures (speed, density, and other "rates"); read scales with appropriate rounding; record and order measurements using decimal notation; change between related units—in numerical and algebraic contexts; solve **word problems** involving money, time, length, and compound measures

Bounds and estimation

(a) understand the limits of accuracy implied by a given measurement in decimal form and interpret the result of an arithmetical calculation

(b) establish bounds on the accuracy of an **estimate** and understand how this affects a calculation

Integer factorisation, fractions, and surds

(a) use the terms factor, multiple, common factor, common multiple; find the *HCF* and *LCM* of given integers

(b) recognise (or test quickly) prime numbers to 120; use the "square root test" to identify primes to 1000

(c) obtain the prime power factorisation of a given integer; list all factors of a given integer

(d) move freely between "mixed" fractions and fractions in standard fractional form $\frac{p}{q}$; reduce a given fraction to lowest terms; rewrite two given fractions with a common denominator; order a list of fractions

(e) use factorisation to simplify surd expressions [e.g.

$$\sqrt{12} = \sqrt{2^2 \times 3} = 2 \times \sqrt{3}]$$

Fractions

(a) understand the **unit fraction** $\frac{1}{q}$ as "that part, of which q identical copies make 1"; understand a general fraction $\frac{p}{q}$ as a multiple $p \times \frac{1}{q}$ of a unit fraction; move freely from a given fraction to a suitable equivalent fraction

(b) add and subtract fractions; multiply and divide fractions; simplify, and hence evaluate, compound expressions involving fractions

Fractions and decimals

(a) move freely between terminating decimals and decimal fractions

(b) know the equivalence of the **exact** (unevaluated) fraction notation $\frac{p}{q}$ and the result of evaluating $p \div q$; find the decimal of any given fraction; understand why the decimal form of $\frac{p}{q}$ must terminate, or recur

(c) change any terminating decimal into a fraction in its lowest terms; change any recurring decimal into a fraction

Surds

(a) recognise $\sqrt{k}$ (for $k > 0$) as the **exact** positive real number whose square is equal to k; given $k > 0$ find the exact or approximate value of $\sqrt{k}$; use the algebra of surds—including rationalising denominators [e.g.

$$\frac{1}{\sqrt{2}+1} = \sqrt{2} - 1];$$

use surds (and π) to calculate *exactly* in geometric contexts; give lengths arising from applications of *Pythagoras' Theorem* and solutions to quadratic equations in exact (mixed surd) form

(b) use the standard notation for, and calculate with, cube roots;

Powers, roots, and the index laws

(a) factorise instantly any output from multiplication tables to 10×10; recognise square numbers to 25×25; recognise cubes to 6^3.

(b) recognise powers of 2, 3, 4, 5; recognise square and cube roots of familiar squares and cubes; extend powers and roots to simple fractions and decimals; find, or estimate, the square root or cube root of any positive number

(c) know, understand, and use the index laws; use index notation to present expressions in simplified power form; calculate freely with numerical and algebraic expressions involving powers

(d) write any given number in standard form and translate a given standard form into the (approximate) number it represents; calculate with numbers given in standard form "as though they are exact"

Fractions, decimals, and percentages

(a) find and recognise fractional parts of shapes and quantities; express one quantity as a fraction of another

(b) understand percentage as a fractional operator with denominator 100; know and use the percentage equivalents of familiar fractional parts;

work freely with percentages; use the multiplicative character of percentage increase and decrease; solve problems involving percentage change (including inverse problems and compound interest)

Sequences

(a) work with standard integer sequences; generate terms given a **term-to-term** rule, or a **position-to-term** rule; guess the simplest position-to-term rule for the nth term given the first few terms of a sequence

(b) use a given term-to-term rule to find a **closed formula** for the position-to-term rule

(c) find the term-to-term rule and the position-to-term rule for sequences **defined intrinsically**

(d) understand that when $x < 1$ (or $|x| < 1$) the sequence of powers (x^n) tends rapidly to 0, and when $x > 1$ (or $|x| > 1$) the sequence of powers (x^n) grows rapidly without bound; link to compound interest, to population growth, to doubling times and to radioactive half-life

Ratio and proportion

(a) divide a given quantity into two parts in a given part-to-part, or part-to-whole **ratio**; express the division of a quantity into two parts as a ratio; work with separate quantities in a given (external) ratio; reduce a ratio to its simplest form

(b) calculate the result of a change of units; draw and use scale diagrams and maps; understand the effect of scaling and enlargement on different quantities (including angles, lengths, areas, and volumes)

(c) solve proportion problems (where three of the four variables are given, determine the fourth); use the **unitary method**, and then the general method, to solve *proportion* problems

(d) understand and use "X is inversely proportional to Y" as meaning "X is proportional to $\frac{1}{Y}$"

Algebraic expressions

(a) substitute numerical values into **formulae** and **expressions**

(b) multiply out brackets, collect like terms, and take out common factors to simplify linear, quadratic and higher order expressions; *simplify* general expressions (possibly involving powers and roots) by using additive simplification, the distributive law, and cancellation—giving answers in factorised form; work with algebraic fractions having linear and quadratic denominators

(c) rearrange formulae; solve problems using standard formulae

(d) set up linear equations; solve the general linear equation in one unknown

(e) set up linear equations in two unknowns; interpret a linear equation in two unknowns in the coordinate plane as representing a straight line; draw the graph of a linear function, identifying its gradient, and interpreting its position; find the gradient from an equation given in any form; transform a given equation into the form $y = mx + c$ (or $x = a$); construct linear functions arising from real problems, sketch and interpret their graphs; establish the link to **ratio and proportion**

(f) solve any pair of simultaneous linear equations by eliminating a variable; interpret the analytic solution as "finding the point of intersection" (if any) of the two lines

(g) factorise quadratic expressions in one variable; solve quadratic equations by factorising; interpret solutions as those points where the graph crosses the x-axis; solve fractional equations that reduce to quadratics [e.g.

$$\frac{1}{x+1} = \frac{x-1}{x}];$$

(h) factorise and use the difference of two squares; conclude that, if $k > 0$, the equation $x^2 = k$ has two solutions ($\pm\sqrt{k}$); interpret this as a statement about the graph of $y = x^2 - k$

(i) know and use the expansion of $(x + a)^2$; extend to $(x + a)^3$; use this to "complete the square" for any given quadratic; obtain the formula for the solutions of the general quadratic

$$y = ax^2 + bx + c;$$

use this formula to solve quadratic equations; deduce the symmetry of the graphs of quadratic functions

(j) solve two simultaneous equations where one is linear and the other quadratic; use completing the square to find the centre and radius, given the equation of a circle; find the points where two circles intersect

(k) understand the difference between an equation and an **identity**; decide whether two given expressions are identical or not—then **prove** they are, or show that they are not

(l) solve linear inequalities in one and two variables; interpret the solution graphically

3. *Coordinates, graphs, and functions*

Pupils should:

(a) read and plot coordinates in all four quadrants; move freely between straight lines in the coordinate plane and linear equations in x and y; derive the equation of a line through two given points, and the equation of a line through a given point with a given gradient

(b) find the coordinates of the midpoint of a line segment; calculate the distance between two points in 2D or 3D

(c) interpret straight line graphs arising in real situations

(d) know and use the general form $y = mx + c$ (or $x = a$) for a straight line; use gradient and intercept; find the point of intersection of two given straight lines

(e) know that parallel lines have the same gradient; prove and use the fact that two lines with gradients m and m' are perpendicular precisely when $m \cdot m' = -1$

(f) for particular values of m and c interpret the standard form $y = mx + c$ as '$Y = mX$' relative to an origin at $(0, c)$ or at $(-\frac{c}{m}, 0)$

(g) sketch the graph of any given quadratic function by completing the square

(h) sketch other graphs—including simple cubic functions, the reciprocal function $y = \frac{1}{x}$, the exponential function $y = k^x$ for easy (positive) values of k, the circular functions $y = \sin x$, $y = \cos x$, and $y = \tan x$

(i) use coordinates to solve simple problems in 3D

4. *Processing, representing, and interpreting data*

Pupils should:

(a) engage in practical and theoretical work to construct and interpret tables, lists, and information presented graphically; use precise measures of "centre" and spread; sort, classify, and organise information

(b) discuss variability; distinguish between data representing a single idealised measure and informal "random variables" **sampled** from a **population** or distribution

(c) calculate the mean of a set of numbers or measures; use mode or median as appropriate to summarise the "centre"; identify the modal class for grouped data; refine measures of spread and "central tendency"

(d) introduce ideas of **probability** via standard examples of discrete **sample spaces** in which each outcome is equally likely; explore the general notion of an "event"

(e) understand why

$$prob(A \cup B) = prob(A) + prob(B)$$

for disjoint events A, B; use simple counting to calculate probabilities in discrete sample spaces; understand and use the inclusion/exclusion formula

$$prob(A \cup B) = prob(A) + prob(B) - prob(A \cap B)$$

for events which are not necessarily disjoint

Ma2: Geometry

1. *Using and applying "Geometry"*

Pupils should:

Solving problems

(a) know and understand basic **ruler and compass constructions**; use these to devise simple constructions

(b) use standard units in geometry; solve geometrical problems in 2D and 3D involving calculation, construction, and deduction

(c) measure and calculate accurately to construct and analyse 2D and 3D figures in terms of triangles; use known results to construct simple proofs

Communicating

(a) use geometrical language, notation, terminology, and symbols correctly

(b) work in all four quadrants of the coordinate plane; interpret a given equation as the graph of a function or a circle

(c) lay out calculations, constructions, and **proofs line-by-line**

Reasoning

(a) use the basic principles of **Euclidean geometry** and results derived from them to justify each step in a calculation, construction, or deduction

(b) analyse 2D and 3D configurations [e.g. by singling out, and using known properties of triangles]

2. *From naïve construction to Euclidean geometry*

Pupils should:

Ruler and compass constructions revisited and organised

(a) know that two points A, B determine a line AB, a line segment $\overline{AB}$, and a circle with centre A and radius $\overline{AB}$; relate this to ideal **ruler and compass constructions**

(b) know and use the conventional notation for labelling the angles and sides of $\triangle ABC$

(c) accept and use the SAS, SSS, ASA (and later RHS) congruence criteria; prove the basic properties of isosceles triangles; justify the basic ruler and compass constructions and use them to devise other constructions

(d) prove that the perpendicular bisector of a given line segment $\overline{BC}$ is the locus of points X equidistant from B and C; construct the circumcentre of any triangle

(e) recognise the "perpendicular distance" from a point X to a line as the (shortest) distance to the line; prove the angle bisector of $\angle BAC$ is the (part-) locus of points equidistant from the lines AB and AC; construct the incentre of $\triangle ABC$

(f) prove that the three altitudes of a triangle are concurrent

Parallel lines and angles in a triangle

(a) know that angles at a point total 360°, and that angles at a point on a straight line total 180°; conclude that "vertically opposite angles are equal"

(b) recognise that "two lines are parallel precisely when alternate angles (or equivalently, when corresponding angles) created by any transversal are equal"; derive the basic properties of a parallelogram and of a rhombus; where possible prove the converse results; prove and use the *Midpoint Theorem*

(c) prove that the angles in any triangle add to 180° and that the exterior angle at any vertex is equal to the sum of the two interior opposite angles; deduce that the angles in any quadrilateral add to 360°; calculate the angle-sum in an n-gon, and the angle size in a regular n-gon

(d) combine known results about angles to find unknown angles, and to show that certain pairs of lines are parallel

(e) know and use the fact that the tangent and radius at a point on a circle are perpendicular; conclude that tangents from an external point are equal; prove that the angle subtended by a chord on the major arc is half the angle subtended at the centre O; conclude that angles subtended in the same segment are equal, and that opposite angles of a cyclic quadrilateral add to $180°$; prove and use the *Alternate Segment Theorem*

(f) prove that the area of a parallelogram is equal to that of a rectangle on the same base and between the same parallels and deduce the formula for the area of a triangle; use this to prove *Pythagoras' Theorem*

Similarity

(a) establish and use the AAA similarity criterion and the SAS similarity criterion for general triangles; prove basic results using similarity

(b) extend the *Midpoint Theorem* to divide a given segment into any number of equal parts; prove and use the *Intercept Theorem*

3. *Geometric calculation*

Pupils should:

Trigonometry

(a) show that the standard trig ratios for acute angles θ depend only on the angle θ; understand that $\sin\theta$, $\cos\theta$ take values between 0 and 1

(b) find the exact values for $\theta = 0°, 30°, 45°, 60°$; plot graphs of $y = \sin\theta$, $y = \cos\theta$, and $y = \tan\theta$ for $0° \leqslant \theta < 90°$; understand why $\cos\theta = \sin(90° - \theta)$

(c) calculate missing lengths and angles in a given triangle ABC

(d) given triangle ABC, derive and use the formula

$$\text{area}(ABC) = \frac{1}{2}ab\sin C;$$

deduce the *Sine Rule* and use it to "solve triangles"; prove that

$$\frac{a}{\sin A} = 2R,$$

where R is the circumradius of triangle ABC

(e) show that on the unit circle with centre at the origin O, the point P for which the radius OP makes an angle θ with the positive x-axis has coordinates $(\cos\theta, \sin\theta)$; apply *Pythagoras' Theorem* to derive the identity

$$\sin^2\theta + \cos^2\theta = 1;$$

use this identity to find values of $\cos\theta$ given the value of $\sin\theta$ (and *vice versa*), and the value of $\tan\theta$ given the value of $\cos\theta$

(f) prove the *Cosine Rule*, and use it to find unknown lengths and angles in triangles and other 2D and 3D figures

(g) extend the definition of $\sin\theta$ and $\cos\theta$ to $\theta > 90°$; extend the graphs of $y = \sin\theta, y = \cos\theta$ to $180° < \theta < 0°$, and to $-180° < \theta < 0°$

(h) show that in the "ambiguous (ASS) case", the data may determine two possible triangles

2D and 3D figures

(a) work freely with standard 2D figures

(b) draw figures to scale; interpret maps and other scale drawings; apply similarity in analysing problems; understand how enlargement and scaling (or similarity) affects angles, lengths, areas, and volumes

(c) find lengths and angles in 3D figures by considering 2D cross-sections; calculate the angle between two planes

(d) calculate surface areas and volumes of standard figures

Circles

(a) understand and use the terms centre, radius, chord, diameter, circumference, tangent, arc, sector, segment

(b) understand and use the formula for the circumference of a circle; calculate the length of circular arcs

(c) relate the formula for the area of a circle to the formula for the circumference; calculate the area of a sector

(d) calculate the circumradius and inradius of a triangle

(e) use *Pythagoras' Theorem* to find the equation of a circle of radius r centred at the origin and at the point (c, d); complete the square to identify easy quadratic equations as circles and find their centre and radius

(f) find the equation of the tangent to a given circle at a specified point

Permissions

All chapters in this book were first published in TMSL, by Open Book Publishers by Tony Gardiner; hereby published with permission under the Creative Commons Attribution License or equivalent. Every chapter published in this book has been scrutinized by our experts. Their significance has been extensively debated. The topics covered herein carry significant information for a comprehensive understanding. They may even be implemented as practical applications or may be referred to as a beginning point for further studies.

We would like to thank the editorial team for lending their expertise to make the book truly unique. They have played a crucial role in the development of this book. Without their invaluable contributions this book wouldn't have been possible. They have made vital efforts to compile up to date information on the varied aspects of this subject to make this book a valuable addition to the collection of many professionals and students.

This book was conceptualized with the vision of imparting up-to-date and integrated information in this field. To ensure the same, a matchless editorial board was set up. Every individual on the board went through rigorous rounds of assessment to prove their worth. After which they invested a large part of their time researching and compiling the most relevant data for our readers.

The editorial board has been involved in producing this book since its inception. They have spent rigorous hours researching and exploring the diverse topics which have resulted in the successful publishing of this book. They have passed on their knowledge of decades through this book. To expedite this challenging task, the publisher supported the team at every step. A small team of assistant editors was also appointed to further simplify the editing procedure and attain best results for the readers.

Apart from the editorial board, the designing team has also invested a significant amount of their time in understanding the subject and creating the most relevant covers. They scrutinized every image to scout for the most suitable representation of the subject and create an appropriate cover for the book.

The publishing team has been an ardent support to the editorial, designing and production team. Their endless efforts to recruit the best for this project, has resulted in the accomplishment of this book. They are a veteran in the field of academics and their pool of knowledge is as vast as their experience in printing. Their expertise and guidance has proved useful at every step. Their uncompromising quality standards have made this book an exceptional effort. Their encouragement from time to time has been an inspiration for everyone.

The publisher and the editorial board hope that this book will prove to be a valuable piece of knowledge for students, practitioners and scholars across the globe.

Index

CPSIA information can be obtained
at www.ICGtesting.com
Printed in the USA
LVHW082034020122
707669LV00001B/15

9 781639 89141